AF473813

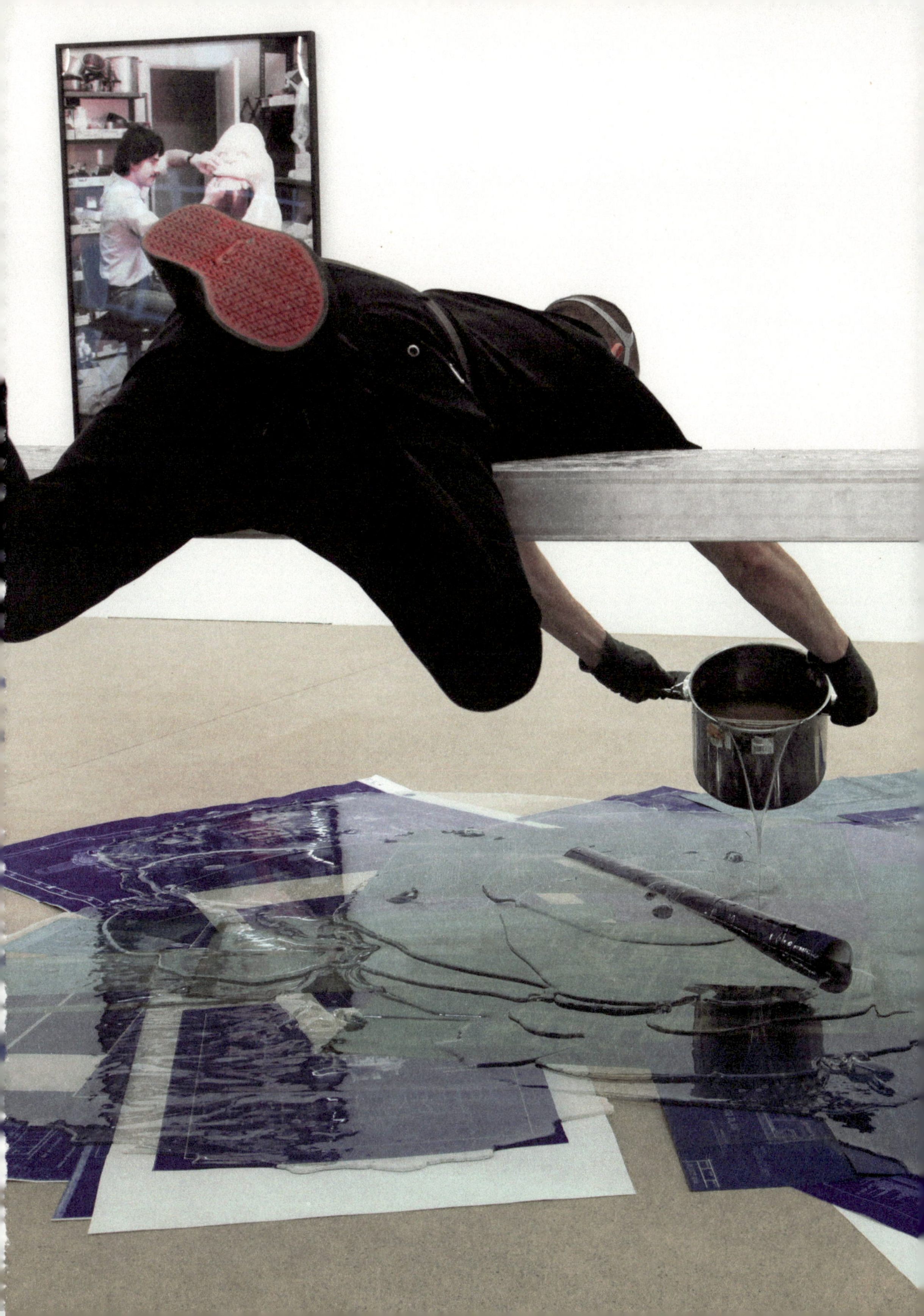

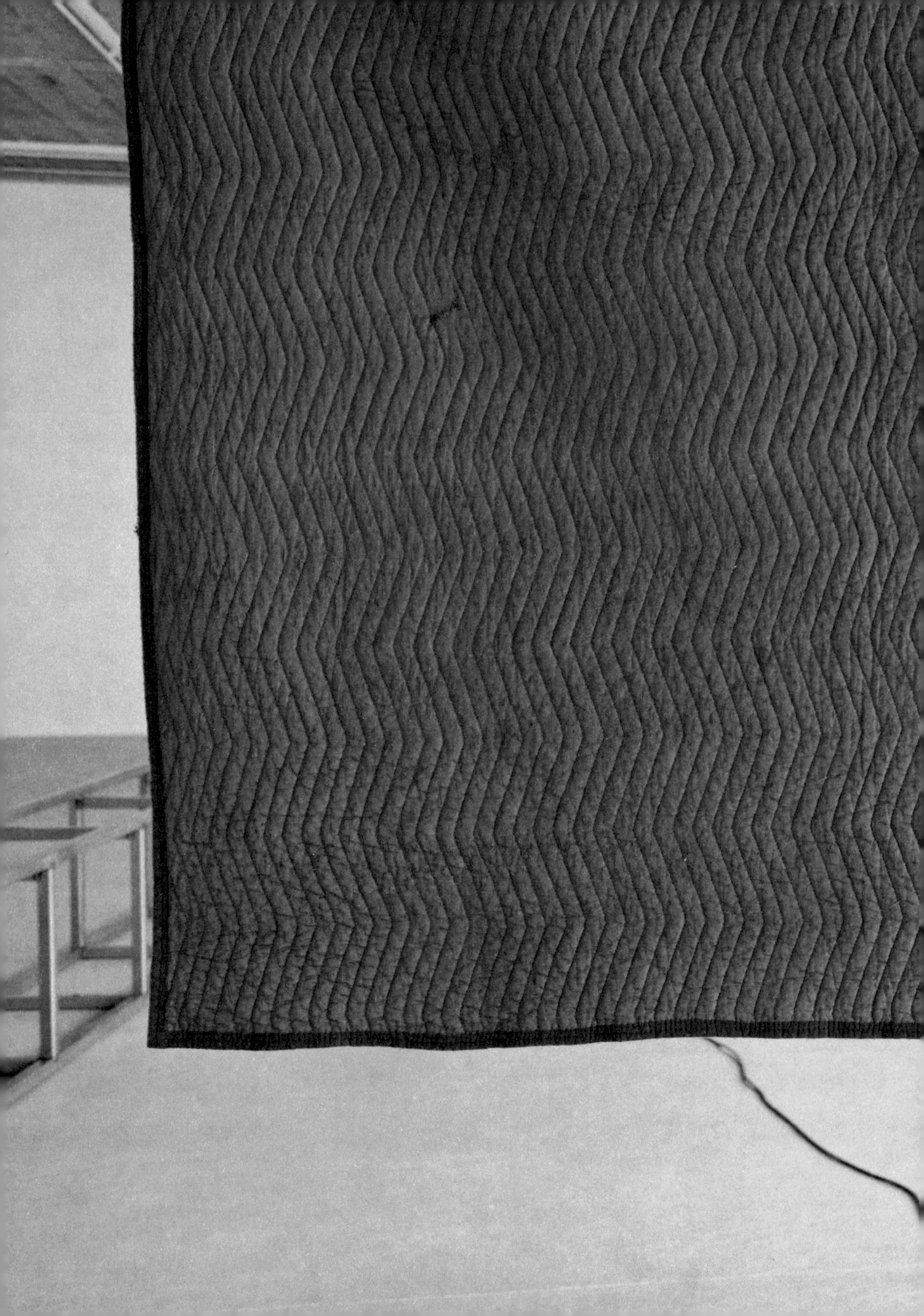

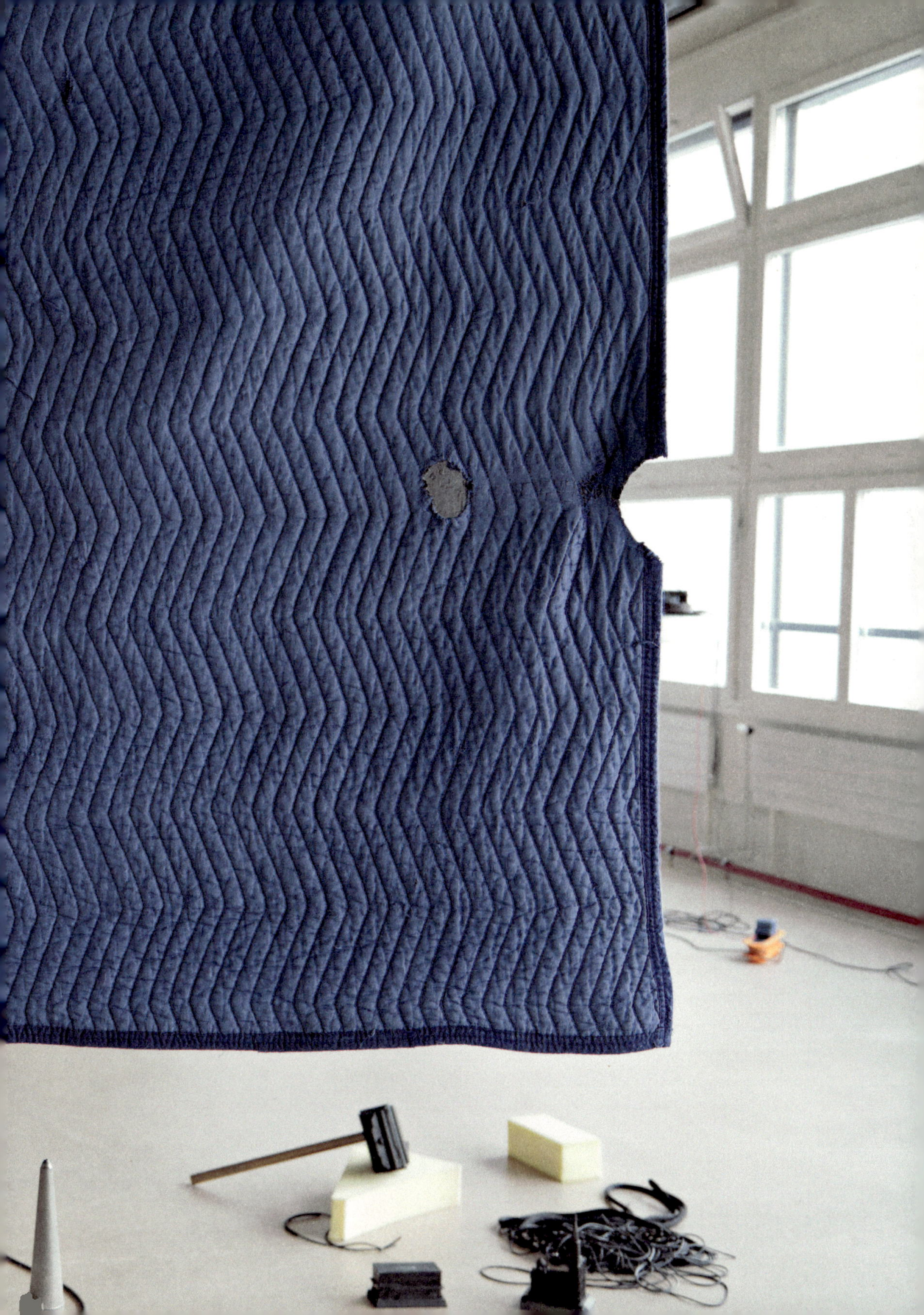

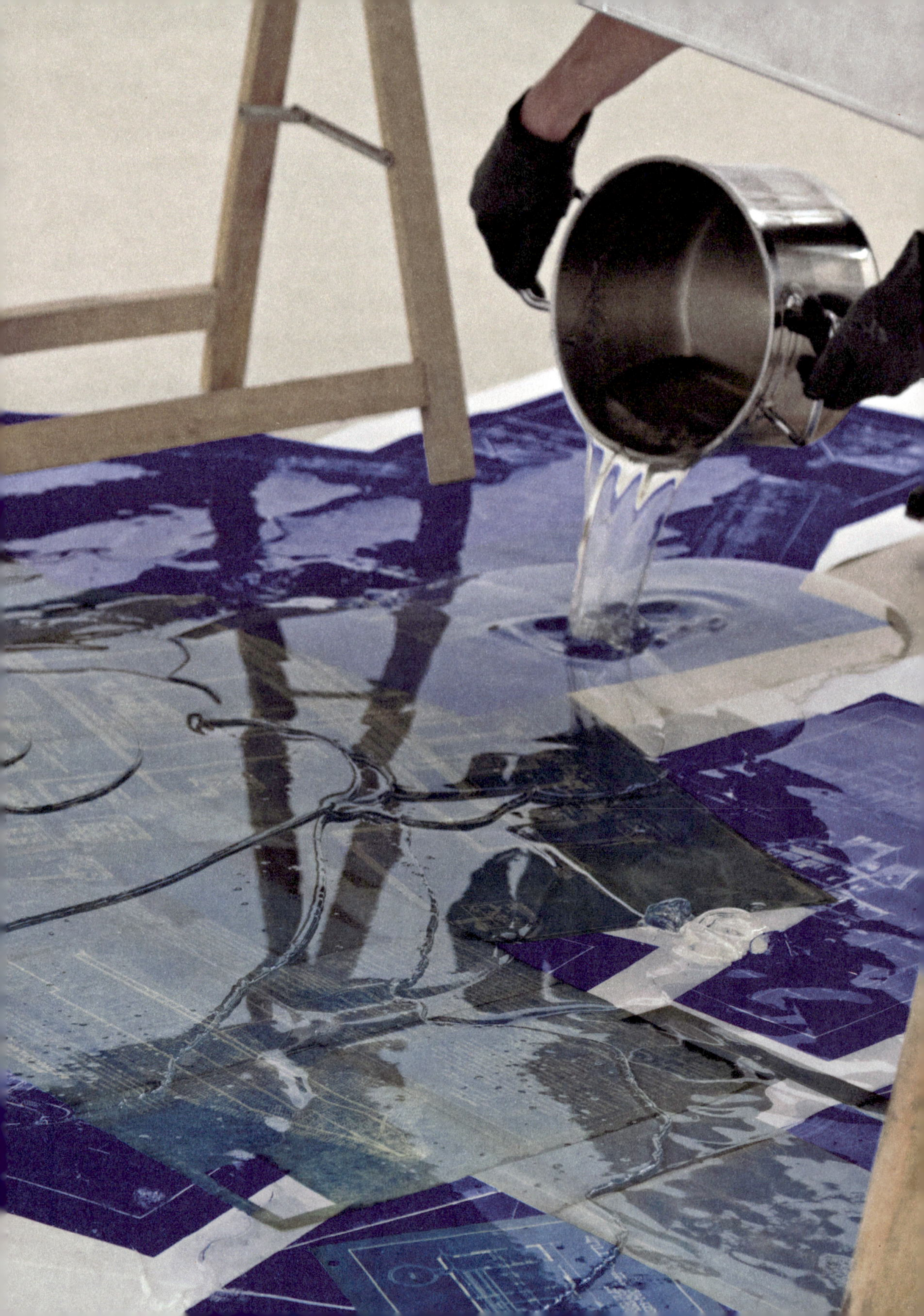

The Poltergeist Experimental Group (PEG) Applied Spirituality and Physical Spirit Manifestation

2011

St. Helena / Reichtümer aus den Tiefen der Berge

2010

Der Werwolf von Wien

2009

Published by

migros museum für
gegenwartskunst Zürich
&
JRP|Ringier

Table of Contents

Crossmapping Germann — Ein Vorwort zum Werk von Florian Germann

Raphael Gygax

Für die Ankündigung seines Werkzyklus *The Poltergeist Experimental Group (PEG) Applied Spirituality and Physical Spirit Manifestation*, den er im Rahmen seiner Einzelausstellung im migros museum für gegenwartskunst erarbeitete, benutzt Florian Germann eine Fotografie, die einen Mann bei der Arbeit an einer Skulptur zeigt. Der mediensozialisierte Betrachter erkennt diese sogleich als Modell des freundlichen grünen Ektoplasma-Geists aus dem Film *Ghostbusters* (1984). Damit spielt Germann einerseits mit einem Pop-kulturellen Zitat – andererseits verzahnt er den Zyklustitel mit einem aus der Kunstgeschichte bekannten Motiv: der Künstler in seinem Atelier. Durch diese Bildappropriation verweist Germann jedoch nicht nur auf die Frage nach der Rolle des Künstlers, sondern öffnet auch einen Denkraum zwischen den Feldern Kultur, Wissenschaft und Natur und deren scheinbarer Gegensätzlichkeit. Gerade der «Geistermacher», der mit seinen eigenen Händen, also physisch, und seinen wissenschaftlichen Kenntnissen sich an das «Übernatürliche» heranwagt, damit herumexperimentiert und es schliesslich selbst erschafft, kann als Oxymoron und damit als Figur angesehen werden, welche die vermeintliche Divergenz zwischen den genannten Feldern aufhebt. Im 20. Jahrhundert haben Künstler immer wieder den Graben zwischen Kultur, Wissenschaft und Natur diskutiert und zu überwinden versucht; sei es Marcel Duchamp in den 1910er Jahren mit seinen Überlegungen zum «grossen Glas» *(La mariée mise à nu par ses célibataires, même [Le grand verre]*, 1915–23), sei es Joseph Beuys in den 1970er Jahren mit seinem Multiple *Rose für direkte Demokratie* (1973). Es handelt sich dabei um einen gläsernen Labormesszylinder, der eine Rose enthält. Beuys deutete die Gegensätzlichkeit dieser Materialien zu einer Losung um: ein Gesellschaftsmodell (die direkte Demokratie), die spirituelle Kultur (die Rose) und die Wissenschaften (der Messzylinder) als Errungenschaften, in denen sich eine positive Entwicklung spiegelt. Die von Germann verwendete Fotografie ist also nicht nur ein künstlerisches Selbstporträt, sondern steht auch für eine Denkfigur, die in seinem Schaffen zentral ist – die Absage an Hegels Diktum vom Ende der Kunst als Wahrheitsfindung –, und distanziert sich von der Idee von Kunst und ihrer Autonomiebewegung als Reflexionsprozess, der sich nur noch auf sie selbst bezieht. Dementsprechend sind die Felder Kunst und Wissenschaft in seinem Werk nicht voneinander isoliert, sondern gehen ineinander über und bilden durch ihre Verbindung eine eigene «Wahrheit».

Germanns Arbeiten sind meist grössere Werkzyklen: Aus formalästhetischer Sicht wirken sie wie eine Mischung aus physikalischen Instrumenten und modernistischen Skulpturen, die sich im Ausstellungsraum ausnehmen wie eine Versuchsanordnung, deren Sinnzusammenhänge sich erst allmählich, wie ein feines Netz, darüberlegen. Als inhaltliche Ausgangspunkte für diese Versuchsanordnungen dienen Germann oftmals historische Figuren wie etwa Napoleon oder mythologisch-fantastische Motive wie das der Lykanthropie (von griechisch «lykos», «Wolf», und «anthropos», «Mensch», also dem Werwolf-Motiv) oder Geistererscheinungen. Diese unterwirft er einer Umschreibung, wobei er faktische und fiktive Momente miteinander verwebt. In diese Erzählungen mit eingebunden ist für Germann auch immer das Interesse an physikalischen Prozessen und an der Transformation von Energien. Dieses Interesse widerspiegelt sich auch in der Haptik seiner Werke: Germanns Objekte und Skulpturen – oftmals dienen ihm Metalle wie Messing (*St. Helena/Reichtümer aus den Tiefen der Berge*) oder Silber (*Der Werwolf von Wien*) als Material – durchlaufen in Form von «Aktionen» häufig einen (Aktivierungs-)Prozess, der für den Betrachter nur noch als Spur an den Objekten ablesbar ist.

Im Werkzyklus *The Poltergeist Experimental Group (PEG) Applied Spirituality and Physical Spirit Manifestation* tritt – wie im Titel impliziert – ein anonymes Kollektiv in Erscheinung, das sich mit dem Phänomen des Poltergeists beschäftigt, dessen Wirken sich im Feld der Parapsychologie ansiedelt. Unter einem «Poltergeist» versteht man das Auftreten von Klopfgeräuschen, elektrischen Störungen, Bewegungen von Gegenständen, die nicht durch eine unmittelbare physikalische Einwirkung verursacht werden. Den beiden amerikanischen Parapsychologen Joseph Gaither Pratt und William G. Roll zufolge treten Poltergeist-Phänomene vor allem in der Gegenwart pubertierender oder medial veranlagter Personen und bezeichnen das Geschehnis als wiederkehrende spontane Psychokinese («recurrent spontaneous psychokinesis»).[1] Demnach handelt es sich also nicht um einen «realen Geist», sondern um eine mentale Projektion, die sich unter anderem bei Jugendlichen als «psychokinetischer Effekt» entladen kann. Auf Germanns geistiger Landkarte des aktuellen Werkzyklus bildet dieses paranormale Phänomen das Zentrum, von dem aus er verschiedene Verbindungen zieht und rückkoppelt – so etwa zur Ritualkultur der Pfadfinderbewegung (man denke an die nächtlichen Taufrituale) oder auch zur Materialität von Orgelpfeifen.[2] Letztere zeichnet sich aufgrund der Metalllegierung aus Blei und Zinn durch ihre leichte Verformbarkeit schon bei geringer Hitze aus. Gleichzeitig nehmen die Orgelpfeifen in ihrem Verbund

1—See William G. Roll, *The Poltergeist* [1979], Paraview, New York 2004.
2—Robert Baden-Powell, *Scouting for Boys: A Handbook for Instruction in Good Citizenship*, Oxford 2004 (erstmals erschienen: 1908).

als Instrument eine zentrale Stellung als musikalisches Leitinstrument für die Gemeinde in der Liturgie ein – durch ihre Klänge kann eine ganze Gruppe von Menschen in Trance versetzt werden –, und sie stehen so auch als Symbol für Geistlichkeit.

Das Vorgehen Germanns, der literarische, filmische, historische, aber auch wissenschaftliche Figuren, Motive und Wissensfelder aufgreift, als schlichtes «Sampling» zu bezeichnen, wäre zu kurz gegriffen, da der Künstler sich insbesondere für die Zwischenräume interessiert, die sich durch solche Verbindungen öffnen. Ebenso wenig kann man Germanns Arbeitsweise als intertextuelles Verfahren bezeichnen, wo das in und zwischen den Texten bereits Vorhandene herausgearbeitet wird. Unter dem Begriff «Crossmapping» stellt die Literatur- und Kulturwissenschaftlerin Elisabeth Bronfen in ihrer gleichnamigen Studie eine Methode vor, die versucht, «ähnliche Anliegen» von Texten «unterschiedlicher Medialitäten» herauszuarbeiten, indem sie «entlang der Achse einer von ihnen geteilten Bildsprache» verglichen werden – sich also aus der Bildtheorie der Pathosformel Aby Warburgs entwickelt.[3] Anhand dieses Verfahrens führt Bronfen beispielsweise Charlotte Perkins Gilmans Erzählung *The Yellow Wallpaper* (1890), Francesca Woodmans Fotoarbeiten aus den 1970er Jahren und den Hollywood-Film *The Others* (2001) von Alejandro Amenábar zusammen, verbindet die Bildformeln und Denkfiguren und macht diese miteinander «fruchtbar». Dieses Verfahren, dessen Ausgangslage die vergleichend-assoziative Seherfahrung ist, hat den «Anspruch, einen Denkraum zu entfalten, der ästhetische Bildformeln neben theoretische Denkfiguren setzt, um das kulturelle Nachwirken innerer Ergriffenheiten sowie die Korrespondenz zwischen den unterschiedlichen Formalisierungen, die diese Intensitäten erfahren haben, aufzuzeichnen», indem er das «Aufflackern kultureller Intensität zu verschiedenen historischen Zeiten sowie in verschiedenen Medien vergleichend betrachte[t]».[4]

Vielleicht könnte man sich als Betrachter Germanns Schaffen – das sich einem «Erkenntnisgewinn» verschreibt – entsprechend nähern, indem man seine Werkzyklen als künstlerische Form eines Crossmappings versteht: eine Arbeitsmethode, die Themen und Motive miteinander verbindet, Parallelen herausarbeitet, Linien zieht, die vorher unsichtbar waren, wo faktische und fiktive Momente sich miteinander verweben und zu einem Ganzen werden.

3—Elisabeth Bronfen, *Crossmappings – Essays zur visuellen Kultur*, Zürich 2009.
4—Ebd. S. 7–41.

Crossmapping Germann—A Foreword to the Work of Florian Germann

Raphael Gygax

For the announcement of his cycle of works *The Poltergeist Experimental Group (PEG) Applied Spirituality and Physical Spirit Manifestation*, which he developed for his solo exhibition at the migros museum für gegenwartskunst, Florian Germann used a photograph of a man working on a piece of sculpture. As anyone socialized by today's media immediately recognizes, the sculpture is a model of the friendly green ectoplasm ghost from the movie *Ghostbusters* (1984). On the one hand, Germann is playing with a quotation from pop culture; on the other hand, he weaves a motif familiar from art history into the title of his cycle: the artist in his studio. Yet Germann's appropriation of a visual source not only points to the question of the artist's role, it also opens up an intellectual space for the motif between the fields of culture, science and nature, and their apparent contradictions. The figure of the "ghost-maker" who, taking a hands-on approach, blends physical labor with scientific knowledge to venture into the "supernatural," experimenting with it and finally making it his own creation, can be read as a poignant oxymoron, a figure that dissolves such apparent contradictions. Many artists of the twentieth century addressed the chasm between culture, science and nature, and sought to bridge it; see, for instance, Marcel Duchamp in the 1910s with the deliberations that led him to the *Large Glass* (*La mariée mise à nu par ses célibataires, meme [Le grand verre]*, 1915–23), or Joseph Beuys in the 1970s with his multiple *Rose for Direct Democracy* (1973). The latter is a glass measuring cylinder from a laboratory, which contains a rose. Beuys reinterpreted the sharp contrast between these materials as a rallying cry: a social model (direct democracy), spiritual culture (the rose), and the sciences (the measuring cylinder), as achievements that reflect a positive development. So the photograph Germann uses is not just an artist's self-portrait; it also represents a figure of thought that is central to his art—the rejection of Hegel's dictum that art as a vehicle of the quest for truth has come to its end—and distances itself from the idea that art's efforts to achieve autonomy are a process of reflection whose only reference is now art itself. In the world of Germann's art, the fields of art and science, far from being isolated, fluidly pass over into each other; their marriage allows a genuine kind of truth to emerge.

Germann usually presents his works as parts of larger cycles. From the perspective of their formal aesthetics, these look like an assortment of physical instruments and modernist sculptures that, in the exhibition room, take on the appearance of an experimental arrangement whose overarching meaning slowly spreads over them like a finely spun web. At the content level, Germann often uses historic figures, like Napoleon, as points of departure for these experimental arrangements, or motifs from mythology and fantasy, such as lycanthropy (which is to say, the werewolf motif, from the Greek *lukos*, wolf, and *anthropos*, man), or spirit apparitions. He subjects these motifs to a revision that interweaves factual and fictional elements. The resulting narratives always also respond to Germann's interest in physical processes and the transformation of energies. The same interest is apparent in the tactile qualities of his works: many of Germann's objects and sculptures—often made out of materials such as brass (*Saint Helena/Riches from the Depths of the Mountains*) or silver (*The Werewolf of Vienna*)—undergo processes (of activation) in the form of "actions," legible to the beholder only in the residual traces they have left on the works.

As the title implies, the cycle *The Poltergeist Experimental Group (PEG) Applied Spirituality and Physical Spirit Manifestation* is the creation of an anonymous collective that investigates the phenomenon known as a "poltergeist," a spirit whose operation belongs to the realm of parapsychology. The term is used to describe knocking sounds, electrical disturbances, or movements of objects that cannot be traced to an immediate physical cause. Two American parapsychologists, Joseph Gaither Pratt and William G. Roll, have argued that poltergeist phenomena primarily occur in the presence of the pubescent and people with paranormal gifts, and described these manifestations as "recurrent spontaneous psychokinesis."[1] The poltergeist, in other words, is not a "real spirit" but rather a mental projection, a discharge of energy that can take the form of a "psychokinetic effect" in teenagers and others. This paranormal phenomenon marks the center of the mental landscape on which Germann's current cycle of works is based. From this center, he draws a variety of connections and feedback loops that extend, for instance, to the rituals practiced in the boy scout movement (such as the nocturnal baptism ceremonies), but also to the material qualities of organ pipes.[2] The latter are made of an alloy of lead and tin that is highly malleable even at low heat. But an ensemble of organ pipes also forms an instrument that occupies a central position in community life during the liturgy—its sounds can entrance an entire group of people—and so they are a symbol of spirituality as well.

It would be overly simplistic to call Germann's approach, which takes up literary, filmic, historical, and also scientific figures, motifs, and fields of knowledge, mere "sampling": the artist is particularly interested in the

1—See William G. Roll, *The Poltergeist* [1979], Paraview, New York 2004.
2—Robert Baden-Powell, *Scouting for Boys: A Handbook for Instruction in Good Citizenship* [1908], Oxford University Press, Oxford 2004.

interstitial domains such associations open up. Nor can we describe Germann's method as an intertextual procedure that serves to bring out what is already present in and between the texts. In a study entitled "Crossmapping," the literary and cultural scholar Elisabeth Bronfen has proposed that term to describe a method that seeks to reveal "similar concerns" in texts "in different media" by comparing them "along the axis of a shared visual language"—a method, that is to say, that builds on Aby Warburg's iconographic theory of the pathos formula.[3] Bronfen applies this method, for instance, to relate Charlotte Perkins Gilman's short story *The Yellow Wallpaper* (1890) to Francesca Woodmann's photographic works from the 1970s and the Hollywood movie *The Others* (2001) by Alejandro Amenábar, combining their visual formulae and figures of thought in a "fertile" conjunction. This approach, whose initial inspiration lies in the experience of comparative and associative seeing, is dedicated to "unfolding a space of thinking that places aesthetic visual formulae alongside figures of theoretical thought in order to register the cultural aftereffects of forms of internal affect as well as the correspondence between the various formalizations these intensities have undergone" in order to "arrive at a comparative perspective on how cultural intensity has flared up at different times in history as well as in different media."[4]

As beholders, we might perhaps similarly approach Germann's art—which aspires to "cognitive gains"—by reading his cycles as artistic forms of such "crossmapping": a method that connects themes and motifs, bringing out parallels and tracing hitherto invisible lines, where factual and fictional elements interweave to create a new whole.

3—Elisabeth Bronfen, *Crossmappings: Essays zur visuellen Kultur*, Scheidegger & Spiess, Zurich 2009.
4—Ibid., pp. 7–41.

Werwolf, Napoleon, Poltergeist und die Wissenschaft

Ein Gespräch zwischen Florian Germann und Raphael Gygax

RG Du gliederst deine künstlerische Arbeit in grosse Werkzyklen mit Titeln wie etwa *Der Werwolf von Wien* (2009), *St. Helena/Reichtümer aus den Tiefen der Berge* (2010) oder *The Poltergeist Experimental Group (PEG) Applied Spirituality and Physical Spirit Manifestation* (2011) – ein Zyklus, den du gerade für deine Ausstellung im migros museum für gegenwartskunst entwickelst. Allen deinen Arbeiten ist gemeinsam, dass sie für den Betrachter auf den ersten Blick wie eine Art wissenschaftlich-enigmatische Versuchsanordnung wirken. Man hat das Gefühl, dass hier etwas erforscht wird. Wie wichtig ist dir ein «Erkenntnisgewinn» durch deine Arbeit?

FG Für mich persönlich ist ein Erkenntnisgewinn sicherlich zentral – daher spreche ich in Bezug auf meine Arbeit auch gerne von einem «geistigen Ertüchtigungsprogramm». Mich interessiert dementsprechend auch das Künstlerbild der Renaissance: der Universalgelehrte. Jedes Projekt bringt mir Inputs für neue Arbeiten. Es ist vielleicht wichtig, zu sagen, dass es mir weniger um das einzelne Ergebnis geht als vielmehr darum, eine Enzyklopädie von Resultaten zu schaffen, die durch die einzelnen Arbeiten erst ermöglicht wird.

Bei den Themen, die mich als «Untersuchungsgegenstände» interessieren und die auf den ersten Blick teils gegensätzlich erscheinen, versuche ich, eine gemeinsame Mitte «herauszuspüren». Die Zwischenräume sind für mich wichtiger als das Materialisierte. Oder vielleicht könnte man sagen, dass ich die von mir gewählten Thematiken und Phänomene in einen technologischen Prozess umzuwandeln suche, um deren «Geistlichkeit» sichtbar zu machen. Diese Mitte könnte man als Hauptstrang meines Interesses bezeichnen. Mich interessiert es, herauszufinden, was das Ganze zusammenhält. Man könnte diese Arbeitsmethode auch erkenntnisphilosophisch erklären: Du siehst zwei Dinge, und daraus entsteht etwas Drittes. Es gibt dieses Phänomen auch bei der Beulenpest. Da setzen sich zwei Stoffe unter der Haut fest, und durch die Drüse der Pestbeule werden sie zusammen wieder ausgeschieden. Aus zwei Stoffen entsteht also ein dritter – eine warme Fusion eigentlich.

RG Wie arbeitest du? Gehst du wie ein Wissenschaftler von einer These aus, die du beweisen willst? Und welchen Stellenwert hat die Recherche, das heisst die Phase der Untersuchung in deinem Schaffen?

FG Was ich mache, entspricht keiner klassisch-wissenschaftlichen Vorgehensweise, sondern einer intuitiven. Meine Arbeiten funktionieren nach eigenen Prinzipien: Sie bauen zwar auf wissenschaftlichen Erkenntnissen auf, folgen jedoch ihren eigenen Gesetzen.

Die Triebfeder für meine Projekte ist immer die Frage, wieso etwas so ist, wie es ist, und eben nicht anders. Zudem arbeite ich additiv und prozesshaft. Ich beginne an einem Punkt und gehe von diesem zum nächsten. Am Schluss steht dann eine Art Schaltungsschema wie bei einem Stromkreislauf. Dieses erzeugt die geistigen Energien zwischen den einzelnen Teilen. Zu Beginn des Arbeitsprozesses weiss ich jedoch nicht, wohin es führen und wie dieses Schaltungsschema aussehen wird.

Die Recherche dient mir dazu, eine spezifische Form zu schaffen. Am Anfang gibt es lediglich eine skulpturale Hülle, die ich als eine Art weichen Ballon verstehe, den ich dann mit Informationen fülle – daraus ergibt sich die konkrete Form. Ich bin versucht, den Begriff «literarische Plastik» zu benutzen. Vielleicht macht eine solche Bezeichnung jedoch wenig Sinn. Aber man kann sagen, dass sich dank des Recherchematerials ein Körper zu bilden beginnt.

RG Für deine Arbeiten benutzt du häufig Metalle wie Messing oder Silber – also Materialien, die für ihre Formbarkeit bekannt sind und die in der Literatur eine aussergewöhnliche Psychologisierung erfahren haben – man denke etwa an die Rolle des Silbers im Werwolf-Mythos. Gerade die Alchemie – am bekanntesten sind wohl die Versuche der Goldsynthese – hat sich immer mit einer Art Psychologisierung von Metallen beschäftigt.

FG Mich interessiert tatsächlich nicht die reine Oberflächenbeschaffenheit des Materials, obwohl ich ursprünglich von der Bildhauerei her komme. Mein Augenmerk liegt eher auf dessen physikalischen und psychologischen Merkmalen. Oder genauer gesagt: Es geht mir um die spezifischen Eigenschaften eines Materials – zum Beispiel seine elektrische Leitfähigkeit, seine «Giftigkeit» oder Formbarkeit. Messing etwa hat die Fähigkeit, Spuren und Absonderungen des Körpers aufzunehmen. Jede körperliche Absonderung, beispielsweise Schweiss, jede Berührung schreibt sich in dieses Material ein. Das geht nicht mehr weg. Dieser Oxidationsvorgang spielt auch in meiner neuen Arbeit eine grosse Rolle. Ich habe ein Fahrzeug konstruiert, welches eine Sitzoberfläche aus Messing hat, jedoch keine Bremse. Dies löst während der Fahrt einen Angstzustand aus, welcher die Angsttranspiration durch die Pobacke und die Füsse direkt auf die Messingoberfläche überträgt. Dadurch entstehen Abdrücke und Spuren, welche sich auf der Oberfläche einschreiben – Aktionsspuren.

Das Silber wiederum dient in der Medizin als Katalysator – als Element, das den eigentlichen Wirkstoff des Medikaments transportiert.

RG Fast alle deine Arbeiten thematisieren die Transformation von Energien und Materialien. Zudem stellen sie einen Gegenentwurf zur klassisch-linearen Erzählung dar. Dadurch können deine Arbeiten in einer kunsthistorischen Linie verortet werden, die von Positionen wie der von Joseph Beuys und Chris Burden bis hin zu derjenigen von Jason Rhoades und Matthew Barney reicht.

FG Ja – ich könnte diese Künstler alle als meine «Freunde» bezeichnen. Deren Arbeiten haben sowohl in formalästhetischer als auch in inhaltlicher Sicht mein Schaffen enorm geprägt, und eigentlich gibt es für mich seither nichts richtig Gutes mehr. Zudem ist das Selbstverständnis dieser Künstler dem meinen sehr verwandt: Auch ich möchte von dem, was ich mache, permanent umgeben sein. Sich als Teil seines Werks zu sehen, ist Bestandteil meiner Arbeitsweise und gibt einen gewissen Schutz beziehungsweise bietet ein Versteck. In der Auseinandersetzung mit anderen künstlerischen Positionen trifft man fast automatisch auf Denkansätze, die dem eigenen Ansatz ähneln – etwa die von Beuys oder Burden.

RG In deinen älteren Arbeiten wie etwa dem *Werwolf*-Zyklus hast du eine Reihe von Zeichnungen als Teil der Ausstellungen gezeigt. In der letzten Zeit hast du darauf jedoch verzichtet. Welche Rolle spielt das Medium Zeichnung momentan in deinem Werk?

FG Zu Beginn meiner künstlerischen Tätigkeit habe ich meine Zeichnungen oft als Serien im Ausstellungskontext gezeigt oder als Buch veröffentlicht. Die Zeichnungen des *Werwolf*-Zyklus entstanden ursprünglich als Storyboard für einen Film. Ich hatte für den ORF – es geht ja um einen Werwolf, der in Wien ist – eine *Tatort*-Folge geplant. Leider wurde mein Vorschlag abgelehnt.

Zeichnungen dienen dazu, dem Betrachter Strukturen schnell aufzuzeigen und für ihn nachvollziehbar zu machen. Für meine aktuelle Arbeit sind sie jedoch überflüssig – ich zeige sie daher nicht mehr im Ausstellungskontext. Ich zeichne aber noch privat. Momentan bevorzuge ich dieses Moment der Leerstelle. Ich denke, die Zeichnungen lenken zu sehr ab und die Leute können sich zu wenig auf die anderen Arbeiten konzentrieren.

RG Das Moment der Leerstelle, von dem du eben gesprochen hast, steht in Verbindung mit einem weiteren Thema, das mich im Zusammenhang mit deinen Arbeiten interessiert: dasjenige der Lesbarkeit deiner Werke für den Betrachter. Wie sehr interessiert dich dieser Aspekt?

FG Es gibt schon erklärende Momente in meinen Arbeiten, mit denen ich versuche, die einzelnen Teile zusammenzuhalten beziehungsweise zu verbinden. Einerseits habe ich den Anspruch, dass das Publikum die Zusammenhänge in meiner Arbeit nachvollziehen kann – andererseits ist mir aber auch daran gelegen, dass es einen eigenen Zugang zu den Arbeiten entwickelt. Es geht mir nicht darum, dass der Betrachter meine Gedanken vollständig nachvollzieht. Zudem handelt es sich ja auch um Bildstrukturen, die über ein «assoziatives Sehen» funktionieren. In Bezug auf die Lesbarkeit meiner Arbeit ist auch wichtig, festzuhalten, dass ganz vieles gar nicht aufgeht. Es handelt sich nicht um eine klassische Erzählung, die mit einem Anfang und Ende versehen ist. Meine Arbeiten sind vielmehr durch eine «Pseudologie», nennen wir es mal so, also durch eine individuelle Logik gekennzeichnet. Sie gehen von meinem Wissen und Nichtwissen aus. Bei jeder Arbeit handelt es sich um ein Experiment – dementsprechend können sich auch Sackgassen ergeben, die ich bewusst stehen lasse. Manchmal knüpfe ich an eine solche auch an, woraus dann ein weiteres Projekt entsteht.

RG Während deiner Ausstellungen hast du auch immer wieder Führungen gemacht, die eine Art «lecture performance» darstellen. Dabei hast du meist ein Narrationsnetz zwischen den einzelnen Arbeiten gesponnen sowie die Grenzen zwischen Fakten und Fiktion verwischt. Sind diese Führungen ein integraler Bestandteil deiner Arbeiten?

FG Die Führungen habe ich von Beginn meiner Ausstellungstätigkeit an gemacht, und ich habe sie auch immer als integralen Bestandteil meiner Arbeit angesehen. Das Format ist jedoch nicht gegen Misserfolge gefeit, und so zweifle ich auch immer wieder an ihm. Für mich ging es bei den Führungen in erster Linie um (Wissens-)Vermittlung – was jedoch immer in Konflikt mit meiner Sprachfähigkeit stand, die manchmal versagt hat. Ich habe auch schon Führungen gemacht, bei denen die Leute nur noch gelacht haben. Aber ich meine das eigentlich schon ernst. Wenn man so lange an etwas arbeitet, beginnt man ja auch, daran zu glauben. Im Moment beschäftigt mich die Frage, wie ich dieses Format in Zukunft handhaben möchte oder ob nicht eher jemand anderes das für mich übernehmen könnte. Aber ich halte dieses Vermittlungsmoment für äusserst interessant und wichtig, sodass es auch in Zukunft in der einen oder anderen Form Bestandteil meiner Arbeit sein wird. In meiner neuen Installation für das migros museum für gegenwartskunst wird es zum Beispiel über Tonband Stimmen aus dem Off geben, die einen solchen Beitrag ersetzen werden.

RG Für deinen neuen Werkzyklus hast du zudem geplant, dass er vor Ausstellungseröffnung durch eine Reihe von Aktionen aktiviert wird. Jede Arbeit wird dabei einem Prozess unterworfen – und das unter Ausschluss der Öffentlichkeit.

FG Die Aktionen stehen in einem zeitlichen Verhältnis zu den Objekten. Die Objekte brauchen eine Aktivierung, und diese muss an dem Ort stattfinden, an dem die Werke ausgestellt werden. So bleiben auch die Spuren sichtbar. Vielleicht wird es eine Rauchstelle an der Decke geben oder Bremsspuren von Gummi auf dem Boden. Es gibt beispielsweise eine Arbeit von Jannis Kounellis in der Halle für Neue Kunst in Schaffhausen, für die er einen Kamin mit Holz aus Schaffhausen eingeheizt hat. Dabei bildete sich an der Museumsdecke ein Russfleck, der immer noch sichtbar ist. Einige meiner Arbeiten funktionieren ähnlich.

Es gibt das Objekt, seinen Platz in der Geschichte, dadurch entsteht seine Handlung. Oftmals werden giftige Stoffe bei der Aktivierung von Motoren freigesetzt, oder manche Materialien zersetzen sich, verändern sich, und das birgt auch immer eine Gefahr. All das möchte ich dem Betrachter ersparen. Ich gehe aber davon aus, dass die Spannung erhalten, dass der Entstehungsprozess weiterhin spürbar bleibt.

RG Ich würde gerne noch einmal auf das erzählerische Moment in deinen Arbeiten zurückkommen. Wie würdest du deine Erzählungen in ihrer strukturellen Anordnung beschreiben?

FG Ich bediene mich keines feststehenden Erzählkonzepts. Es ist jedes Mal ein anderes, und es ergibt sich aus der Arbeit heraus. Während des Entstehungsprozesses zeigt sich, ob und welche verschiedenen Teile noch ausgearbeitet werden müssen und welche nicht. Der neue Zyklus beispielsweise besitzt einen strangartigen Aufbau mit verschiedenen Zweigen. Ausgehend von einer Mittellinie, bilden sich verschiedene Narrationen. Beim *St. Helena*-Zyklus war die Erzählung eher wie ein Kreis angeordnet: Sie konnte von jedem Objekt aus beginnen.

Oftmals orientiere ich mich auch an unterschiedlichen Erzählgenres. Für den *Werwolf von Wien* beispielsweise habe ich mir viele Filme von Alfred Hitchcock angeschaut und analysiert, wie man einen Spannungsbogen aufbaut. Der Begriff «MacGuffin», den Hitchcock geprägt hat, wurde für mich wichtig. Darunter versteht man, dass mehr oder weniger beliebige Objekte oder Personen in einem Film dazu dienen, die Handlung voranzutreiben oder gar aufzulösen, ohne selbst von besonderem Interesse zu sein. Die Personen zeichnen sich dementsprechend meist durch eine sehr flache Psychostruktur aus. Dieses Stilmittel ist weit verbreitet, um Spannung über eine gesamte Handlung hinweg aufrechtzuerhalten. Hitchcocks Filmsprache hat mich dazu angeregt, die Gestalt des Werwolfs im Zyklus selber gar nicht vorkommen zu lassen – sozusagen die Abwesenheit des titelgebenden Protagonisten, um den sich jedoch alles dreht.

RG Und beim *St. Helena*-Zyklus?

FG Beim *St. Helena*-Zyklus habe ich mich von amerikanischen Folk-Art-Museen inspirieren lassen. Dort habe ich eine Ausstellung über den amerikanischen Mathematiker John Nash gesehen, der für seine Forschung über Spieltheorien bekannt ist. In den 1990er Jahren gewann er sogar den Nobelpreis für seine Untersuchungen. Er selbst erkrankte mit 30 Jahren an Schizophrenie. Den meisten wird John Nash wohl durch das Biopic *A Beautiful Mind* (2001) bekannt sein. Als Arbeitsinstrument nutzte er rauminstallative Pinboards, an denen er sich obsessiv abarbeitete. In der Ausstellung gab es unterschiedliche Exponate, beispielsweise Kleider von ihm und eine Rekonstruktion seines Arbeits- und Schlafzimmers. So etwas wollte ich auch machen – einfach mit der Figur von Napoleon. Die Strategie der Umschreibung einer Person mithilfe von einzelnen Gegenständen hat mich fasziniert.

RG In welchem Verhältnis stehen bei dir Fakt und Fiktion? Woher weiss der Betrachter, was erfunden ist und was nicht? Und wie führst du ihn aufs Glatteis?

FG Meine Arbeiten werden oftmals mit «das ist ja alles nur erfunden» kommentiert, was jedoch gar nicht stimmt. Würde sich jemand die Mühe machen, die Dinge selber zu recherchieren, würde er herausfinden, dass mindestens drei Viertel, wenn nicht sogar alles stimmt. Im Zuge meiner Recherchen für den *St. Helena*-Zyklus etwa, bei dem Napoleon als Protagonist fungiert, habe ich herausgefunden, dass dieser fast 20 Jahre lang Besitzer des Mount Rushmore war. Das wollte so mancher gar nicht glauben. Auf dieser Tatsache aufbauend, habe ich dann meine *Mount Rushmore-Gutzon Borglum*-Aktion erarbeitet. Mithilfe einer Schaukelkonstruktion, die an der Decke angemacht war, habe ich an der nahen Wand ein Napoleon-Relief modelliert, welches sich auf die Geschichte von Gutzon Borglum, des Bildhauers und Ingenieurs des Memorials, bezieht.

Für meine Arbeiten bediene ich mich aber immer auch fiktiver Momente, um die Fakten anzureichern; damit man sich diese überhaupt anschaut. Vielleicht könnte man auch die Brücke als Metapher benutzen: Die Brückenpfeiler sind die Fakten, und der Überbau beziehungsweise die Überspannung ist die Fiktion, die überhaupt erst einen «Spannungsbogen» erzeugen kann. Die Fiktion benutze ich im Grunde nur, um die Form zu vollenden. Als Künstler habe ich natürlich die Freiheit, das zu tun, und ich muss mich nicht an eine wissenschaftliche Methodik halten.

RG Der neue Werkzyklus ist – wie der Titel schon impliziert – dem Poltergeist gewidmet. Was interessiert dich an dieser Figur beziehungsweise diesem Phänomen?

FG Der Poltergeist ist ein unfassbares, meines Erachtens jedoch wahrnehmbares Phänomen, dem ebenso physiologische wie psychologische Ursachen zugrunde liegen. Es kann in Form von telekinetischen Erscheinungen auftreten, sich aber auch als räumliche Temperaturveränderung zeigen. Es tritt vor allem bei männlichen Personen zwischen dem 13. und dem 17. Lebensjahr auf und ist auf die schnelle Entwicklung eines jungen Menschen in der Pubertät zurückzuführen.

Beim Poltergeist handelt es sich um eine Form der Imagination. In der Literatur werden diese Erscheinungen als körperlos beschrieben; das Medium kann aber als physikalisches Phänomen sichtbar werden – etwa indem es Gegenstände verschiebt oder eine Spur aus Ektoplasma hinterlässt. Der Titel des Werks bezieht sich aber eher auf die Arbeit des Parapsychologen als auf die Erscheinungen selbst. Die Tätigkeit des Parapsychologen ist dem Beruf des Künstlers nämlich nicht unähnlich.

RG Im Zusammenhang mit dem Poltergeist hast du eben das Phänomen des Ektoplasmas erwähnt – die Stofflichkeit oder Absonderung eines Geistes. Ich als mediensozialisierter Betrachter verorte diese Phänomene eher in Geisterfilmen.

FG Das Ektoplasma ist ein synästhetisches Material, das auf körperliche Stimmungen reagiert. Die Beschäftigung mit diesem Phänomen war für mich der Ausgangspunkt, um Körper zu schaffen, die physikalisch auf ihr Umfeld reagieren. Ektoplasma kommt natürlich auch in Filmen wie *Ghostbusters* (1984) vor, in dem es eine Hauptrolle spielt. Es ist aber vor allem ein wichtiges «Untersuchungsmaterial» in der Parapsychologie, findet sich aber auch in der Zellbiologie, wo es die gleichen Eigenschaften aufweist: Auch dort handelt es sich um ein Material, das sich durch sein Umfeld verändert. Generell sind für mich eher Materialien interessant, die ein Eigenleben besitzen beziehungsweise entwickeln. Nur so können Dinge und Spuren entstehen, die sich meinem Einfluss entziehen.

In mehreren Arbeiten benutze ich beispielsweise Orgelpfeifen, die meist aus einer Blei-Zinn-Mischung bestehen und folglich sehr formbar sind – und deshalb auch in Bezug auf die Energieverlagerung für mich von Interesse sind. Ich habe einen Ofen gebaut, der die Hitze direkt in einen Orgelpfeifenkamin hineinlenkt. Sie werden sich durch diese Handlung deformieren – wie, ist noch unklar. Der Kontrollverlust, der sich aufgrund der Eigendynamik der Materialien vollzieht, widerspricht dabei meiner Vorliebe, Kontrolle über diese zu haben, sie zu beherrschen.

Das Gespräch wurde im August 2011 in zwei Teilen geführt und anschliessend mit Unterstützung von Judith Welter und Stefanie Kleefeld transkribiert und redigiert.

Werewolf, Napoleon, Poltergeist, and Science

A Conversation Between Florian Germann and Raphael Gygax

RG You group your works of art in large series that bear titles such as *The Werewolf of Vienna* (2009), *Saint Helena—Riches from the Depths of the Mountains* (2010), or *The Poltergeist Experimental Group (PEG) Applied Spirituality and Physical Spirit Manifestation*—the last of these is a cycle you are currently developing for your show at the migros museum für gegenwartskunst. All your works have a feature in common, in that they initially strike the viewer as an enigmatic sort of scientific experimental arrangement. There's a sense that some kind of research is being conducted. How important is it to you that your work generates a "cognitive gain?"

FG To me personally, cognitive gain is certainly a central aspect—that's why I also often speak of my work as a "spiritual fitness program." I am accordingly also interested in how the Renaissance pictured the artist: as a universally learned person, a polymath. Every project gives me input for new works. I should perhaps emphasize that my focus is not so much on the individual result; instead, I am trying to create an encyclopedia of results that would not be possible without the individual works.

When I take up the issues that draw my interest as "objects of study"—at first glance, they sometimes seem in contradiction with each other—I try to get a "feel" for their common core. The interstices are more important to me than what is materially present. Or perhaps one might say that I try to transform the issues and phenomena I choose into a technological process, in order to render their "spirituality" visible. One might describe that core as the primary strand running through my interests. I am trying to find out what it is that holds everything together. One might also give an epistemological explanation of this method: you see two things, and a third emerges from them. The same phenomenon exists in the case of the bubonic plague. Two substances take hold beneath the skin before being excreted together through the gland of the bubo. So two substances are transformed into a third—an instance of warm fusion, really.

RG How do you work? Do you begin with a hypothesis that you want to prove, like a scientist? And how important is the research, that is to say, the analytical phase, in your creative process?

FG What I do does not conform to any classical scientific method; my approach is intuitive. My works function in accordance with principles of their own: they build on scientific insight, but follow their own laws.

The driving force behind my projects is always the question: why is something the way it is, and not a different way? My work is also process-oriented and additive. I begin at one point and then proceed from that point to the next. Ultimately, something like a circuit configuration emerges, not unlike an electrical circuit, which generates the spiritual energies between the individual components. But when I begin work on something, I do not yet know where it is going to go, or what this circuit configuration will look like.

Research allows me to create a specific form. At first there is nothing but a sculptural shell, which I see as a sort of soft balloon that I then fill with information—that's how the concrete form emerges. I am tempted to use the term "literary sculpture." But perhaps that sort of label makes little sense. Yet one may say that the research material initiates the formation of a body.

RG You often use metals such as brass or silver for your works—materials, that is to say, that are known for their malleability and have been fraught with extraordinary psychological symbolism in literature; we could, for example, cite the role silver plays in the werewolf myth. Alchemy, in particular—the best-known example of which would be the attempts to synthesize gold—has always been occupied with a sort of psychologization of metals.

FG I am indeed not interested in the pure surface character of the material, even though my original training is in sculpture. My focus is more on its physical and psychological features. Or to put it more precisely: I'm interested in a material's specific qualities—in its electrical conductivity, for instance, its "toxicity," or its malleability. Brass, for example, has the ability to absorb traces and secretions of the body. Any bodily secretion, such as sweat, any physical contact is inscribed in this material. There's no removing it anymore. This process of oxidation also plays a major role in my new work. I've constructed a vehicle that has a brass seat but no brakes. As you ride it, that causes a state of anxiety that transmits the transpiration associated with fear via the buttocks and the feet straight to the brass surface. Imprints and traces result that are inscribed on the surface—traces of action.

Silver, on the other hand, serves as a catalyst in medicine—as an element that transports the actual active ingredient in a medication.

RG Almost all your works address the transformation of energies and materials. They also represent a challenge to the classical linear narrative. That allows us to situate your works in an art-historical line that extends from positions such as those of Joseph Beuys and Chris Burden to those of Jason Rhoads and Matthew Barney.

FG True—I might describe all these artists as my "friends." Their works have had a profound influence on my own creativity in terms both of formal aesthetics and of content, and there hasn't been anything that I think is really good since them. Then, too, the self-conception of these artists is closely akin to my own: I also want to be permanently surrounded by what I do. My approach includes seeing myself as part of the work, which offers me a certain amount of protection or, you might say, a hideout. When you engage the positions of other artists, you almost inevitably encounter approaches that resemble your own—Beuys's and Burden's, for example.

RG In your earlier works, such as the *Werewolf* cycle, you presented a number of drawings as part of the exhibitions. More recently, you have eschewed the inclusion of drawings. What role does the medium of drawing play in your work right now?

FG When I began my career as an artist, I often presented my drawings as series in the context of exhibitions, or published them as books. The drawings in the *Werewolf* cycle were originally created as a storyboard for a film. I had planned an episode of the crime drama *Tatort* for the Austrian public broadcasting station, about a werewolf in Vienna. Unfortunately, they rejected my proposal.

Drawings let me quickly illustrate structures in a way that helps the viewer understand them. For my current work, however, they are unnecessary—that's why I no longer show them in the exhibition context. But I still draw privately. Right now I prefer this idea of a blank. I think the drawings are too much of a distraction; it makes people focus too little on the other works.

RG The idea of the blank you just mentioned is related to another issue that I'm interested in with regard to your art: the question of the legibility of your works for the beholder. How much does that matter to you?

FG There are indeed explanatory features about my works, where I try to hold the individual components together or to connect them. On the one hand I aspire to enable the audience to understand the structural connections in my work—but on the other hand it's also important to me that people develop their own approaches to the works. My aim, after all, is not to make the beholder reconstruct my ideas in every respect. Then, too, these are visual structures that function by way of a form of "associative seeing." With regard to the legibility of my work, I should also note that there's much about it that doesn't add up. This is not a classical narrative that has a beginning and an end. My works are instead defined by a "pseudology," let's use that term, which is to say, by an individual logic. Their point of departure is my knowledge, and what I don't know. Each work is an experiment—and so works I produce may also prove to be cul-de-sacs that I deliberately leave in place. Sometimes I take up such a cul-de-sac later on, which then gives rise to a new project.

RG You've often held guided tours of your exhibitions that may be described as "lecture performances." You have usually spun a narrative network between the individual works, blurring the lines separating fact from fiction. Are these tours an integral component of your work?

FG I've done these guided tours ever since I started exhibiting, and I've also always seen them as an integral part of my work. But the format is not immune to mishap, and so I've repeatedly had my doubts about it. My aim with these tours was primarily to communicate (knowledge)—and that has time and again conflicted with my linguistic abilities, which have sometimes failed me. I've also held guided tours where people ended up laughing the whole time. But at bottom I really am serious about this. When you've worked on something for so long, you also start believing in it. Right now I'm thinking hard about how I want to handle this format in the future, or whether someone else might do the tours in my stead. But I do think that communicating the art is an extraordinarily interesting and important element, and so it will continue to be part of my work in one form or another. My new installation, for example, will include recorded voices played from a tape that will stand in for a live segment.

RG For your new cycle of works, you also plan on activating it in a series of actions before the exhibition opens. Each work will undergo some kind of process—but the events will be closed to the public.

FG There is a relationship of time that exists between the actions and the objects. The objects need activation, and that activation has to take place at the site where the objects are on display. That's how the traces remain visible, too. Perhaps there will be a smoke stain on the ceiling, or rubber skid marks on the floor. For example, there is a work Jannis Kounellis created for the Halle für Neue Kunst, Schaffhausen, for which he fired up a fireplace with wood from Schaffhausen. A soot stain formed on the ceiling of the museum that is still visible. Some of my works function in a similar fashion.

There is the object, its place in history, and that gives rise to its action. The activation of motors often releases toxic substances, or some materials disintegrate or undergo modification, and that always also poses risks. I want to spare the beholders all of that. But I do assume that the tension will be sustained, that the process of a work's genesis will still be palpable.

RG I'd like to come back one more time to the narrative aspect of your works. How would you describe your narratives in their structural arrangement?

FG I don't employ a fixed narrative concept. It's a different one each time, and it grows out of the work. As I work on something, it becomes apparent which individual parts still need more elaboration, and which parts don't. The new cycle, for example, is structured like a central strand with several branches. Departing from a central line, various narratives take shape. In the *Saint Helena* cycle, the narrative was more circular in structure: it might start with any one of the objects.

I often also look to different genres of cinematic narrative for inspiration. For *The Werewolf of Vienna*, for example, I watched many of Alfred Hitchcock's movies and analyzed how you build an arc of suspense. The concept of the "MacGuffin," a term Hitchcock introduced, became important to me. It describes more or less arbitrary objects or characters in a movie that serve to move the action along or even bring about the resolution, without being of particular interest in themselves. These characters are accordingly usually distinguished by very flat psychological structures. It's a stylistic device that's widely used to sustain the tension throughout an entire plot. Hitchcock's filmic language inspired me to have the werewolf not even make an appearance anywhere in the cycle—the absence of the eponymous protagonist, as it were, even as everything revolves around him.

RG And in the *Saint Helena* cycle?

FG For the *Saint Helena* cycle, I drew inspiration from American museums of folk art. In one of them, I saw an exhibition about the American mathematician John Nash, who is known for his research in game theory. He even won the Nobel Prize for his studies in the 1990s. But he suffered from schizophrenia from the age of thirty. Most people will probably know John Nash from the biopic *A Beautiful Mind* (2001). He worked with installations of pin boards filling entire rooms, on which he worked obsessively. The exhibition included a variety of exhibits, including clothes he had worn as well as a reconstruction of his study and bedroom. I wanted to do something similar—just about the character Napoleon. The strategy of portraying a person through simple objects fascinated me.

RG What's the relationship between fact and fiction in your work? How does the beholder know what's invention and what isn't? And how do you lead him up the garden path?

FG Many people respond to my work by saying, "it's all pure fabrication," when that is not true at all. If someone went to the trouble of researching these things for himself, he would find out that at least three quarters are true, if not everything. During my research for the *Saint Helena* cycle, for example, in which Napoleon is the protagonist, I found out that Napoleon had owned Mount Rushmore for almost twenty years. Some people absolutely refused to believe that. Building on that fact, I then developed my *Mount Rushmore–Gutzon Borglum* action. Using a swing construction suspended from the ceiling, I modeled a Napoleon relief on the nearby wall that makes reference to the story of Gutzon Borglum, the sculptor and engineer who created the memorial.

But my work always also includes fictional components to enrich the facts, so that people will look at them in the first place. Perhaps I might also use the metaphor of a bridge: the facts are the bridge's pillars, and the superstructure or suspended structure is the fiction, without which there would be no "arc of suspense." At bottom, I use fiction only to complete the form. Of course, as an artist I enjoy the freedom to do so, not being bound to some scientific methodology.

RG As the title implies, the new cycle of works is devoted to the poltergeist. What was it about this figure, or phenomenon that drew your interest?

FG The poltergeist is an intangible and nonetheless, I believe, perceptible phenomenon that arises from physiological as well as psychological causes. It can take the form of telekinetic apparitions, but also become manifest as changes of temperature in space. It appears most frequently to male adolescents between the ages of thirteen and seventeen, and can be traced to the rapid development a young person undergoes during puberty.

The poltergeist is a form of imagination. The literature describes these apparitions as having no body; but the medium can become visible as a physical phenomenon—by moving objects around, for instance, or by leaving a trace that consists of ectoplasm. The title of the work, however, refers to the occupation of the parapsychologist rather than to the apparitions themselves. For what the parapsychologist does bears some similarity to the artist's trade.

RG In relation to the poltergeist, you've just mentioned the phenomenon of ectoplasm—the substance or secretion of a spirit. As someone who's been socialized by the media, I would tend to think that these phenomena have their place in ghost story movies.

FG Ectoplasm is a synaesthetic material that responds to physical moods. My study of this phenomenon led me to create bodies that would respond physically to their environments. Ectoplasm, of course, also appears in movies such as *Ghostbusters* (1984), where it plays a leading role. But it is first and foremost an important "material of study" in parapsychology, and can also be found in cell biology, where it displays the same characteristics: there too it is a material that changes depending on its environment. I am more generally interested in materials that lead, or begin to lead, lives of their own. That's what makes it possible for things and traces to develop that elude my control.

For example, I use organ pipes in several works; they are usually made of a mixture of lead and pewter, which renders them highly malleable—that's also why they draw my interest with regard to the displacement of energy. I built a stove that conducts the heat directly into a chimney made of organ-pipes. Its operation will deform them, though it is not yet clear how. The loss of control I suffer due to the inherent dynamism of the materials runs counter to my penchant to maintain control over them, to micromanage them.

The conversation was held in two parts in August 2011, and subsequently transcribed and edited with the assistance of Judith Welter and Stefanie Kleefeld.

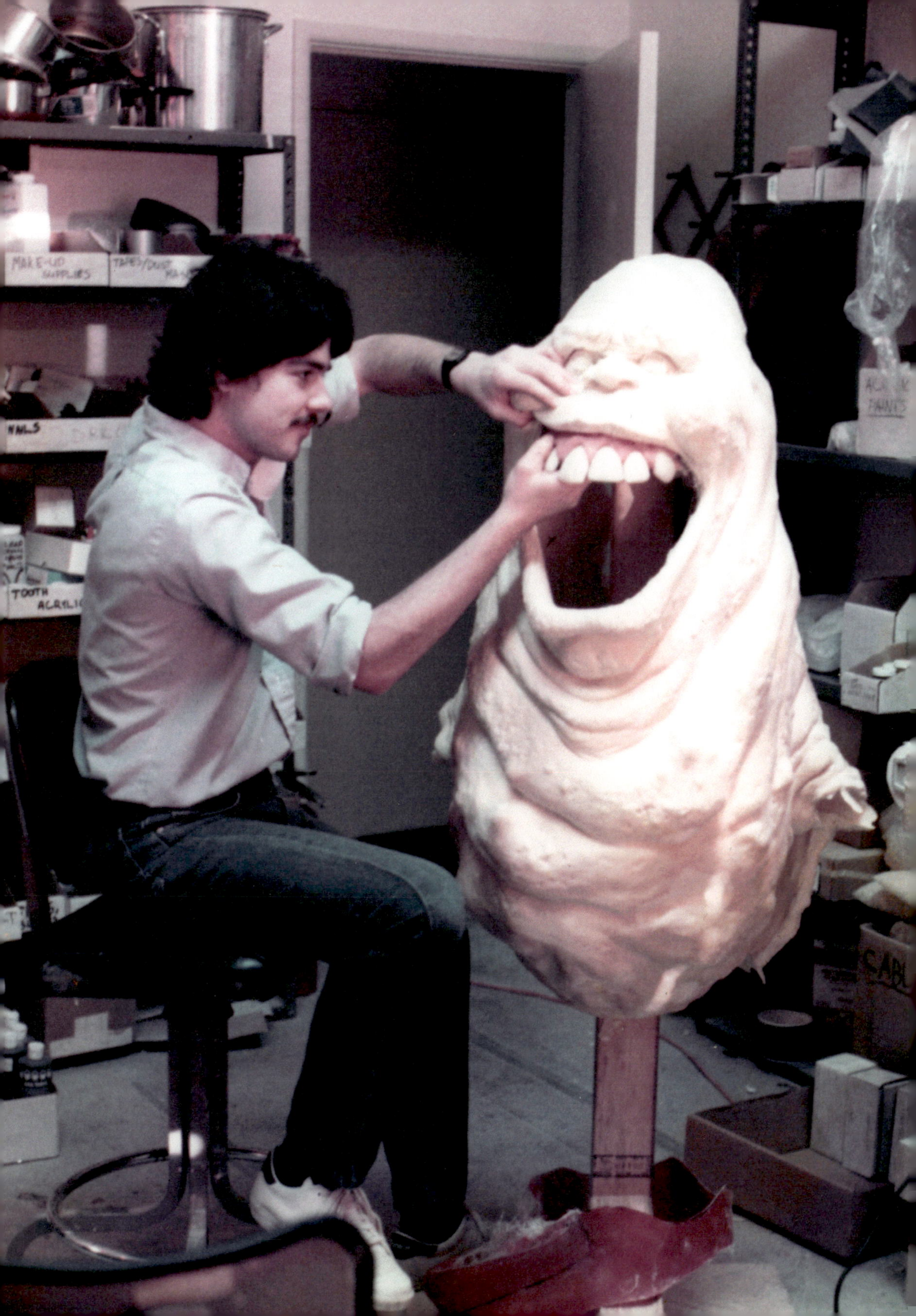
MAKE-UP SUPPLIES
TOOTH

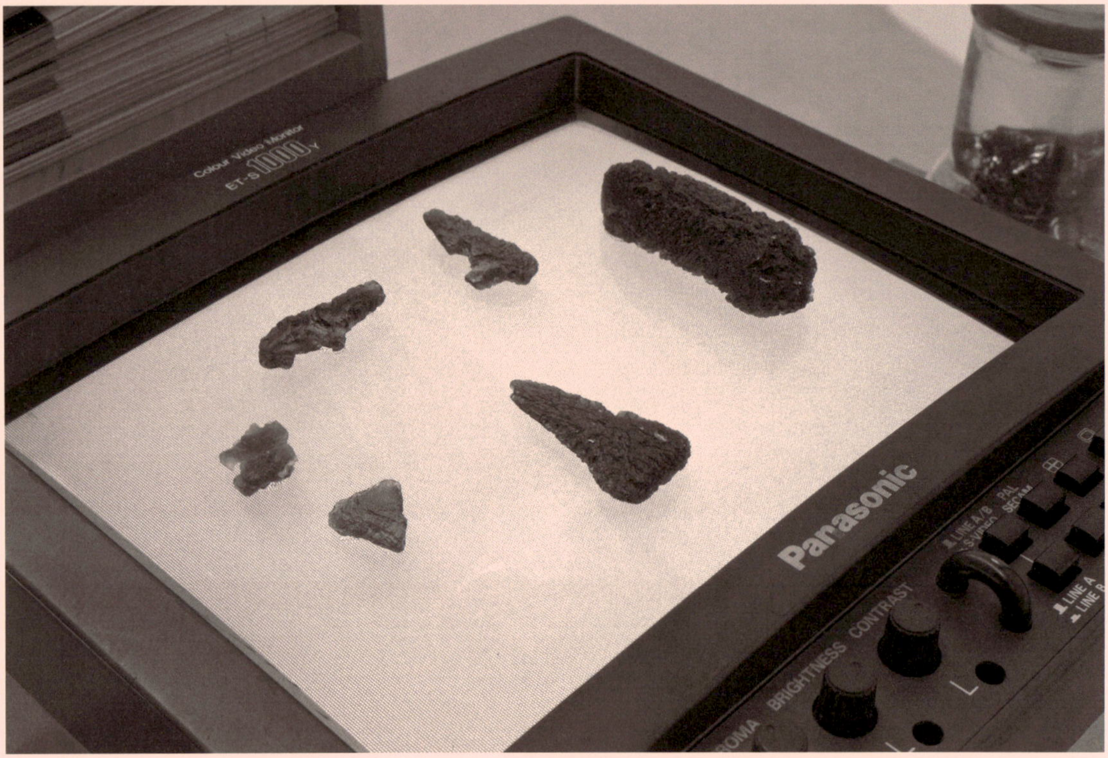

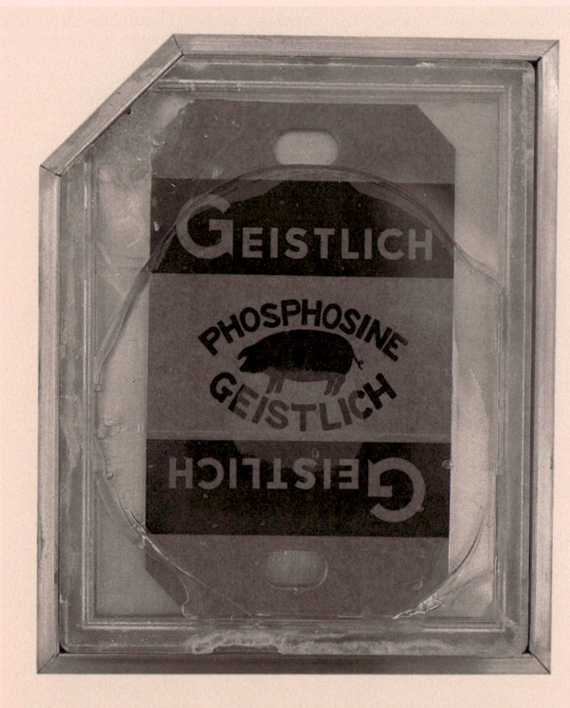
GEISTLICH
PHOSPHOSINE
GEISTLICH
GEISTLICH

The Poltergeist Experimental Group (PEG) Applied Spirituality and Physical Spirit Manifestation

2011

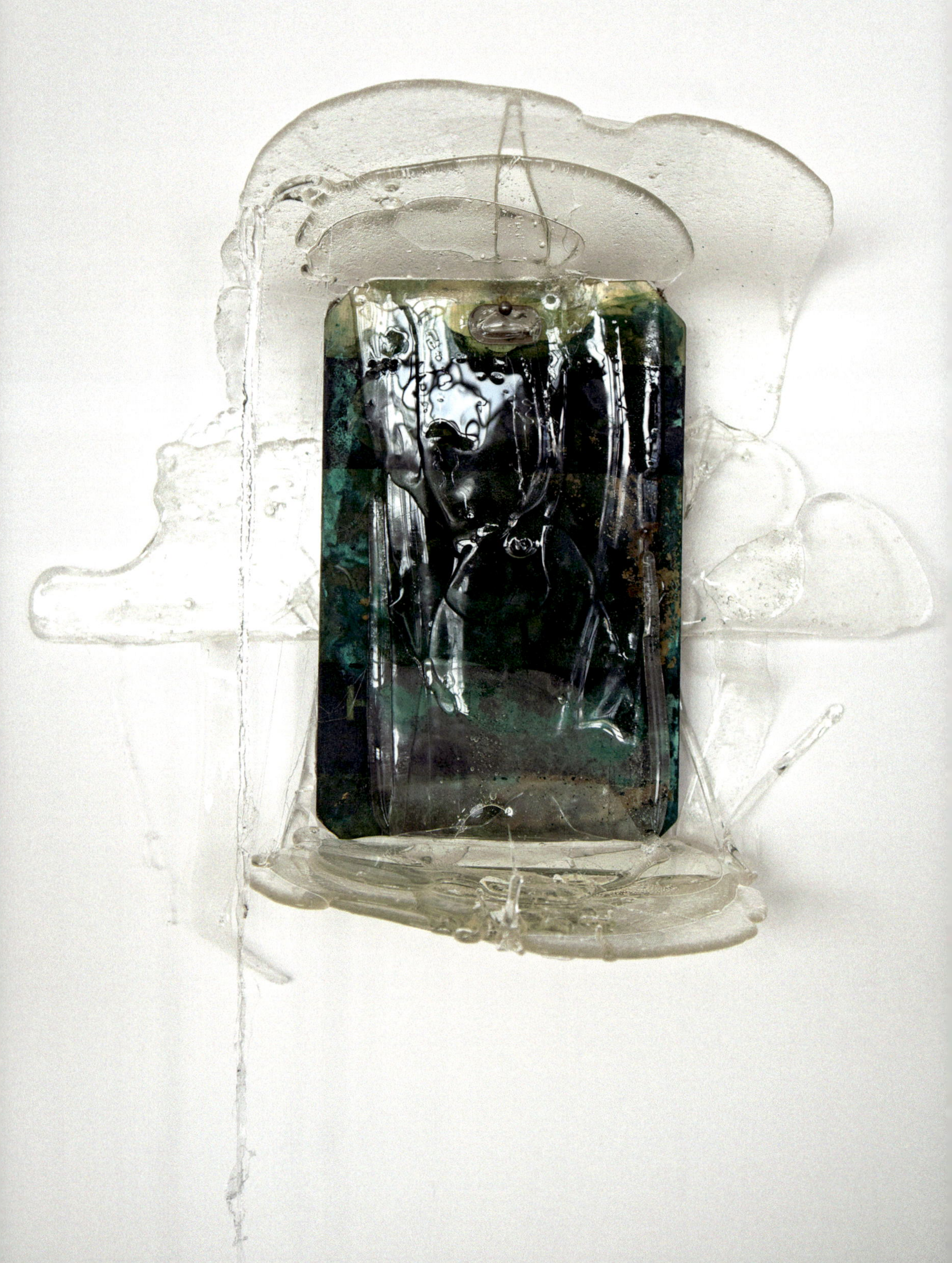

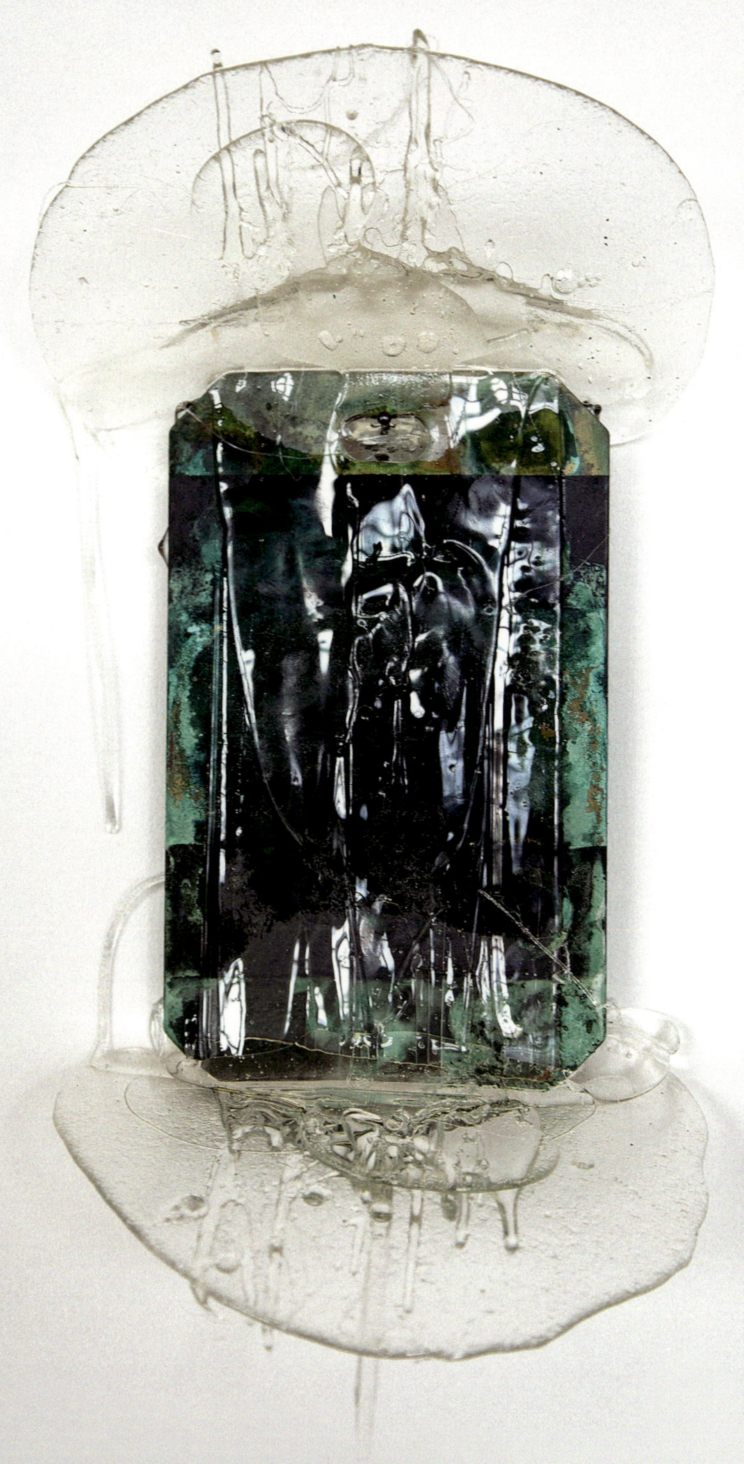

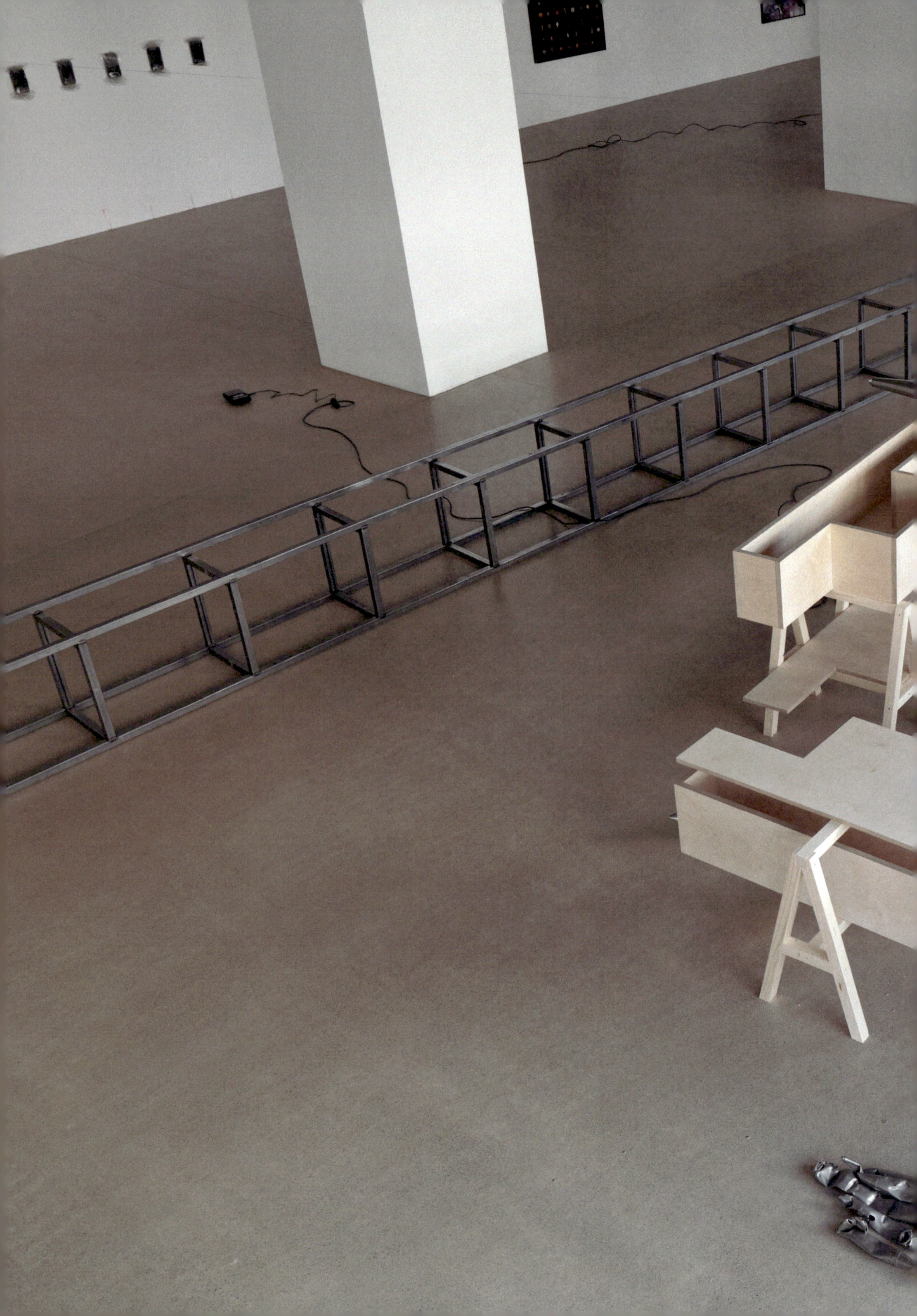

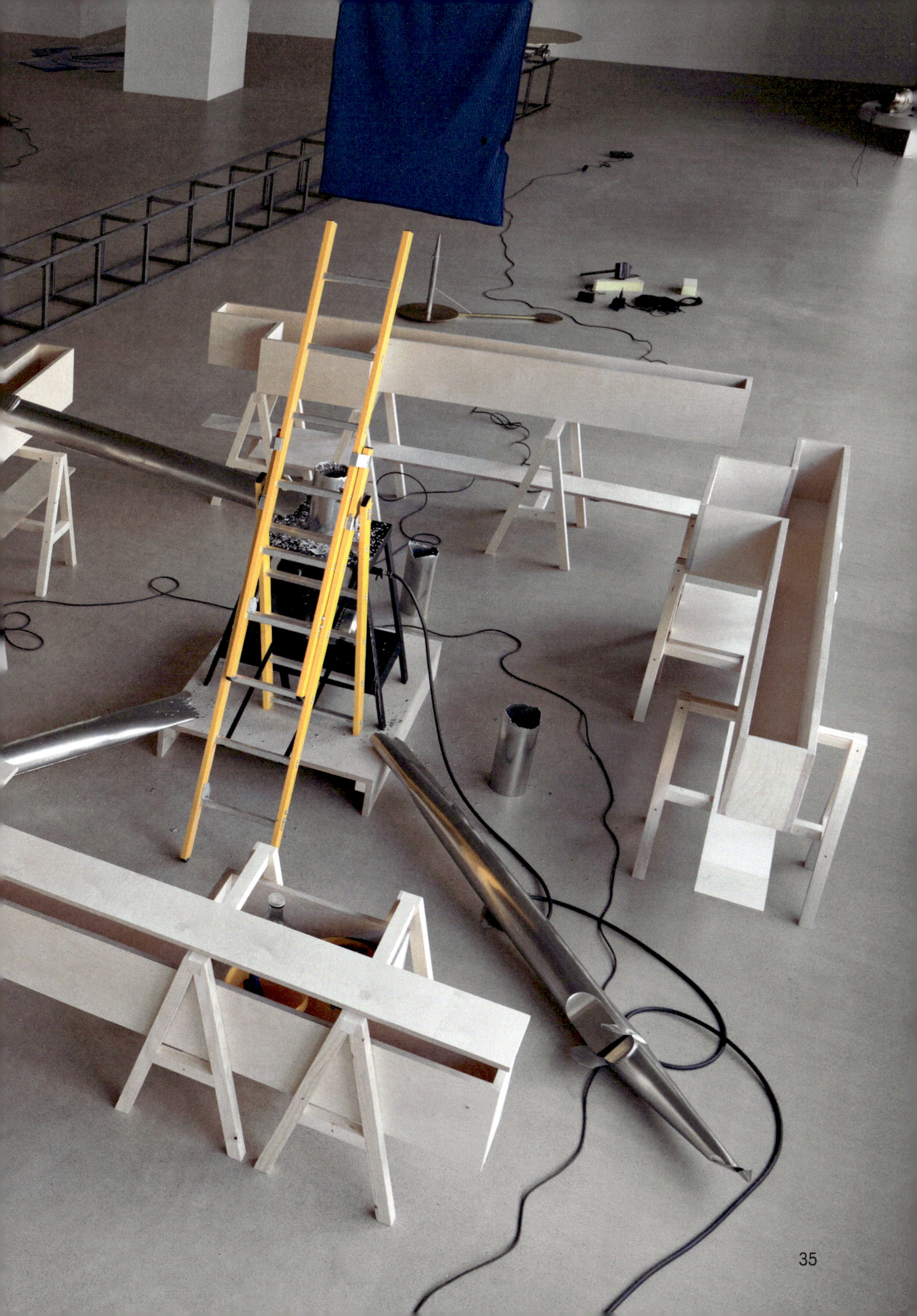

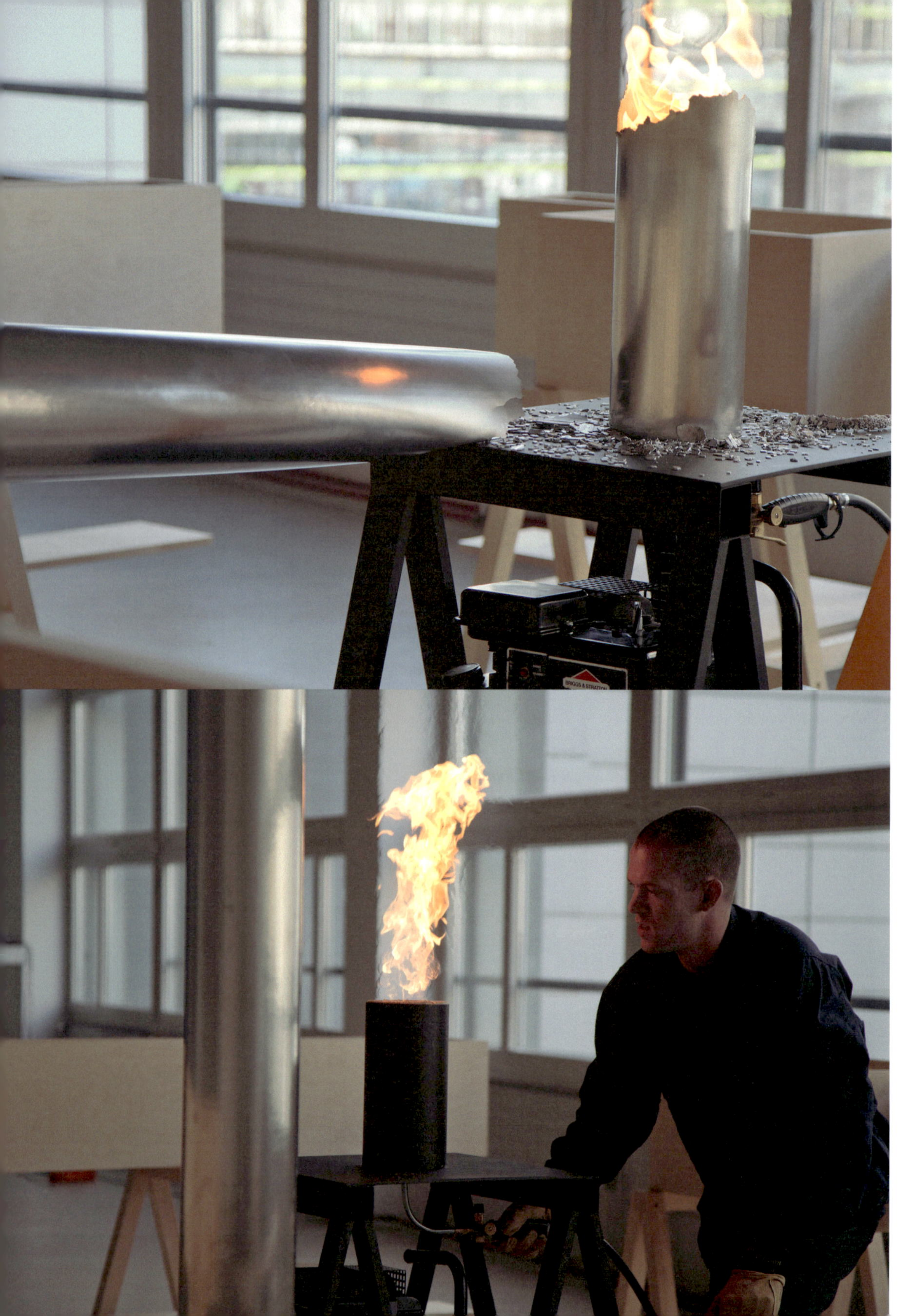
BRIGGS & STRATTON

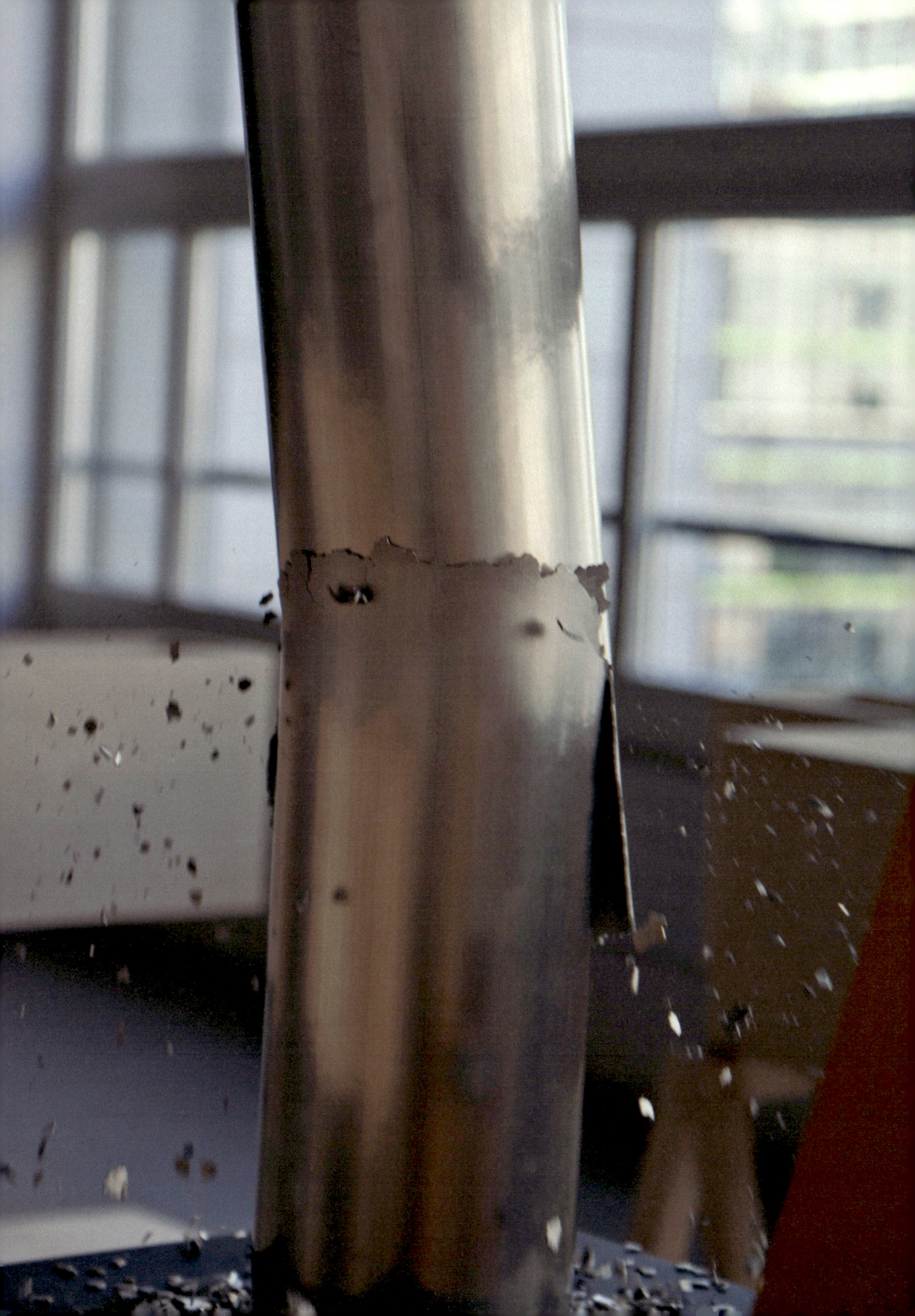

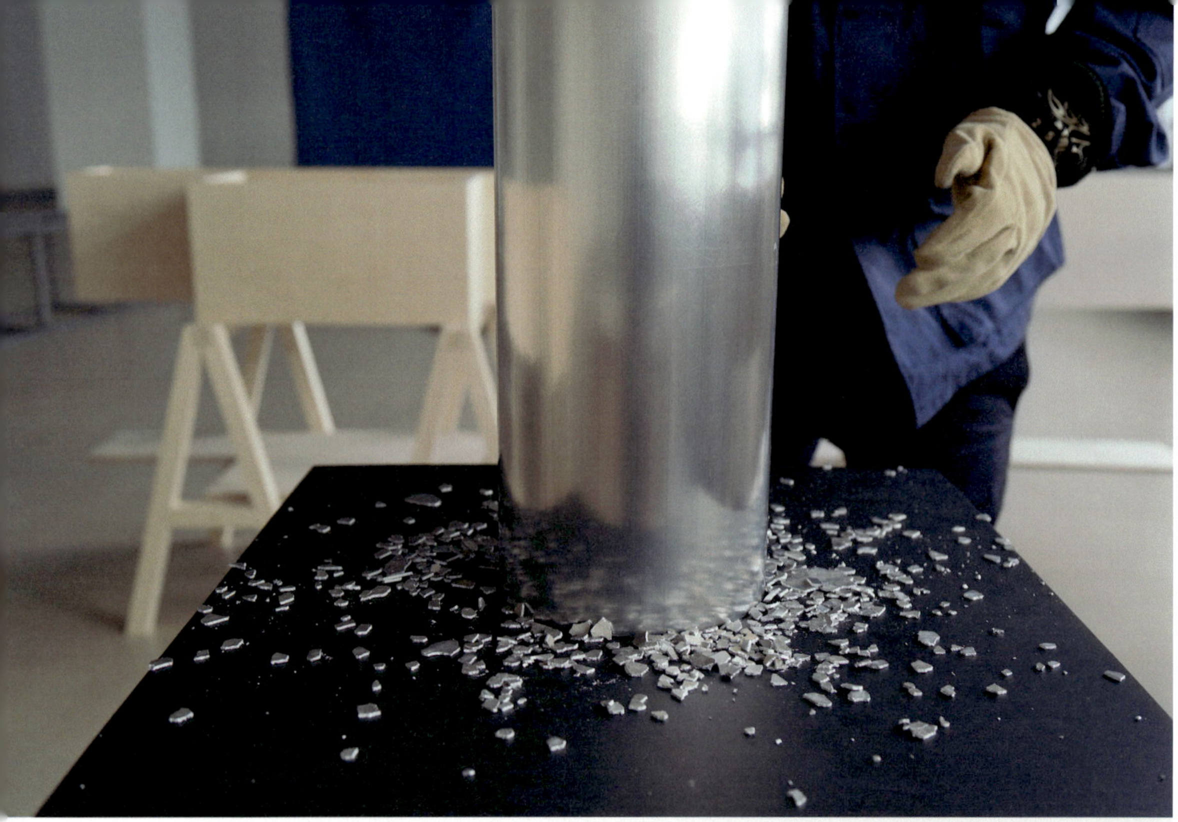

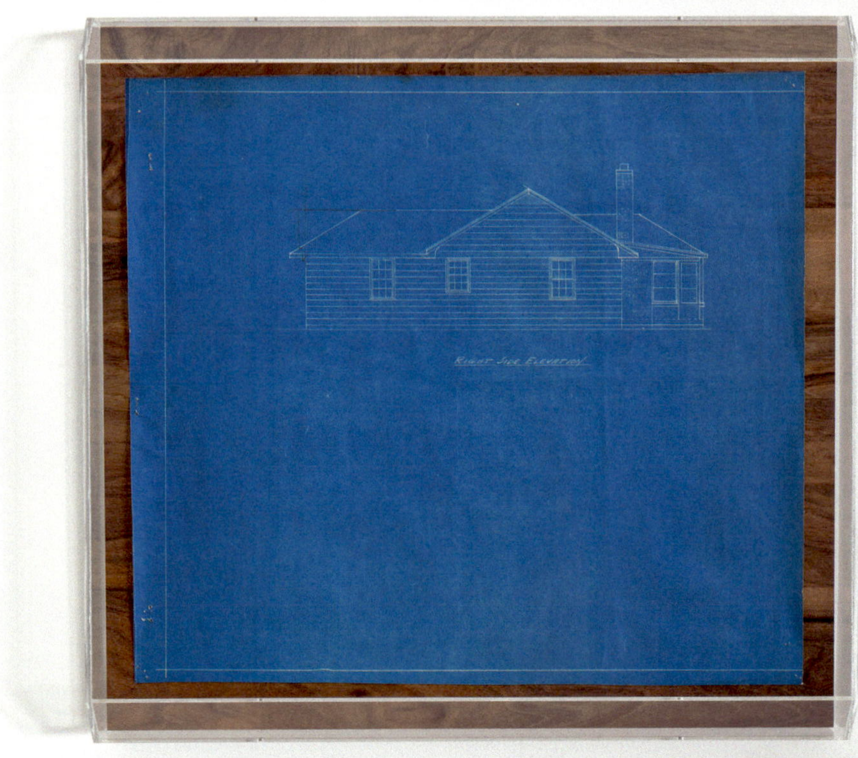
RIGHT SIDE ELEVATION

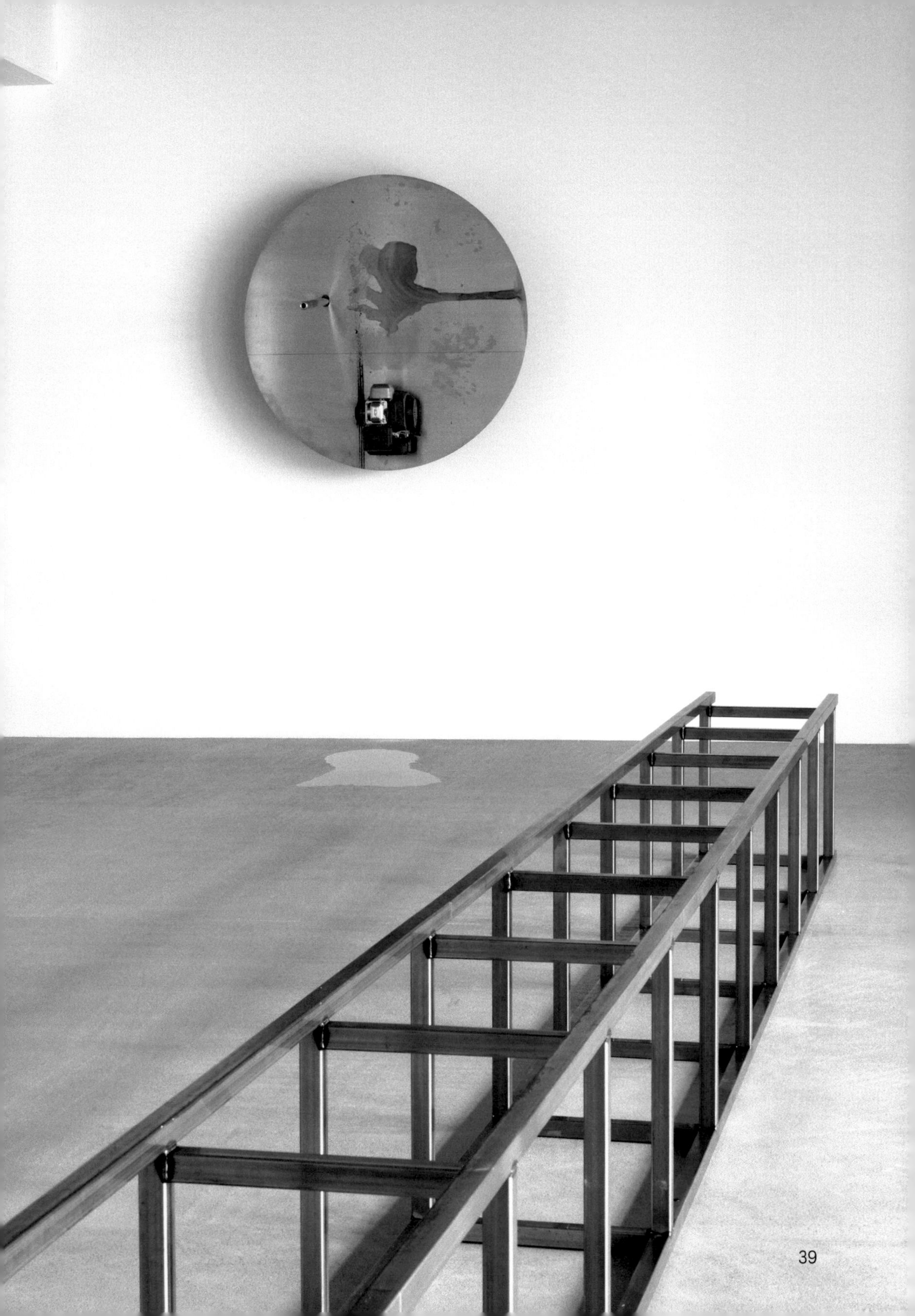

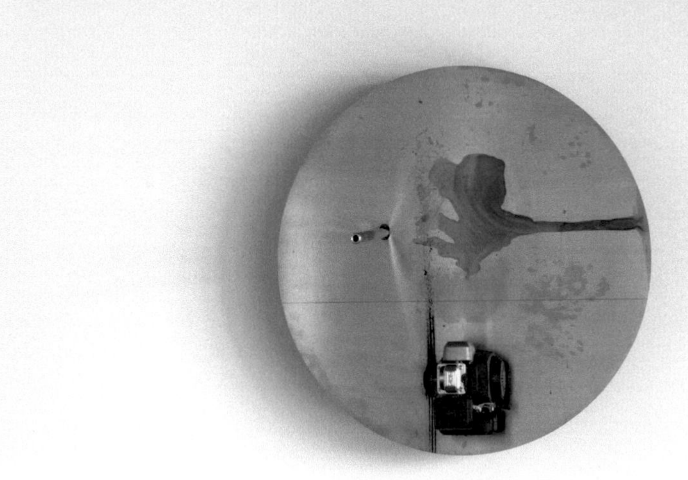

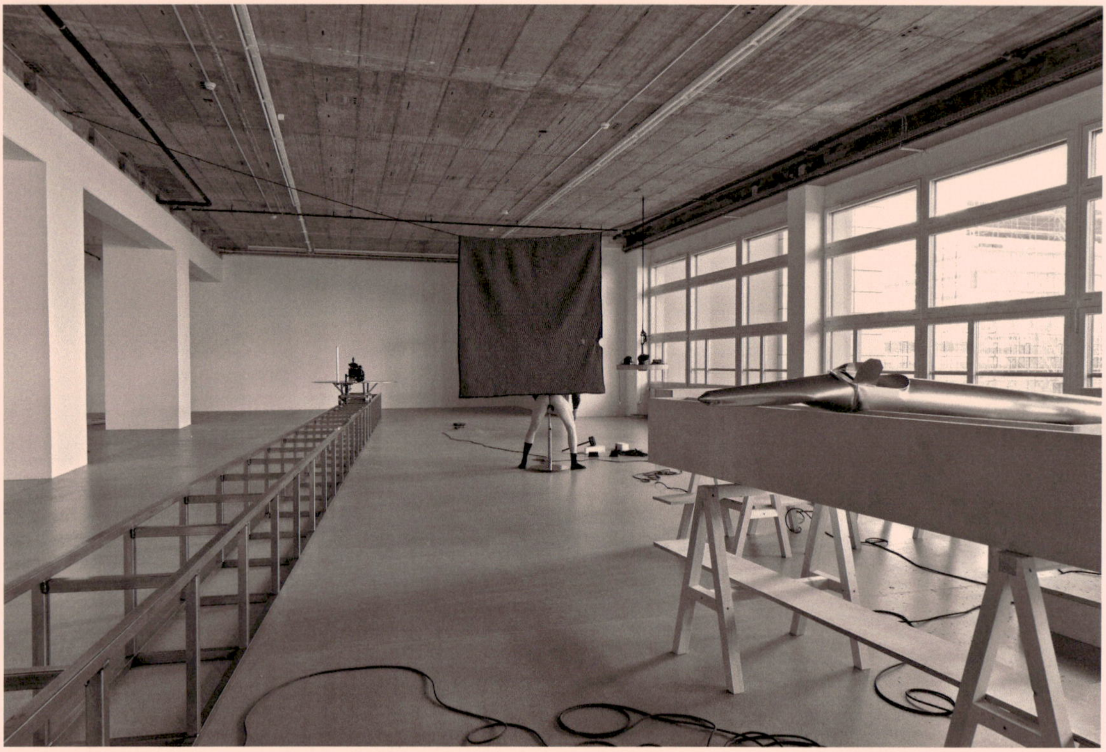

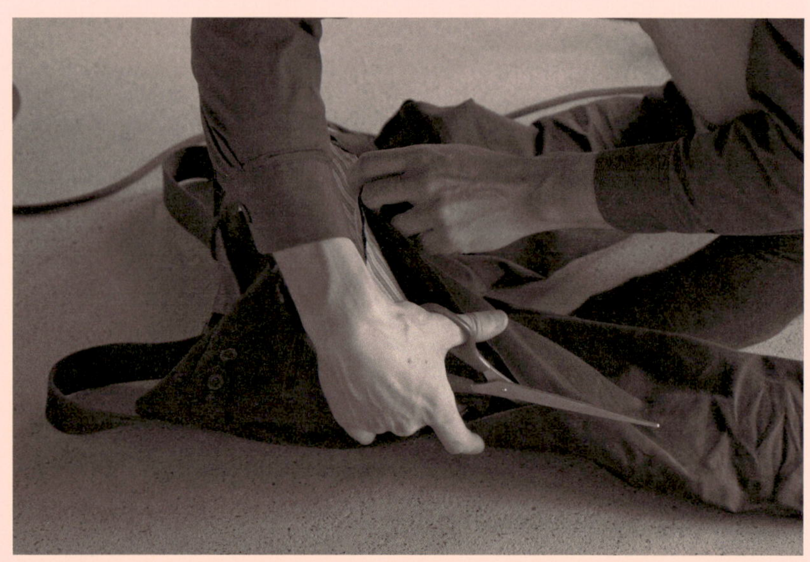

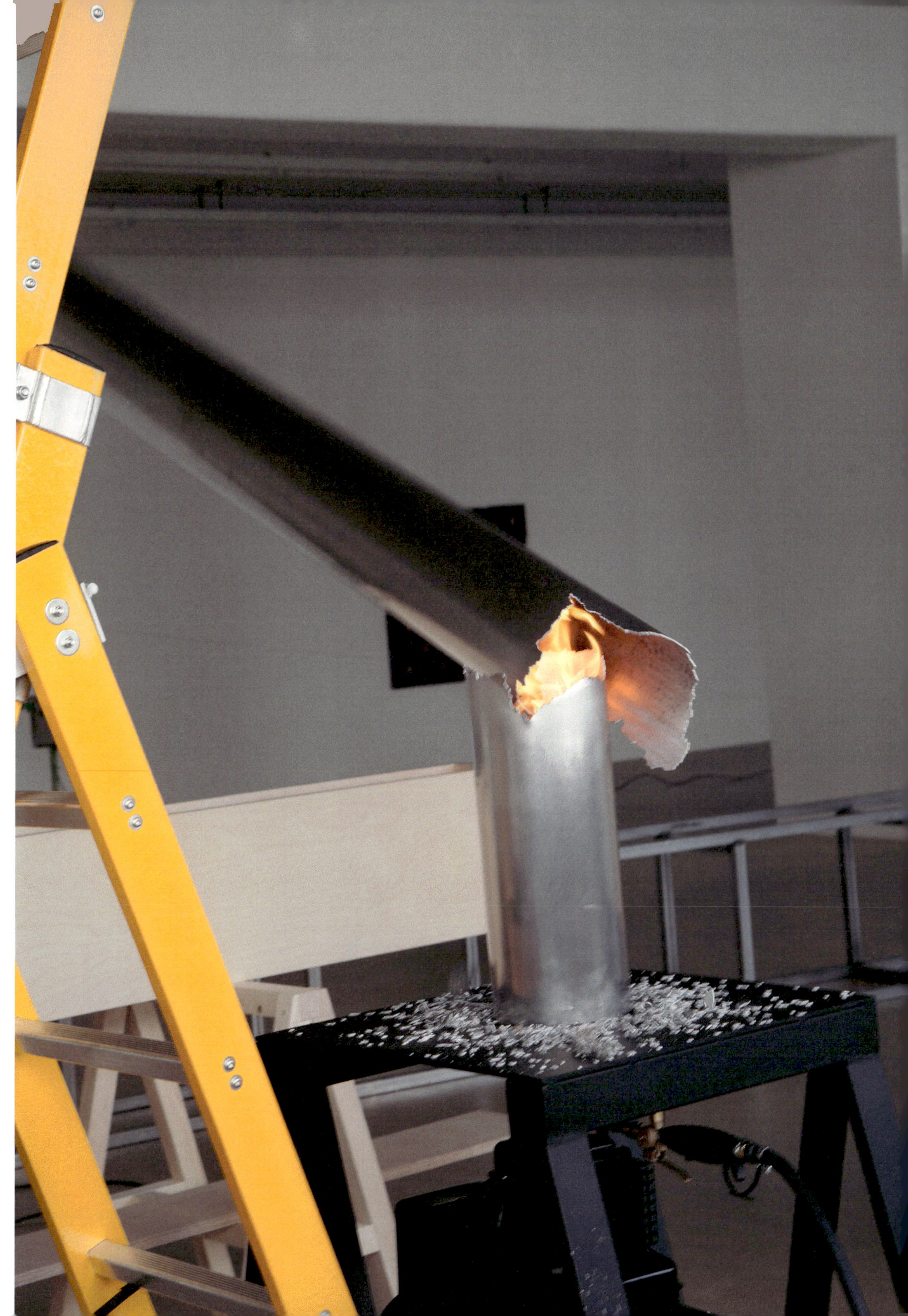

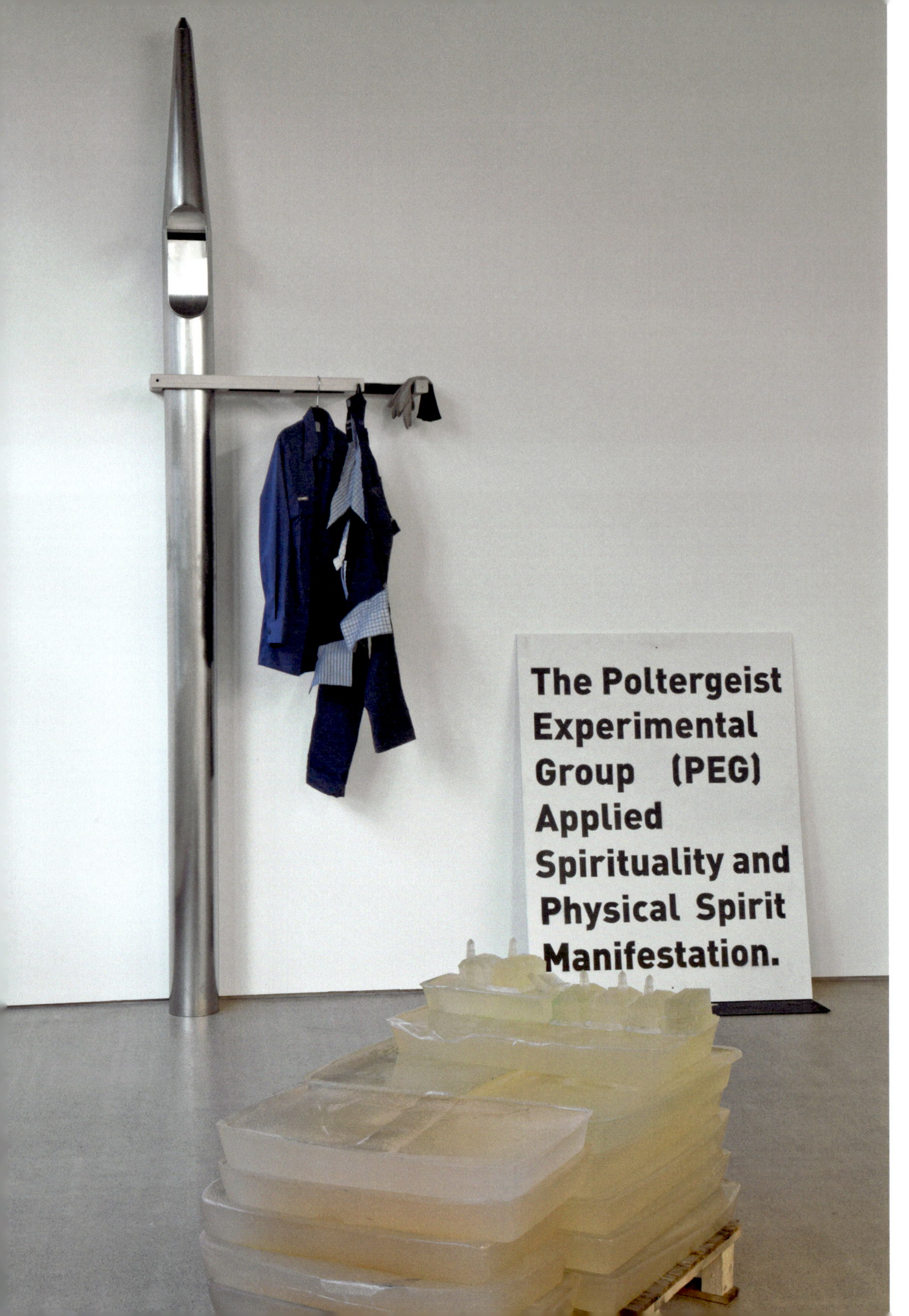
The Poltergeist
Experimental
Group (PEG)
Applied
Spirituality and
Physical Spirit
Manifestation.

Poltergeist are usually associated with an individual. Hauntings seem to be connected with an area.
A house, usually.

Poltergeist disturbances have a fairly short duration, perhaps a couple of months. Hauntings can go on for... years.

Can we talk to you?
Let's go.
Any movement out of those things?
There's been some ionization flux. I'd like to make sure they're not caused by humidity coming from structure leakage, but I'm not going up there to find out.

We have got much more than the paranormal episode taking place here.

There is a measurable physical science in this house that goes far beyond any of the creaking doors or cold spots I've ever experienced.

The voice on the television, where is it coming from?
The absence of a signal on a channel that is not receiving a broadcast means that it's free to receive a lot of noise from all sorts of things, like short waves...
...solar disturbances, car ignitions, barkings, of outer space... or inner space.
Yes. What if these people had an area of bilocation in their own living room, know what I mean?

What do you mean?
If that is the way out... then maybe somewhere in this house there's a way in.

...you master in. There are no certificates of graduation, no licenses to practice. I am a professional psychologist, who spent most of my time engaged in this ghostly hobby which makes me, I suppose, the most irresponsible woman of my age that I know.

This cameo is over a hundred years old...
Yeah... some old, huh?...
...and this watch is only a few years old. And it's not yours.
Well, I'm off. I'm taking these back to the lab along with the tapes.

Would y'all mind hanging back?
You're jamming my frequencies.

I know what you're thinking. But you must take my word for it. She's cleaned many houses. Her gifts have been documented.

I just don't like trick answers.

There is no death. It is only a transition.

These souls, who, for whatever reason, are not at rest, are also not aware that they have passed on. They're not part of consciousness as we know it. They linger in a perpetual dream state... a nightmare from which they cannot awake. Inside this spectral light is salvation. A window to the next plane. They must pass through this membrane, where friends are waiting to guide them to new destinies.

Taylor!
Tangina!
Over here!
I think we finally found the core. We dug under the swimming pool. This is directly below the old graveyard.

Too much power.
I've seen it... in dreams.
What is it?

Well. First the canary died. And then then... the chairs went all funny... and I thought it was kind of exciting, you know. And then...

Nothing really dies ...like a caterpillar becomes a butterfly... death only transforms us into another state of being.

Below the old cemetery... what seems to be a tomb with many bodies in it... directly below your house.
Who are they?
The researchers don't know who these people were. There are no marked graves. There are, however, records of a religious sect that mysteriously disappeared.
What happened?
Their spiritual leader was a medium who led his followers out to California in the early 1800s to start a utopian society. They disappeared near Cuesta Verde... and were believed massacred by Indians.

Here is a photo of those people. I think you should have a look at it... I know this is hard for you, dear, but... I need your verification on something. You see... I don't really trust my instincts anymore. Now... hold this one... and tell me what you feel.

You traveled to a dimension
few people have ever traveled to incarnate!

He is the beast.

...a little demonstration in mass hypnosis. She made me believe I saw a coffee mug fly off my desk into the mirror while giving you a suggestion to smash it.

I'm one of your brother-in-laws.

He's devouring the heat, the energy. He's gathering his strength.

...behind reflections, behind mirrors, stealing images.

Innocence is pure life force. We lose strength as we lose our innocence. You see, innocence is the only gift we're given in life. All else must be fought for.

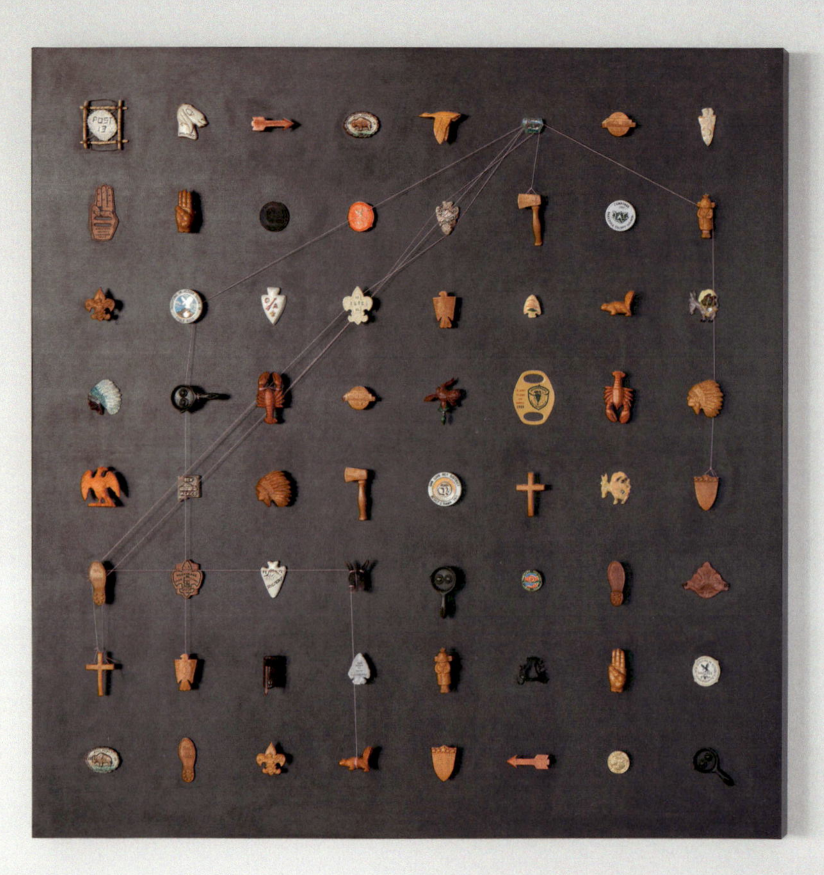
POST
13

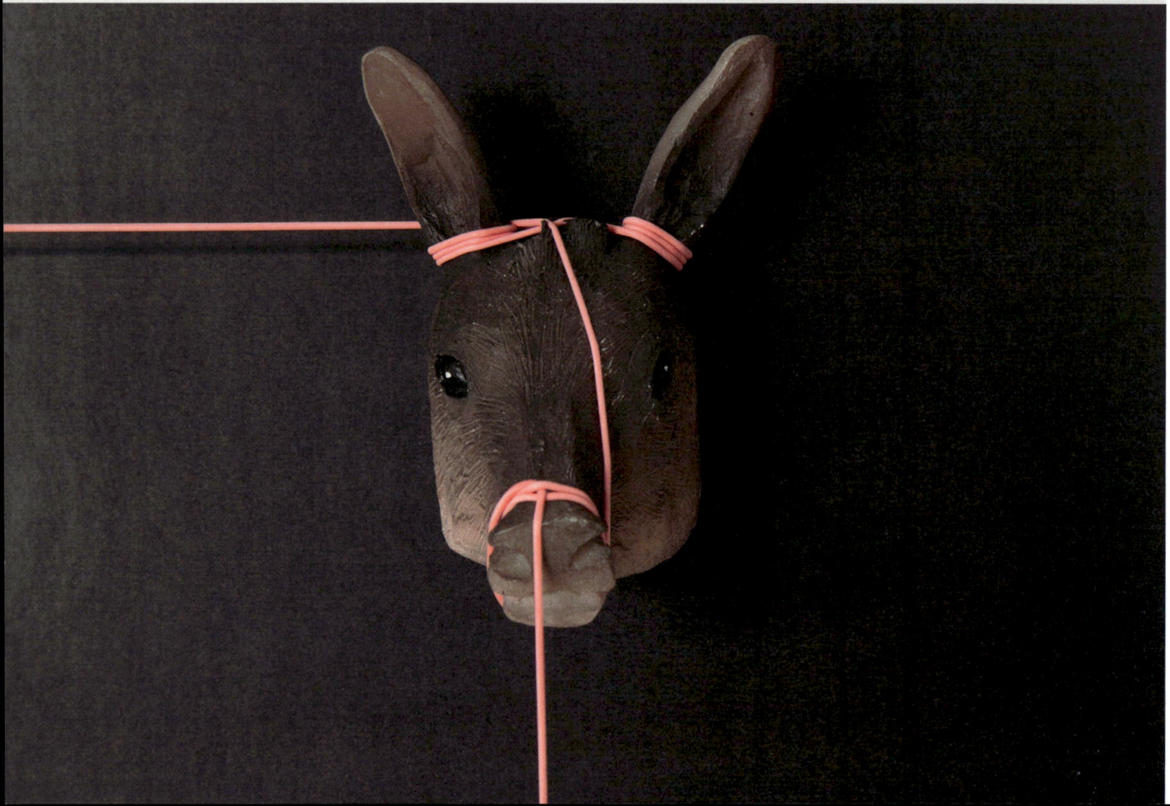

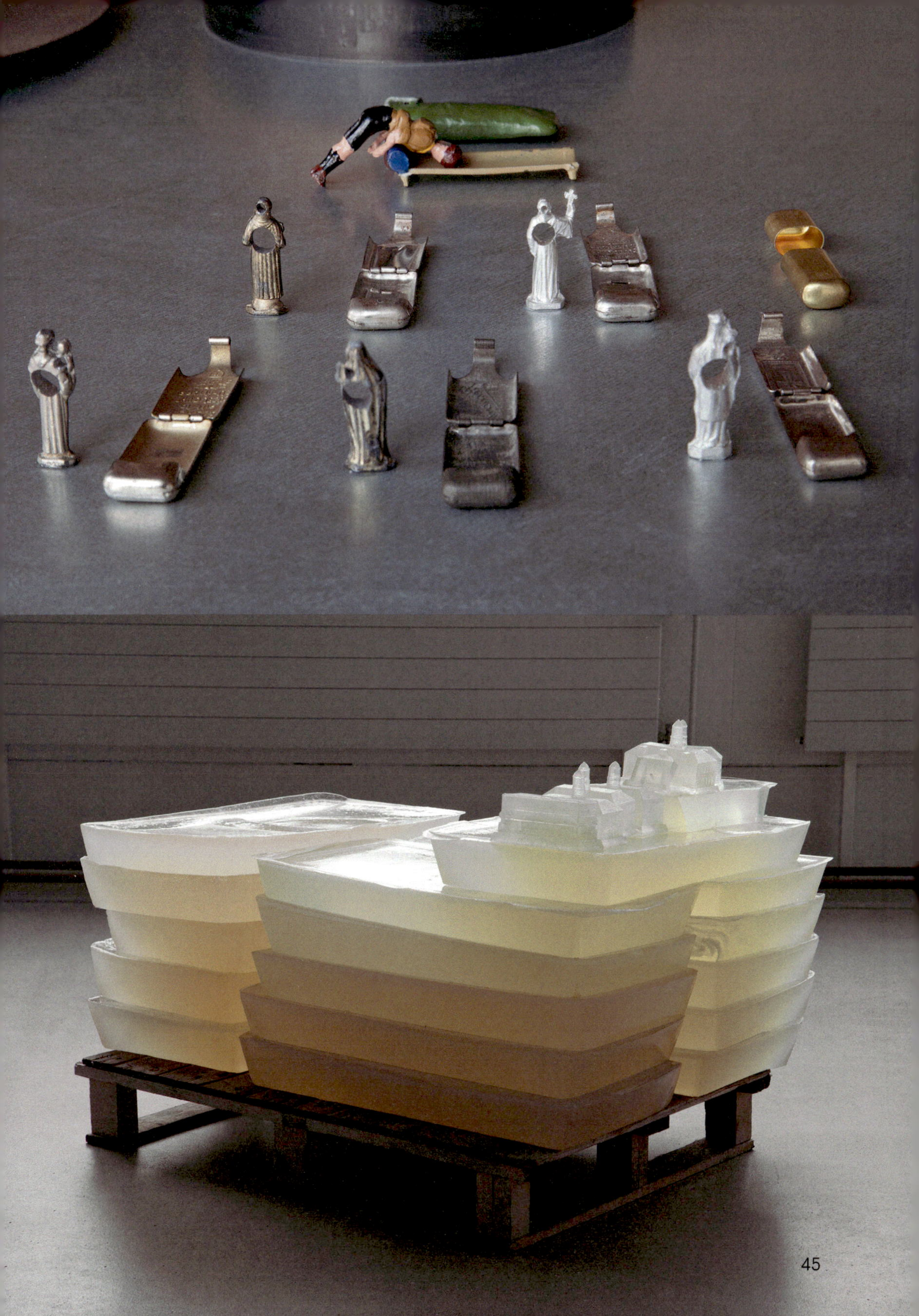

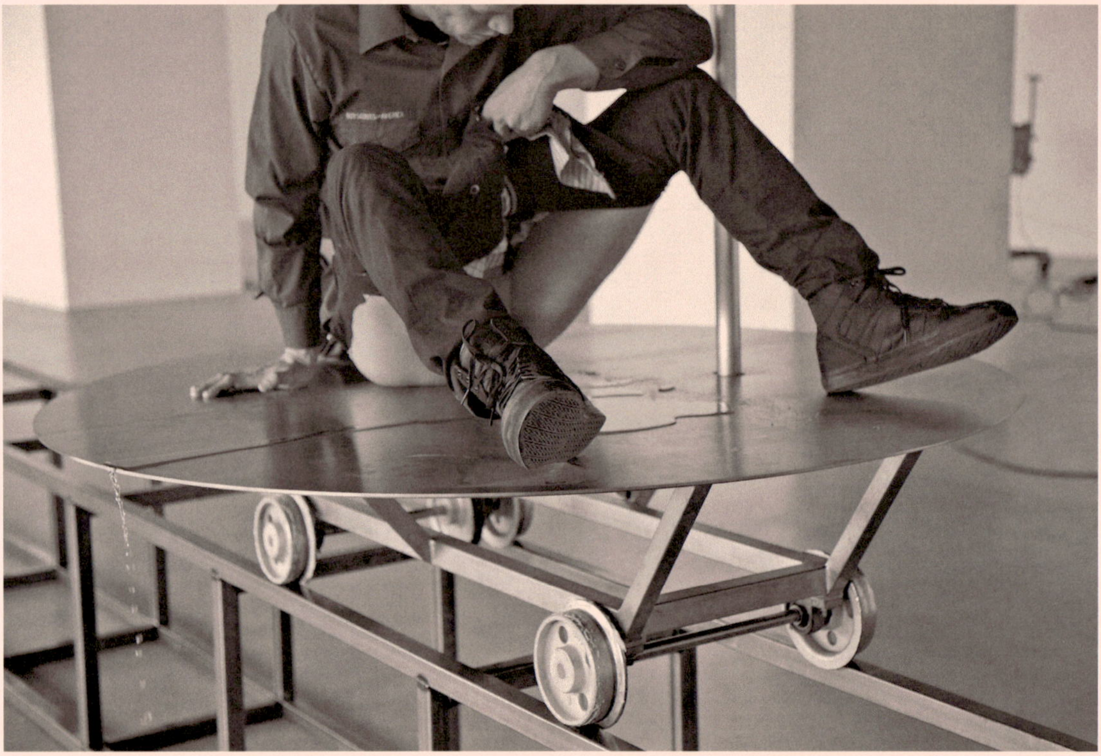

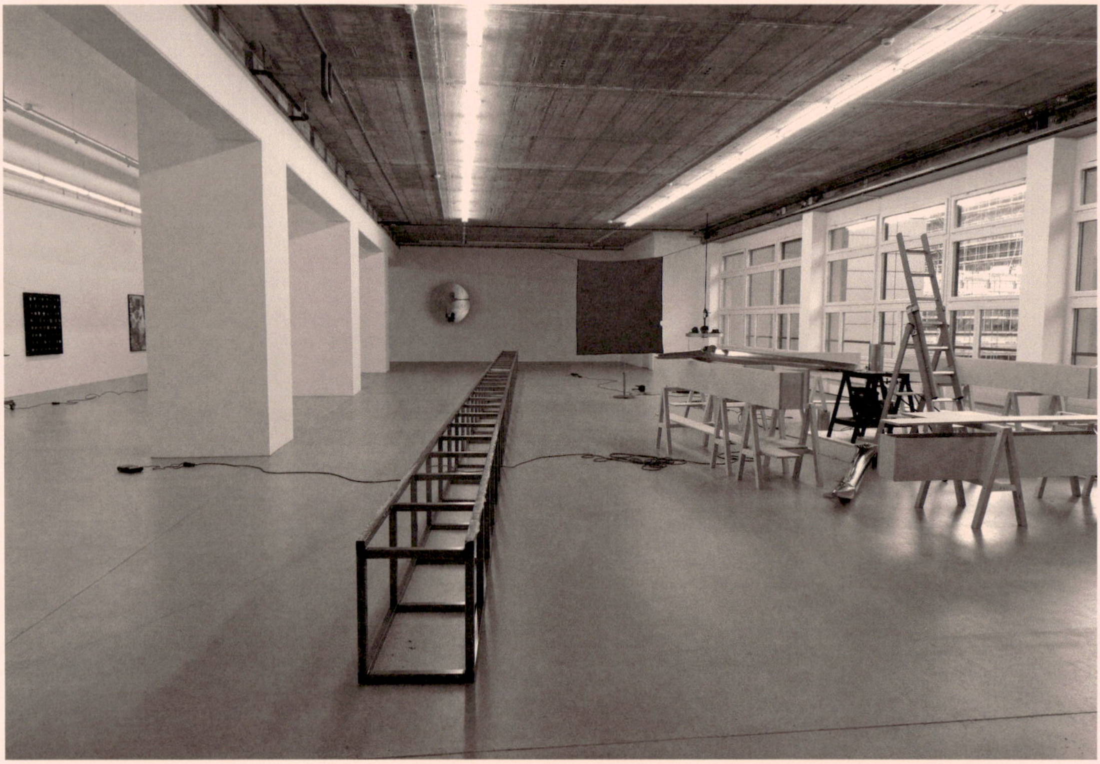

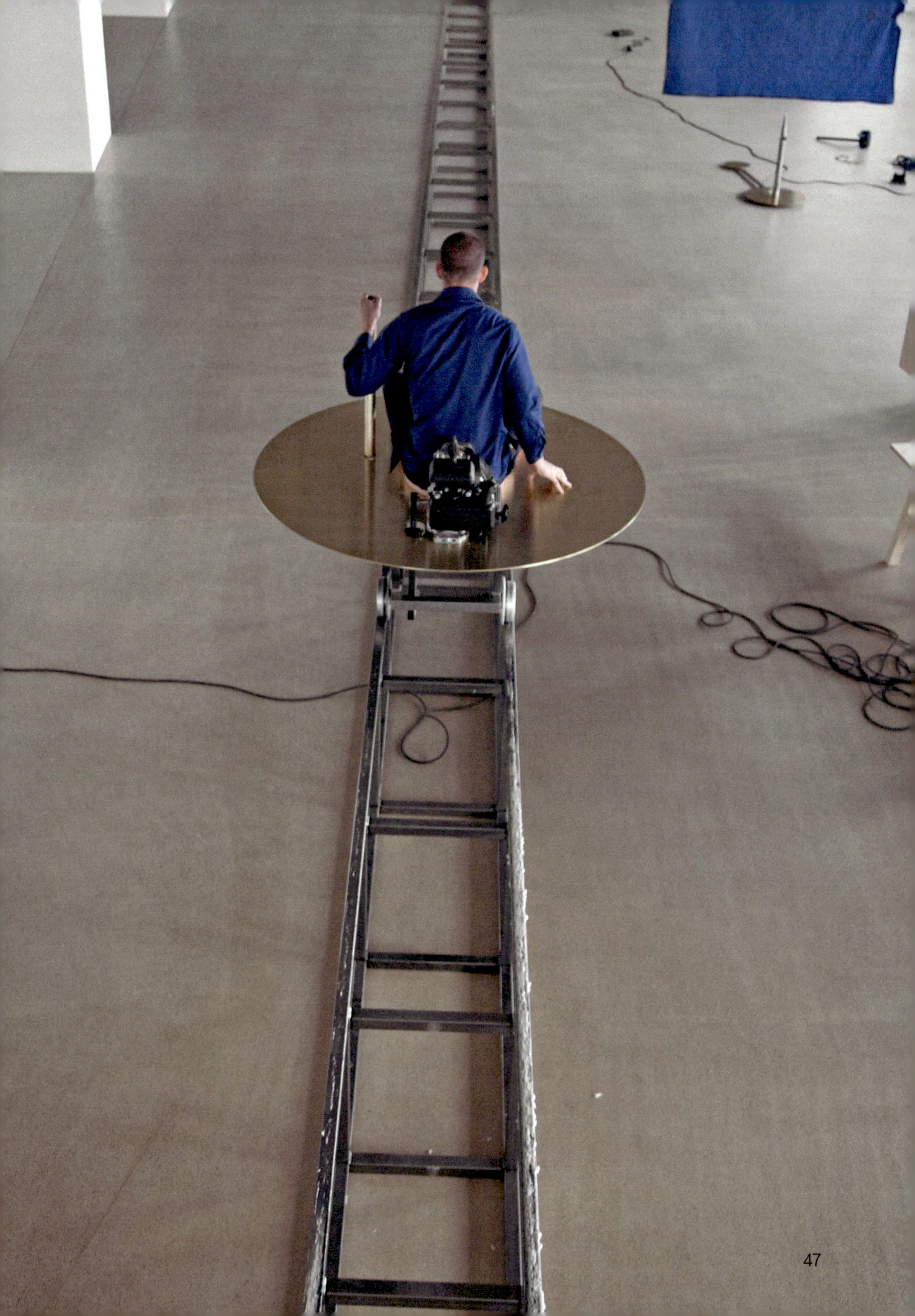

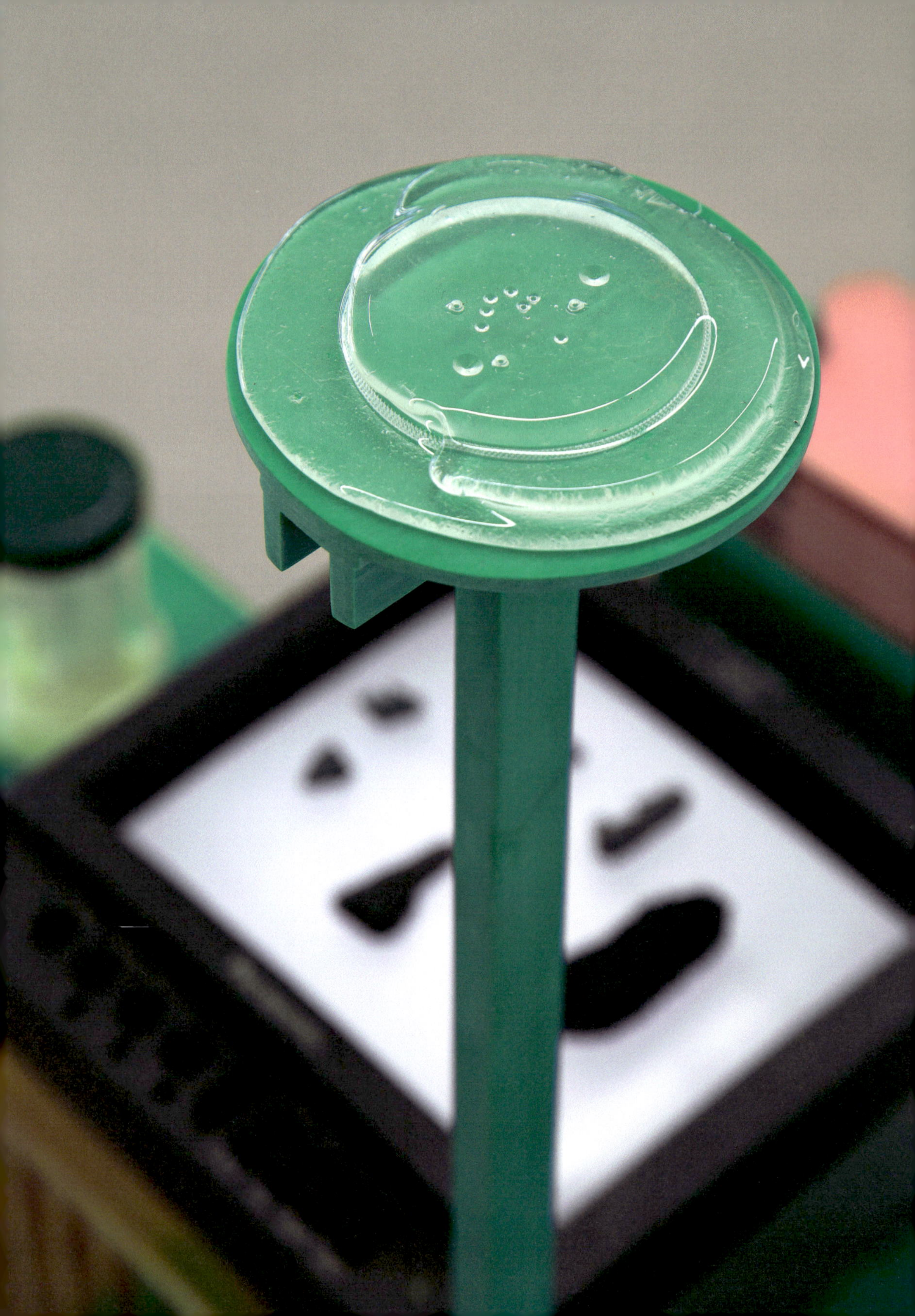

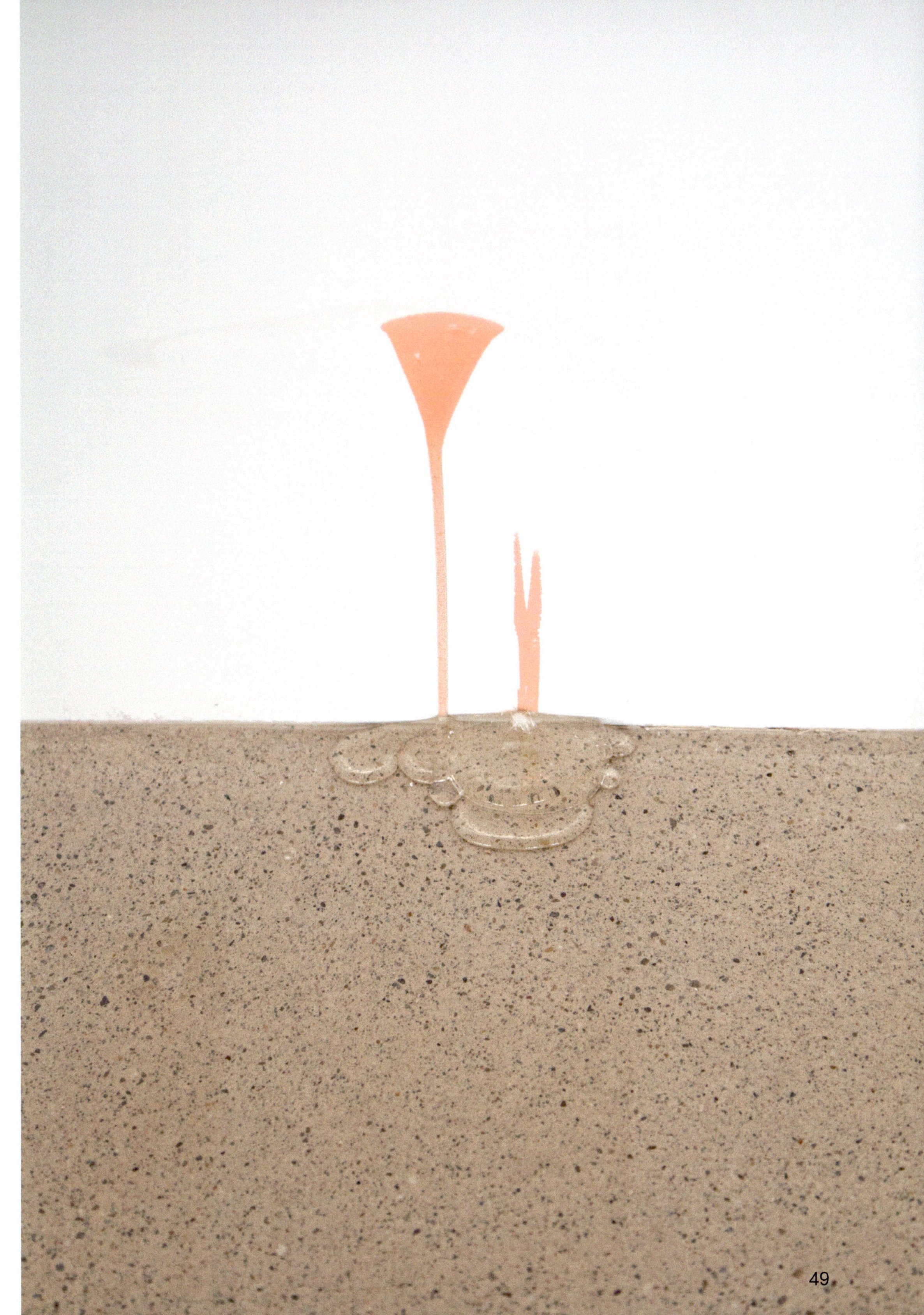

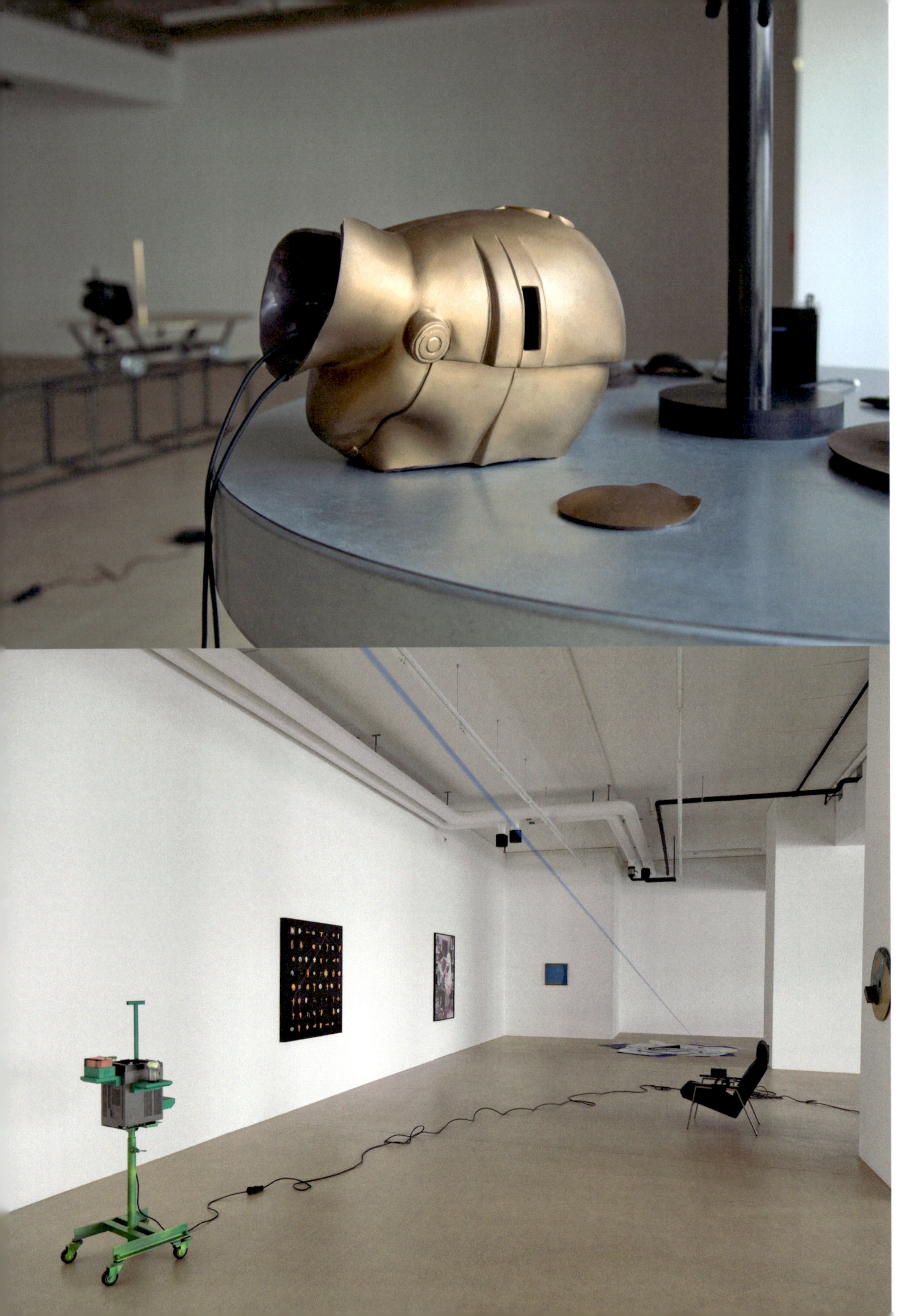

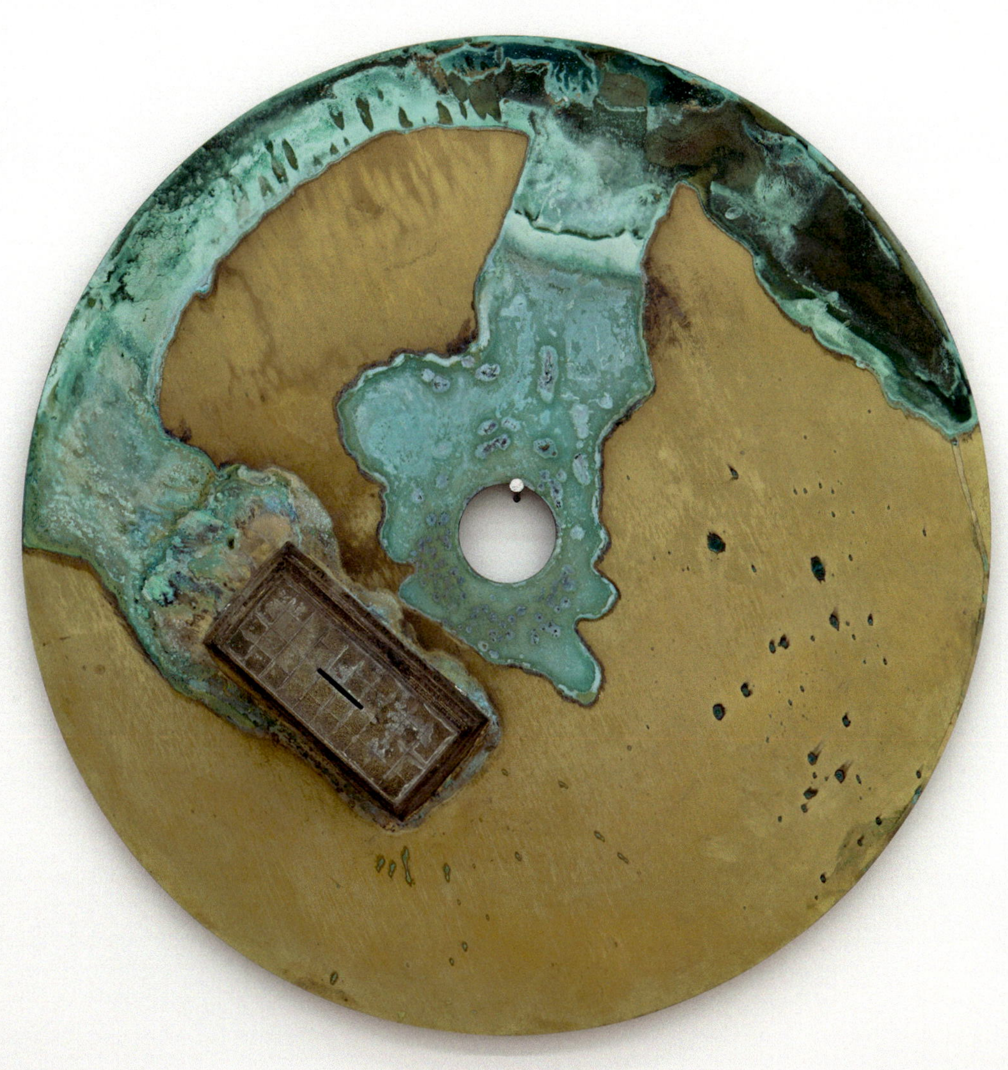

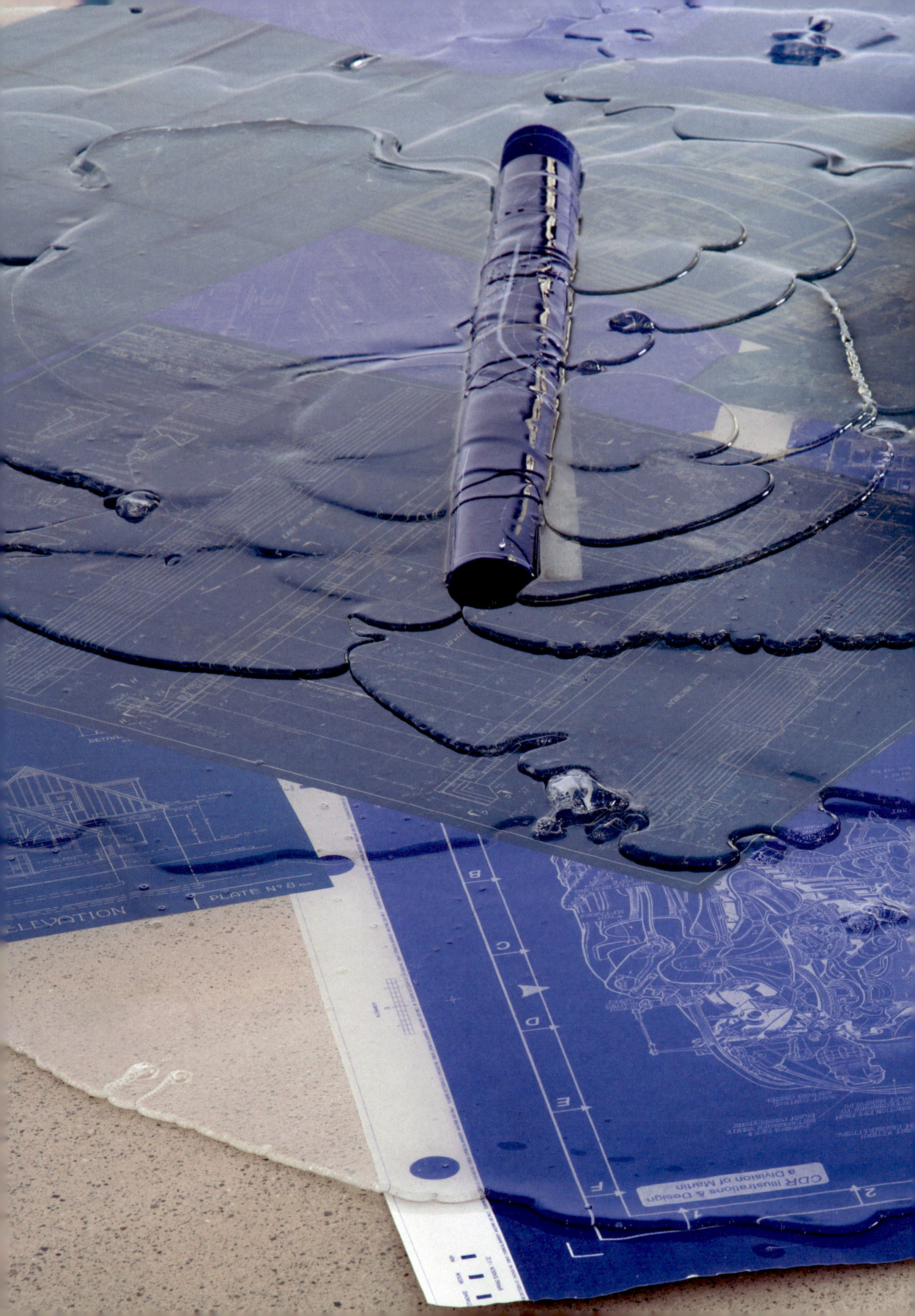
ELEVATION
PLATE Nº 8
CDR Illustrations & Design
a Division of Martin

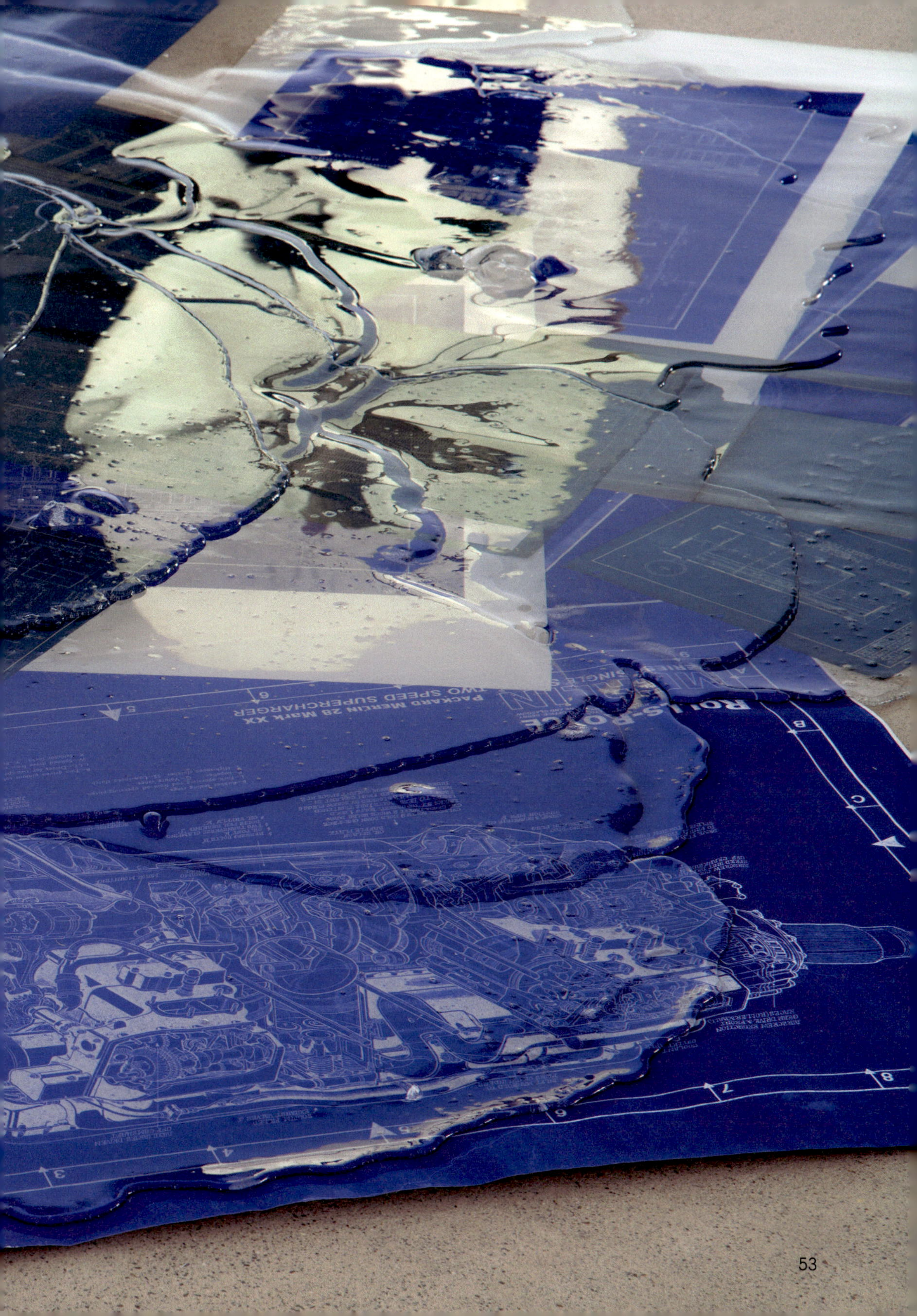
PACKARD MERLIN 28 Mark XX
TWO SPEED SUPERCHARGER

Dante's Inferno, 2010

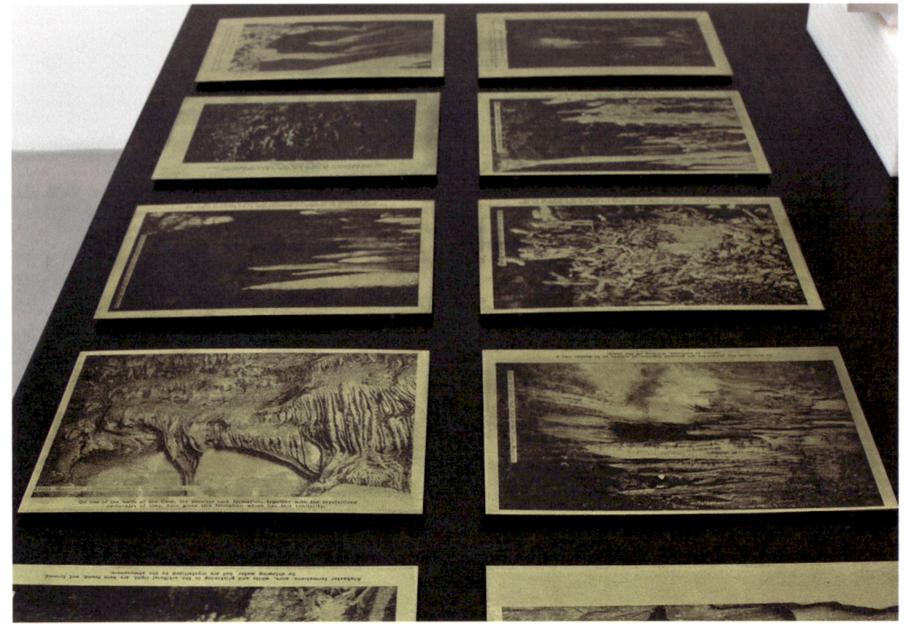

St. Helena / Reichtümer aus den Tiefen der Berge

2010

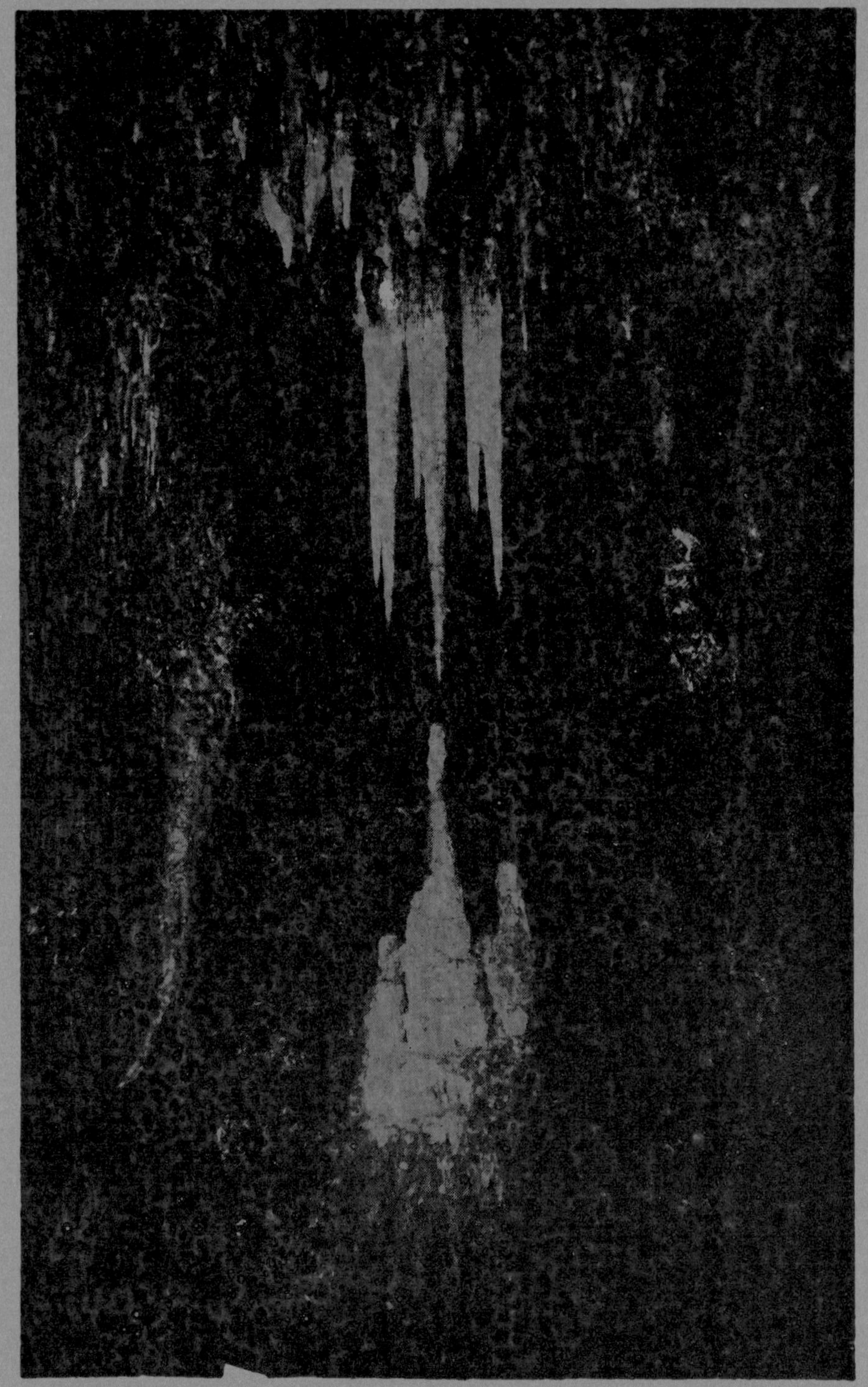

10061. Shafts and Cathedral Spires.

These are stalactites with their stalagmites, beautiful and dazzling white as seen in the interior of the Cave of the Winds.

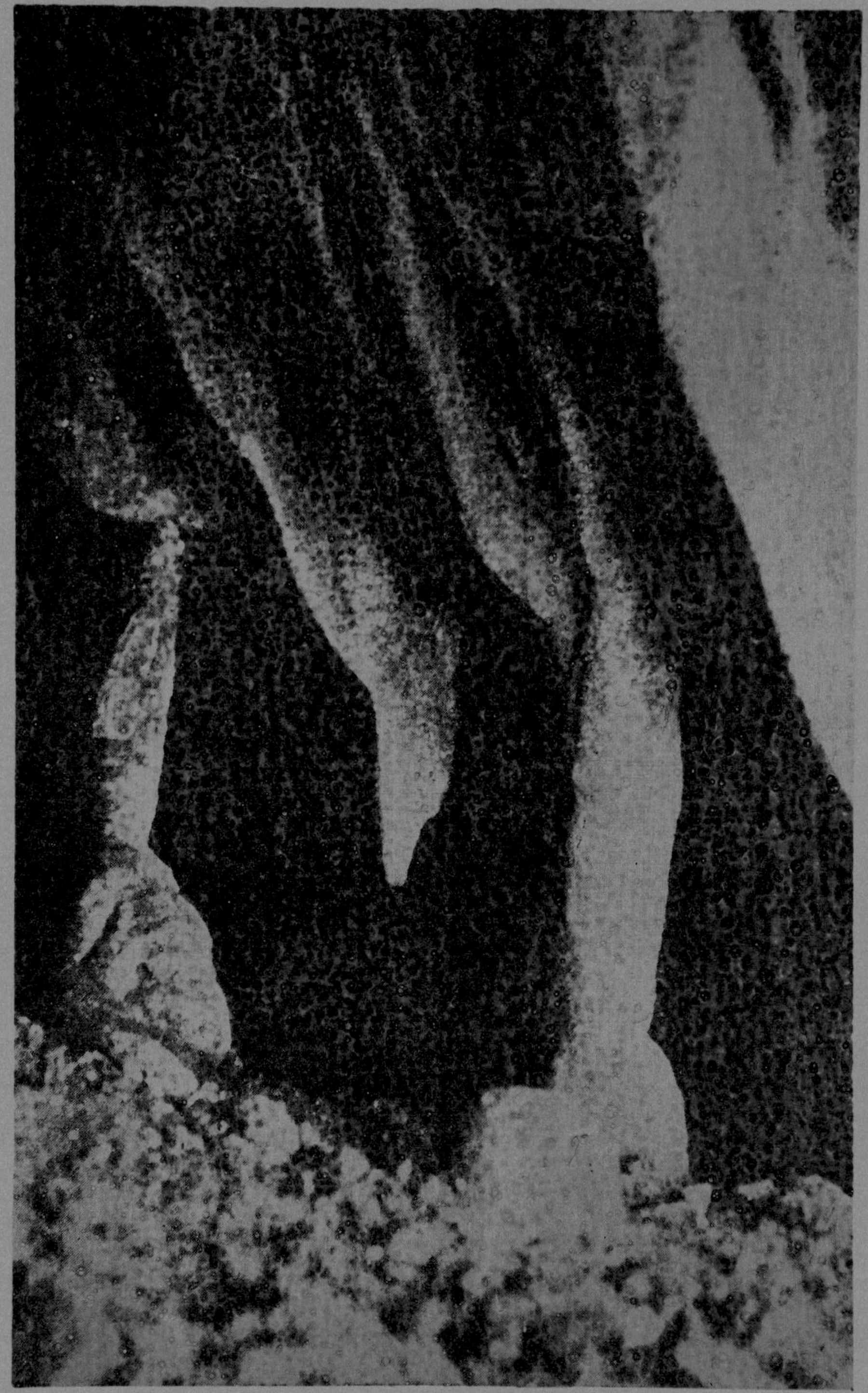

10063. Twin Columns.

Where two sets of stalactites and stalagmites have met and formed into hard white carbonate forms and become crystallized by time.

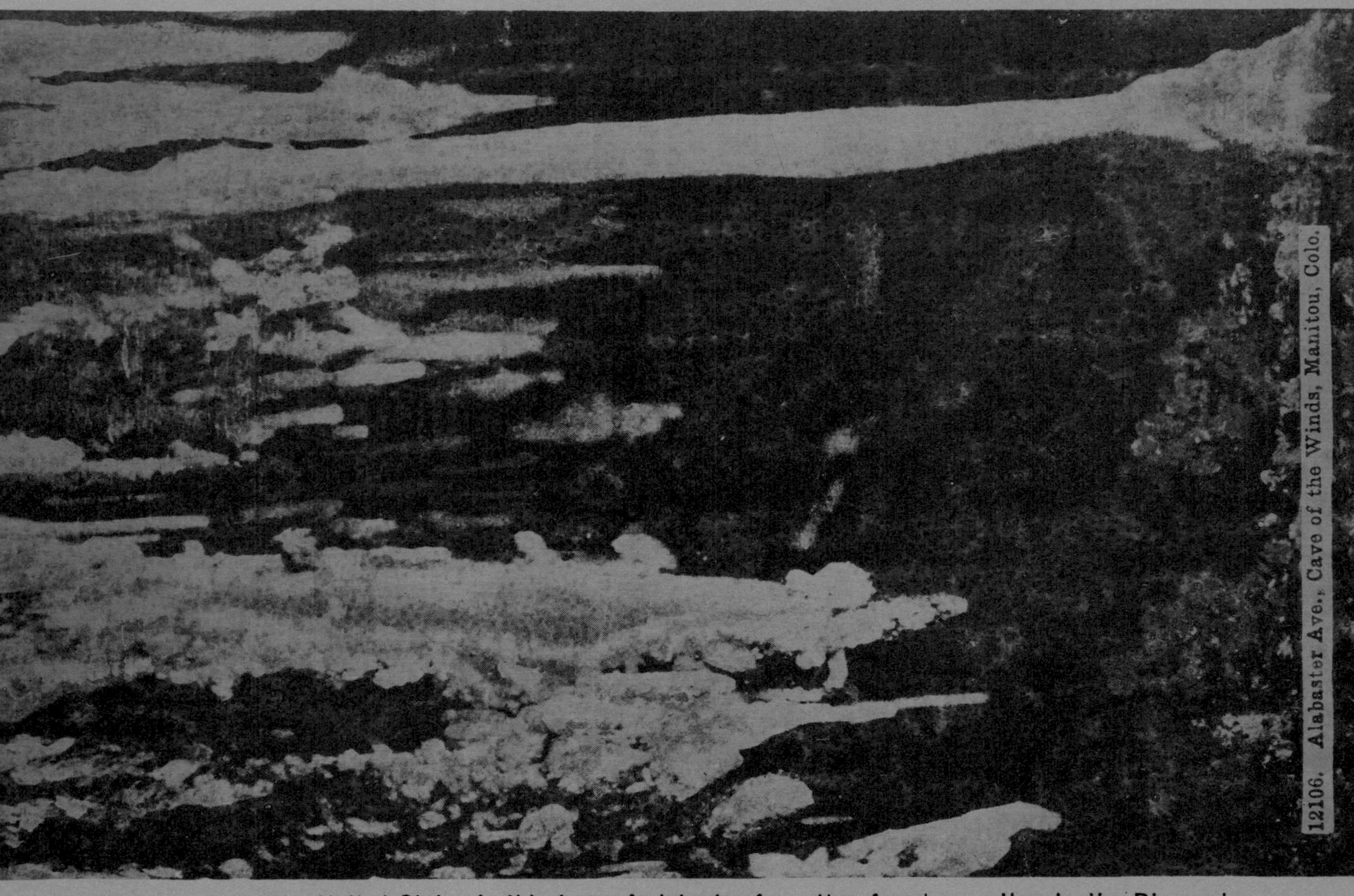

In no cave in the United States is this type of alabaster formation found excepting in the Diamond Hall in Crystal Palace, within the Cave of the Winds.

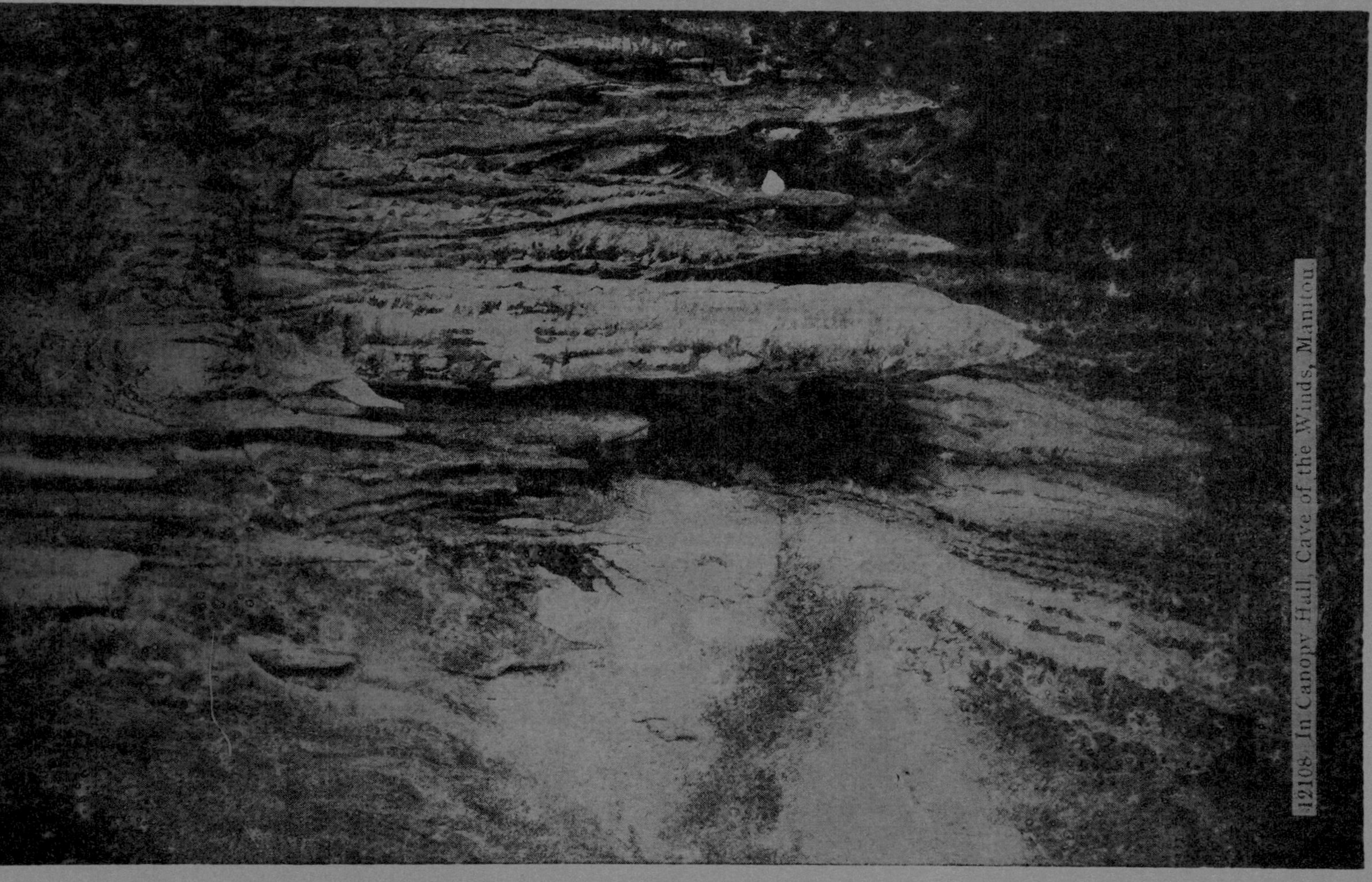

12108 In Canopy Hall, Cave of the Winds, Manitou.

In this room the stalactites are grouped together so closely as to appear like a canopy or portieres, dividing off the space.

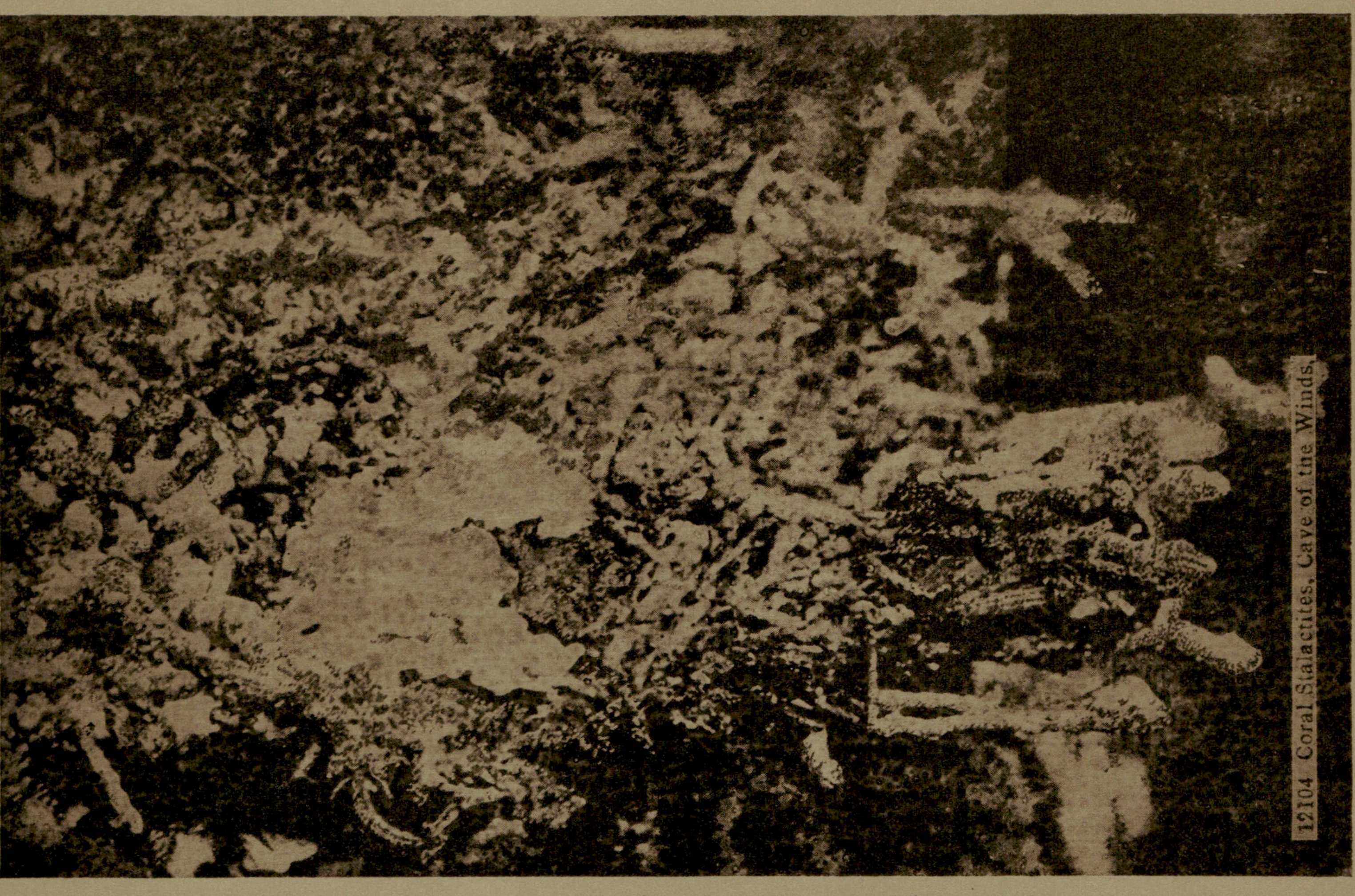

A most unique formation, which has congealed into shapes like sprays of coral, instead of the usual formations like icicles, which are formed by crystallization from drippings produced by gravity.

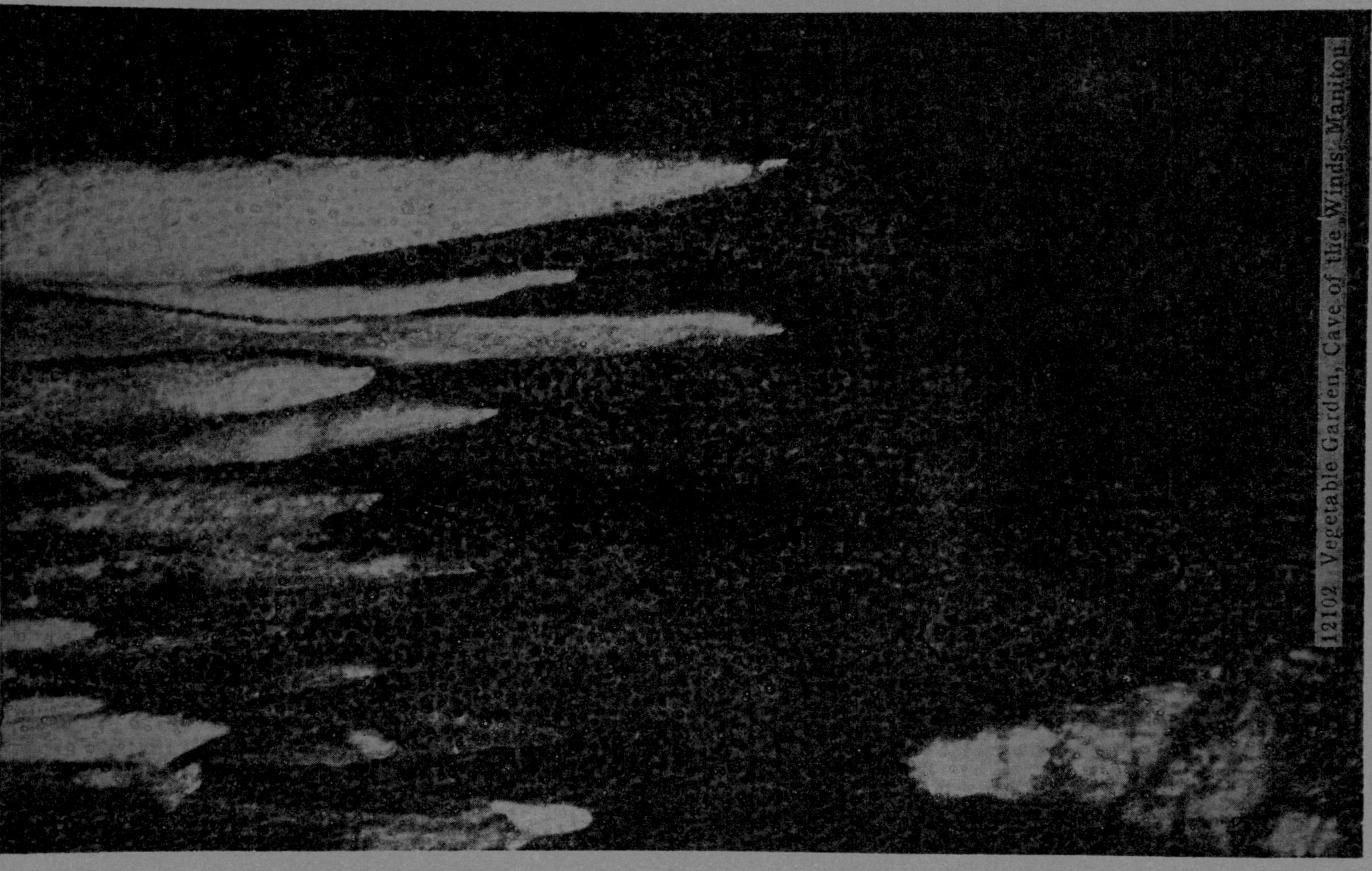

The general outline of the stalactites and stalagmites takes on the appearance in this room of a vegetable garden with its produce upon the ground or on the ceiling.

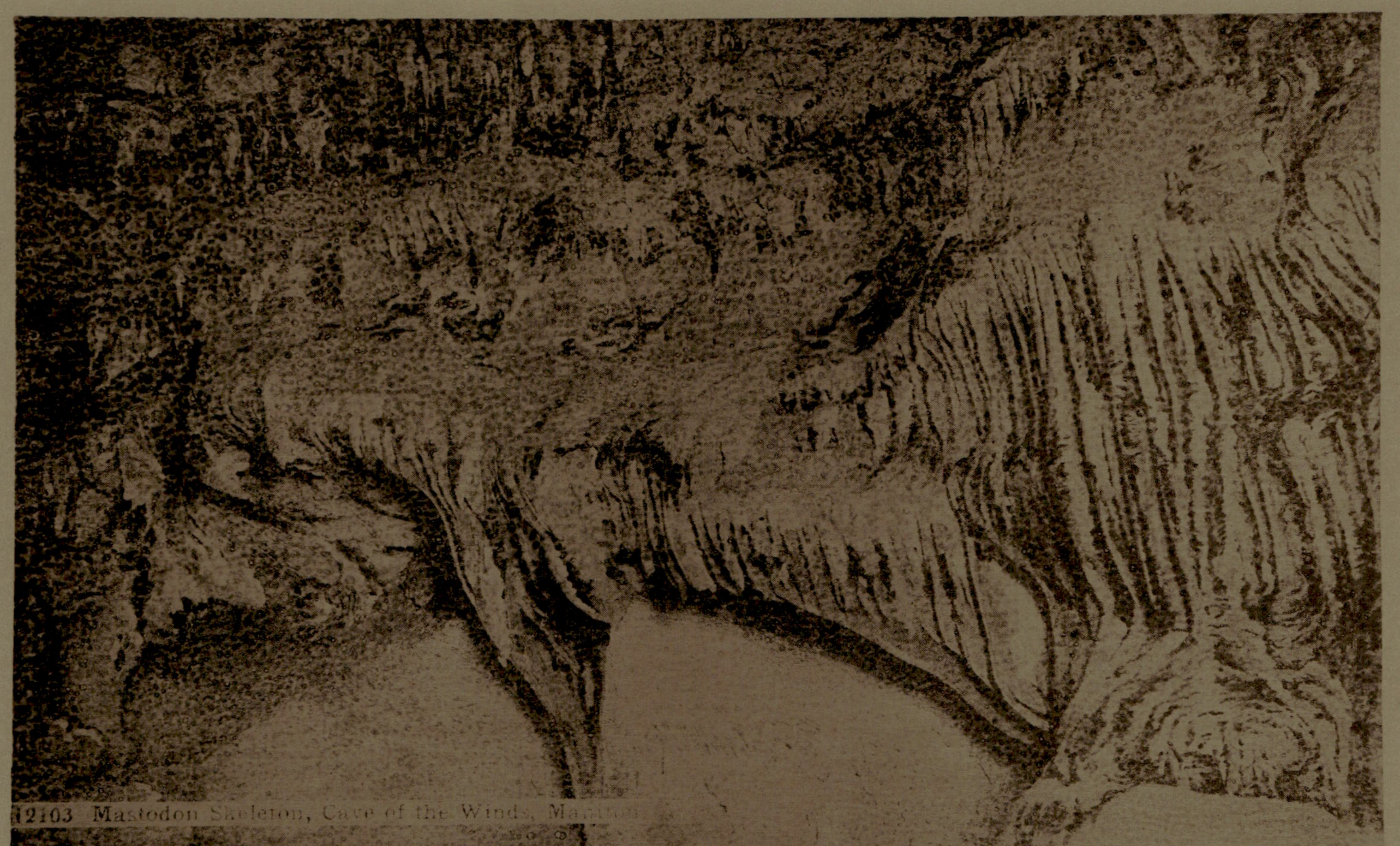

On one of the walls of the Cave, the peculiar rock formation, together with the crystallized carbonates of lime, have given this formation which has this similarity.

St. Helena / Reichtümer aus den Tiefen der Berge

Alexandra Blättler

St. Helena – Arenenberg – Saint-Léonard

Die berühmt-berüchtigte Insel St. Helena hatte aufgrund ihrer Abgeschiedenheit und ihrer Steilküsten nie eine indigene Bevölkerung und blieb bis ins 16. Jahrhundert unbewohnt. Nach ihrer Entdeckung durch die Portugiesen äusserten später auch die Engländer Besitzansprüche. In der Folge kam es zu verschiedenen Auseinandersetzungen, wobei schliesslich die Insel in den Besitz Englands kam. Grosse Farmen wurden gebaut, und Schwarzafrikaner und Chinesen wurden als Arbeitskräfte geholt. So vergrösserte sich der Reichtum St. Helenas – vor allem auch, weil man durch die sichere geografische Lage grosse Mengen von Gold dort aufbewahrte. Die britische Regierung ernannte 1815 St. Helena zum Verbannungsort Napoleons, der im Oktober dessealben Jahres deportiert wurde und bis zu seinem Tod am 5. Mai 1821 in Longwood House residierte.

Es gab aber vorher noch viele andere geografische Stationen im Leben von Napoleon Bonaparte, des französischen Generals, Staatsmanns und schliesslich selbsternannten Kaisers Napoleon I. Eine davon befindet sich in der unmittelbaren Heimat des Künstlers Florian Germann im Kanton Thurgau: Hoch über dem Untersee mit wunderschöner Aussicht liegt das Schloss Arenenberg. Wie ein kostbares Juwel lädt die prachtvolle Anlage zur Entdeckungsreise durch die umliegenden Wälder und zu Ausflügen in die facettenreiche Geschichte des Bodensee-Gebiets ein. Germann muss bereits in seiner Jugend davon fasziniert gewesen sein: Ein Relikt der europäischen Geschichte, das von der Ausstrahlung und Intelligenz Bonapartes zeugte, lag nur einen Steinwurf von seiner Geburtsstätte entfernt. Diese Faszination und das Aufwachsen in unmittelbarer Nähe sollten Germann derart prägen, dass er Jahre später den hier besprochenen Werkzyklus entwickelte.

Ursprünglich als Konstanzer Patriziersitz gebaut, geriet das Schloss im 19. Jahrhundert als Domizil der kaiserlich-französischen Familie ins Blickfeld der Weltgeschichte. Hortense de Beauharnais, Adoptivtochter und Schwägerin Napoleons I., liess das spätgotische Schloss im Sinne des Empire umbauen und gestaltete den Arenenberg nach französischem Vorbild. Im Stil der berühmten Salons ihrer Zeit organisierte Hortense das gesellschaftliche Leben und zog bedeutende Persönlichkeiten an den Bodensee. Dokumente mit Namen wie Dumas, Récamier, Chateaubriand sowie des gesamten europäischen Hochadels füllen das Inventar des Hausarchivs. Das Innere des Schlosses stattete man mit Tapeten, Möbeln, Figuren und Bildern in Erinnerung an Napoleon I. aus. Nach dem Tod von

Hortense 1837 veräusserte ihr Sohn Louis Napoléon das Schloss, eignete es sich jedoch 1855 als Kaiser unter dem Namen Napoleon III. wieder an. 1906 schenkte Eugénie, Witwe Kaiser Napoleons III., das Gut dem Kanton Thurgau, der seither in der Schlossanlage das Napoleonmuseum betreibt – wobei es sich um das einzige deutschsprachige Museum zur napoleonischen Geschichte handelt.[1]

In der geografisch entgegengesetzten Richtung der Schweiz befindet sich der «Lac souterrain» in den Walliser Alpen. Dieser unterirdische See wurde zum ersten Mal 1943 von Jean-Jacques Pittard erforscht und ist seit 1949 der Öffentlichkeit zugänglich. Er misst 300 Meter in der Länge, 20 Meter in der Breite und ist 10 Meter tief. Damit ist der unterirdische See von Saint-Léonard der grösste schiffbare unterirdische See Europas.[2] Auf den ersten Blick mag dieser mythenumwobene Ort nichts mit Napoleon zu tun haben. Nach Auskunft des Künstlers jedoch ist in dieser unterirdischen Grotte unter anderem eine Froschart beheimatet, die blind sein soll und im Volksmund Napoleonfrosch genannt wird – denn zieht der Frosch seine Hinterbeine dicht an seinen Leib heran, so erinnert seine daraus resultierende anatomische Form an die Kopfbedeckung Napoleons, den Zweispitz. Dies, der «Gesang» dieser Napoleonfrösche sowie der Ort der Grotte und weitere mit Napoleon in Zusammenhang stehende Kulturdenkmäler und Naturreservate (Mount Rushmore National Memorial und Alabaster Caverns State Park in Woodward County, Oklahoma) sollen in der Fortsetzung der Geschichte rund um den Werkzyklus *St. Helena* erläutert werden.

Austerlitz – Mount Rushmore – Woodward County

Die einführend genannten Fakten leisten bereits einen wesentlichen Teil zur Beschreibung und Deutung der gross angelegten, komplexen Erzählung im Zyklus *St. Helena/Reichtümer aus den Tiefen der Berge*. In unmittelbarer Konfrontation mit der Installation wandelt und irrt der Betrachter in einem Feld historischer Ereignisse, mythologischer Bezüge, Halbfiktionen, fantastischer Märchenelemente und wissenschaftlicher Fakten. Selber beschreibt Germann seine Arbeitstechnik treffend so, dass er eine «innere Bibliothek durchschreite, um noch nicht kombinierte Möglichkeiten aufzuspüren». Dieser Ausspruch zeugt von jugendlicher Frische voller Entdecker- und Forscherlust einerseits und von einem über Jahre hinweg entwickelten Repertoire an Wissen und Erlebtem andererseits. Der Betrachter wird

1—http://www.napoleonmuseum.ch.
2—http://www.lac-souterrain.com.

Zeuge der Transformation einer historisch-epischen Geschichte und eines dynamischen Arbeitsprozesses gleichzeitig. Mit anderen Worten: Germann lotet nicht nur die Kombinationen verschiedener historischer Gegebenheiten aus, sondern Materialfindung und Transformation von Energie und Material spielen eine genauso grosse, wenn nicht noch grössere Rolle als jene. Der Künstler eignet sich gefundene oder filigran nachkonstruierte Gegenstände und Relikte an und verwebt die damit überlieferten Geschichten, die sich ihrerseits durch die neue Anordnung im Kunstwerk verlieren und neu aufladen.

Mit dem Titel betont Germann seine Faszination für die Bodenschätze und somit für Reichtümer, die aus den Tiefen der Berge in Reinform gewonnen werden können, wie Eisen, Blei, Kupfer, Zink und Schwefel, und die in seinen Arbeiten immer wieder Verwendung finden.

In der Ausstellung *St. Helena/Reichtümer aus der Tiefe der Berge* führte Florian Germann die während 2010 entstandenen Arbeiten vorläufig in einer Installation unter dem gleichnamigen Titel zusammen.[3] Voraus gingen monatelanges Recherchieren, Schnitzen und Schleifen an einer Holzskulptur, das Züchten von russischen und französischen Austern und die Einladung, für das Kunsthaus Glarus eine sogenannte performative Arbeit für die Ausstellung *Performative Attitudes* zu entwickeln.[4] Diese Einladung sollte die Initialzündung für den Werkzyklus *St. Helena* darstellen. Dafür hängte der Künstler in den Oberlichtsaal des Kunsthauses während einiger Monate ein Autowrack, das fast unbemerkt seine skulpturale Erscheinung veränderte. Was davon übrig blieb, ist die Dokumentation einer der Eröffnung vorangegangenen Aktion, die den Titel *Austerlitz I* erhielt. Die Schlacht von Austerlitz ging als wichtigste militärische Errungenschaft Napoleons in die Weltgeschichte ein. Exakt ein Jahr nach seiner Selbstkrönung zum Kaiser der Franzosen, am 2. Dezember 1805, besiegte Napoleon I. am Pratzeberg zwischen Brünn und Austerlitz die österreichischen und russischen Truppen. Für Germanns Werk nun wurde durch Menschenkraft und mittels eines Habegger-Zugsystems die abgetrennte und ausgehöhlte Hinterseite eines Renault 21 zur metallverstärkten Glasdecke hochgezogen. Mit der Befestigung eines zusätzlichen Betongewichts wurde das Autoheck innerhalb weniger Sekunden auseinandergefaltet und erinnerte durch seine Form, die graubeige Farbe sowie seinen Titel *Austerlitz* an eine sich öffnende Auster. Während rund dreier Monate verwies das Relikt auf die Aktion,

3—Galerie BolteLang, Zürich, 28. August bis 2. Oktober 2010.

4—Mit u. a. Nina Beier & Marie Lund, Stefan Burger, Nina Canell, Florian Germann, Navid Nuur – Kunsthaus Glarus, 7. Februar bis 2. Mai 2010, kuratiert von Alexandra Blättler und Sabine Rusterholz.

die in der Folge als filmische Dokumentation unter dem Titel *Austerlitz I* existieren würde, wobei man das restliche Material – ausser einer blauen Halterung, die später in *Austerlitz II* wiederverwendet wurde – entsorgte.

Der erste Akt war somit vollbracht, doch weitere «Bubenstreiche» sollten folgen. Die Nennung der Schlacht von Austerlitz unterstreicht die Bedeutung und dadurch gewonnene Bewunderung und Berühmtheit von Napoleons Kriegsführungsstrategie. Seine bis ins Detail durchdachten Eroberungsaktionen sind dem genauso detailliert konstruierten Erzählstrang von Germanns *St. Helena* in Intensität, Intelligenz und Durchdachtheit verwandt.

Im Folgenden sollen die einzelnen Teile des Zyklus, die faktisch oder assoziativ miteinander in Beziehung stehen, erläutert werden. Im Schaufenster zur Strasse, als Einstieg in die Ausstellung, hing eine vergilbte Postkarte, die John Gutzon de la Mothe Borglum bei der Arbeit zeigt. Borglum wurde 1867 in Idaho geboren und war ein US-amerikanischer Bildhauer. Sein Hauptwerk ist das Mount Rushmore National Memorial in Keystone (South Dakota), das vier monumentale Porträts der US-amerikanischen Präsidenten George Washington, Thomas Jefferson, Abraham Lincoln und Theodore Roosevelt zeigt und das als Heiligenschrein für die Demokratie angesehen wird. Zwischen 1927 und 1941 wurde das Monument in den Granit des Mount Rushmore gesprengt, gehauen und gemeisselt. An den Arbeiten waren rund 400 Mitwirkende beteiligt. Das Gebiet war bekannt für seine grossen Goldvorkommen. Interessant ist an dieser Stelle, dass auch Napoleon Bonaparte einst zu den Besitzern dieses Berges gezählt haben soll – ein für Germann wichtiges und initiales Moment in der Weitererzählung seiner Geschichte. Jedoch muss ihn, der aus dem Berufsstand der Bildhauerei und Restauration stammt, die Megalomanie eines solchen Vorhabens geradezu fasziniert haben. Neben Napoleon wäre somit der zweite nicht unbefleckte Held und Protagonist aus Germanns Geschichte vorgestellt.

Cyprien Gaillard beschäftigte sich 2008 in der Arbeit *Crazy Horse* mit dem Mount-Rushmore-Monument: Er filmte die Entstehung des noch grösser angelegten und in der Nähe in eine Felswand gesprengten Denkmals für den legendären Häuptling der Sioux-Indianer. 1948 begann der Bildhauer Korczak Ziółkowski mit dem Bau dieses Monuments, das nach seiner Fertigstellung zu den grössten Skulpturen der Welt zählen wird und als Antwort der Native Americans auf Mount Rushmore zu lesen ist.

Borglum stieg morgens in eine speziell für Handwerker gefertigte Holzschaukel und liess sich erst abends wieder abseilen. Davon inspiriert, nahm Germann im Innern der Galerie — sozusagen in der Verdoppelung zur Postkarte im Schaufenster — während der gesamten Eröffnungszeit von zirka drei Stunden hoch oben auf einer Schaukel die Position Borglums ein und fertigte – abgeschottet vom Publikum – ein abstrahiertes Napoleon-Emblem als Tonrelief. Während des Vorgangs bröckelte zusätzlicher Ton durch ein Loch in der Wand ins Schaufenster und hinterliess nach getaner Aktion einen kleinen Haufen unterhalb der präsentierten Postkarte, die ihrerseits Borglum am Hang eines Berges zeigt. Relief und Schaukel blieben als Relikte und Verweise auf die Aktion während der Ausstellungsdauer gegenwärtig. Neben der projizierten Dokumentation *Austerlitz I* befanden sich zusätzlich drei weitere Werkgruppen im Raum.

Zehn Silbergelatine-Prints auf Messingplatten mit dem Titel *Dante's Inferno* bilden überlieferte Motive der Alabasterhöhlen in Woodward County in Oklahoma ab. Es handelt sich um eine 1200 Meter lange Gipshöhle mit verschiedenfarbigen Ausformungen von Alabaster. Vor über 200 Millionen Jahren überdeckte ein grosser See die Gegend, wobei beim Austrocknen gipshaltige Ablagerungen zurückblieben. Mit dem Titel des Werks öffnet Germann den Referenzhorizont auf Dantes *Göttliche Komödie* und spielt insbesondere auf die Vorstellung der Hölle (Höhle) an. Die Motivik und Ästhetik der Messingplatten macht den Bezug zu Gustave Dorés 1861 geschaffene Darstellung der *Göttlichen Komödie* und insbesondere des Infernos im Stich naheliegend.

Räumlich befanden sich die Arbeiten *Untitled (Austerlitz II)* und *Untitled (Napoleon's Wife)* auf demselben Tisch wie *Dante's Inferno*. Während längerer Zeit züchtete Germann französische und russische Austern, um im Kontext der Ausstellung die versuchte Kreuzung zweier Austern unterschiedlicher Herkunft zu demonstrieren. Wiederum spielt er hier auf Napoleons Russlandfeldzug an – nimmt jedoch in diesem Zusammenhang auch das in *Dante's Inferno* eingeführte Thema des Alabasters wieder auf. Durch das Experiment der Zusammenführung zweier unterschiedlicher Austernsorten durch die bei *Austerlitz I* verwendete blaue Halterung in einem Nylongefäss soll dargelegt werden, wie der durch die Auster produzierte alabasterartige Kalk über längere Zeit alles überziehen und sich das Material und somit das Objekt verwandeln wird.

Untitled (Napoleon's Wife) vereint auf Nylonsockeln drei Silikonabgüsse von Objekten, die Germann auf dem Schloss Arenenberg vorfand: Es handelt sich dabei um einen Kanonenlauf, den Bleisack eines Gewehrs und einen (an Munition erinnernden) Maiskolben aus dem gross angelegten Garten. Durch die Materialität, die Form und das Wissen um die zahlreichen Liebschaften Napoleons werden durchaus sexuell konnotierte Inhalte transportiert. Einmal mehr weisen Kanonenlauf, Bleisack und Munition auf die mit Napoleon verbundene Waffen- und Kriegsindustrie hin. In diesem Zusammenhang wird überliefert, dass Napoleon nach der Schlacht von Austerlitz die Kanonen der Russen plündern und in Frankreich in einer Metallgiesserei einschmelzen liess, um im Anschluss daran die daraus gefertigte Siegessäule auf dem Pariser Place Vendôme einzuweihen. Deutlich tritt des Künstlers Interesse am Prozess einer ähnlichen Transformation des Materials in der Teilarbeit *Untitled (Napoleon's Wife)* zutage.

In direkter Verwandtschaft mit den Alabasterhöhlen steht die Arbeit *Ansage (aus den Tiefen der Berge)*, bestehend aus einem alten Industriekühlschrank, in dessen Innerem die in der Höhle von Saint-Léonard aufgenommenen Balzrufe der Napoleonfrösche durch ein Abspielgerät hörbar gemacht werden. *Napoleon's Head/Athanor* ist ein hölzerner Körper, der auf den ersten Blick an ein immenses Instrument denken lässt und aus einer gewissen Perspektive wiederum formal auf Napoleons Zweispitz anspielt. Durch die Gussform im Innern – sogenannte Giesskanäle und eine kleine Ader für das Entweichen der Luft – bekommt vor allem der zweite Titel der Arbeit eine konkrete Bedeutung: Vor uns liegt ein für alchemistische Vorgänge gefertigter Ofen. Für die Alchemie wichtige Prozesse sind Erwärmung oder Erhitzung. Fachbegriffe wie «Destillation», «Sublimation» und «Digerieren» beschreiben die drei Hauptprozesse im Reifungsprozess eines neu gewonnenen Materials durch den sogenannten philosophischen Ofen. Konkret handelt es sich um eine Gussform für zwei Kugelgrössen – in der Dimension von handelsüblichen historischen Kanonen.

Germanns Werk lässt sich in seiner Materialverschriebenheit und Prozesshaftigkeit klar in der Tradition von Beuys, der individuellen Mythologien und des Geniekults ansiedeln. Das Erfassen dieser multiplen Vielschichtigkeit kann fast nur in seiner Ganzheit und weniger in der sezierenden Analyse gerettet werden. Zu denken ist hier an die Lektüre Marcel Prousts *À la recherche du temps perdu*, die noch Jahre später ein Gefühl zurücklässt, der Wahrheit für wenige Sekunden direkt ins Auge geblickt zu haben. Dabei bleibt einem jeden die Szene mit der Madeleine in Erinnerung – einer kleinen, unscheinbaren Szene in diesem Meisterwerk der Weltliteratur. Der Geistesblitz einer kurzen Offenbarung der Weltgeschichte liegt auch der Rezeption von *St. Helena* zugrunde, ohne dass das Werk den Anspruch beinhaltet, bis in seine letzten Teilstücke gedeutet werden zu können oder zu wollen.

Ob das Werk *St. Helena/Reichtümer aus der Tiefe der Berge* mit dem besprochenen Zyklus schliessen wird, hängt davon ab, ob Germann nicht nur metaphorisch die Geschichte Napoleons nachzeichnet, sondern, wie geplant, die Biografie Napoleons eigens handschriftlich neu schreiben wird. Dazu reproduzierte Germann durch einen chemikalischen Vorgang die Tinte der wohl berühmtesten und für Napoleons Glorifizierung wesentlichen Biografie aus dem Jahr 1827, geschrieben von Jacques de Norvins (1769–1854), des Barons Marquet de Montbreton – Magistrat, Begleiter und Biograf von Napoleon: «L'examen de la vie de Napoléon, me disais-je, laisse dominer trois grands caractères: l'excès du génie, l'excès de la fortune et l'excès du malheur.»

Saint Helena / Riches from the Depths of the Mountains

Alexandra Blättler

Saint Helena—Arenenberg—Saint-Léonard

Due to its remote location and inaccessible coastline, the notorious island of Saint Helena never had an indigenous population, and remained uninhabited until the sixteenth century. The Portuguese discovered it; later on, the English also laid claim to Saint Helena. Various armed altercations ensued, and eventually the island became an English possession. Large farms were created, and black African and Chinese laborers were brought in. Saint Helena's wealth grew—particularly because its protected geographic situation recommended it for the storage of large quantities of gold. In 1815, the British government selected Saint Helena as the place of exile for Napoleon, who was deported there in October of the same year, and resided at Longwood House until his death on May 5, 1821.

But Napoleon Bonaparte, the French general, statesman, and, finally, self-appointed emperor under the title of Napoleon I, had seen many places before that. One of them is in the immediate vicinity of the place the artist Florian Germann calls home. Since the mid-fifteenth century, the residents of Schloss Arenenberg have enjoyed the gorgeous views from the chateau's perch high above the Untersee, the western branch of Lake Constance. Like a precious jewel, the magnificent grounds invite the visitor to explore the surrounding forests and embark on a tour of the multifaceted history of the region around the lake. The chateau must have fascinated Germann even in his teenage years: a relic of European history that attested to Bonaparte's charisma and intelligence, survived no more than a stone's throw from where he was born. This fascination, and the memory of growing up in close proximity to the castle, made a lasting impression on Germann, so much so that they led him, years later, to develop the cycle of works discussed in the present pages.

Originally built as a country estate for a patrician family from Constance, the chateau entered the focus of world history in the nineteenth century, when it became a residence of the French imperial family. Hortense de Beauharnais, the adopted daughter and sister-in-law of Napoleon I, had the late Gothic chateau reconstructed in the Empire style, and redesigned the park on Arenenberg hill to resemble French models. She hosted social gatherings that emulated the famous salons of her time and drew eminent people to Lake Constance. Documents bearing names such as Dumas, Récamier, Chateaubriand, and those of the entire European high nobility fill the inventory of the chateau's archives. The interiors were decorated with wallpapers, furniture, sculptures, and pictures that commemorated Napoleon I. After Hortense died in 1837, her son Louis Napoléon sold the chateau, but bought it back in 1855—he was now the French emperor, calling himself Napoleon III. In 1906, Eugénie, the widow of Emperor Napoleon III, donated the property to the canton of Thurgau, which has since operated a Napoleon museum in the chateau—the German-speaking world's only museum, it should be noted, dedicated to Napoleonic history.[1]

At the other end of Switzerland, geographically speaking, is the *lac souterrain* beneath the Alps of the Valais. This subterranean lake at Saint-Léonard was first explored by Jean-Jacques Pittard in 1943, and has been open to the public since 1949. At 300 meters (1000 feet) long, 20 meters (66 feet) wide, and 10 meters (33 feet) deep, it is Europe's largest navigable subterranean lake.[2] At first glance, it may seem as though this place, enshrouded in myth, has nothing to do with Napoleon. But as the artist notes, the subterranean grotto is home, among other species, to a kind of frog, said to be blind, whose vernacular name

1—http://www.napoleonmuseum.ch.
2—http://www.lac-souterrain.com.

is "Napoleon frog": when the animal pulls its hind legs up close to its body, the resulting anatomical shape recalls Napoleon's headgear, the bicorn. This fact, the "song" of the Napoleon frogs, and the location of the grotto, as well as other cultural monuments and nature reserves associated with Napoleon (Mount Rushmore National Memorial and Alabaster Caverns State Park, Woodward County, Oklahoma) will be explained in the following history surrounding the cycle of works *Saint Helena*.

Austerlitz—Mount Rushmore—Woodward County

The circumstances laid out by way of introduction above indicate the outlines of a description and interpretation of the wide-ranging and complex narrative at the heart of the cycle *Saint Helena/Riches from the Depths of the Mountains*. When first confronted with the installation, the beholder rambles and wanders through a field of historic events, mythological references, half-fictions, fantastic fairytale-like elements, and scientific fact. Germann himself has aptly described his technique as the "perambulation of an inward library that seeks to detect as yet uncombined possibilities." The remark attests both to the artist's youthful zest for exploration and research, and to the repertoire of knowledge and experience he has built up over the years. The beholder witnesses the transformation of a historic-epic plot as well as a dynamic work process. Germann, in other words, not only probes combinations between different historical circumstances, he also gives an equally significant if not greater role to the identification of materials to work with, and to transformations of energies and materials. The artist appropriates found objects and relics or meticulously made replicas, using them to interweave traditional stories, whose rearrangement in the work of art obscures them or charges them with new meaning.

The title Germann has given to his exhibition emphasizes his fascination with natural resources, and hence with the riches that can be extracted in pure form from the depths of the mountains, such as iron, lead, copper, zinc, and sulfur, substances he has repeatedly used in his works.

In the exhibition *Saint Helena/Riches from the Depths of the Mountains*, Germann brought the works he created over the course of 2010 together, in a provisional installation under the same title.[3] The show represents the culmination of months of research, the carving and sanding of a wood sculpture, cultivating Russian and French oysters, and the invitation to develop a so-called performance work for the exhibition *Performative Attitudes* at Kunsthaus Glarus.[4] This invitation proved the initial stimulus that would lead to the creation of the *Saint Helena* cycle. The artist suspended a wrecked car in the Kunsthaus's skylight hall, where it remained for several months as its sculptural appearance changed almost imperceptibly. What remained of it documents an action under the title *Austerlitz*, which took place before the show opened. The Battle of Austerlitz entered world history as Napoleon's most significant military accomplishment. A year to the day after he crowned himself emperor of the French, on December 2, 1805, Napoleon I vanquished the Austrian and Russian troops at Prace heights between Brno and Austerlitz. For Germann's work,

3—Galerie BolteLang, Zurich, August 28—October 2, 2010.
4—Featuring work by Nina Beier & Marie Lund, Stefan Burger, Nina Canell, Florian Germann, Navid Nuur, and others; Kunsthaus Glarus, February 7—May 2, 2010, curated by Alexandra Blättler and Sabine Rusterholz.

manpower, complemented by a Habegger hoist system, was used to lift the severed and gutted rear half of a Renault 21 up toward the glass ceiling, which had been reinforced with metal elements. By attaching an additional concrete weight, the car tail was unfolded in a matter of seconds; its shape, the gray-beige color, and the title *Austerlitz* now suggested an oyster—the German word is *Auster*—arrested in the act of opening up. For roughly three months, the relic referred to the action, which would survive in the form of a filmic documentation entitled *Austerlitz I*; the remaining material—with the exception of a blue bracket, which would be reused in *Austerlitz II*—was disposed of.

So the first act was done; but more "bad boy's tricks" would follow. Mentioning the Battle of Austerlitz emphasized the significance of Napoleon's war strategy, which earned him admiration and fame. The highly detailed construction of the narrative in Germann's *Saint Helena* is akin, in terms of intensity, intelligence, and elaborateness, to the emperor's carefully thought out expeditions of conquest.

In the following, I will discuss the individual parts of the cycle in their factual or associative interrelation. As a prelude to the exhibition, a yellowed postcard showing John Gutzon de la Mothe Borglum at work, was mounted in the gallery's street-facing window. Born in Idaho in 1867, Borglum was an American sculptor. His chef d'oeuvre is the Mount Rushmore National Memorial in Keystone, South Dakota, which consists of four monumental portraits of the presidents George Washington, Thomas Jefferson, Abraham Lincoln, and Theodore Roosevelt, and is seen as a shrine to the saints of American democracy. The monument was dynamited, carved, and chiseled into the granite face of Mount Rushmore. Around four hundred laborers were involved in the work. The area was known for its large gold deposits, and was accordingly much coveted. An interesting fact that should be noted at this point is that Napoleon Bonaparte is said to have been among the mountain's previous owners—an important aspect of its history that aroused Germann's interest in taking its story further. But what must have positively fascinated him, as a trained sculptor and restorer, was the megalomania of the project. Besides Napoleon, then, we have in Borglum the second hero and protagonist—he, too, not untainted—of Germann's story.

In his 2008 film *Crazy Horse*, Cyprien Gaillard examined the Mount Rushmore Memorial: he recorded work on the monument to the legendary Sioux leader, even grander in design, which is being dynamited into a cliff near Mount Rushmore. The sculptor Korczak Ziółkowski began work on the monument in 1948; it will be among the world's largest sculptures once it is completed, and must be read as a Native American response to Mount Rushmore.

Every morning, Borglum stepped onto a wooden swing stage especially manufactured for the craftsmen, from which he did not rope down until the evening. Inspired by this procedure, Germann took up Borglum's position inside the gallery, on a scaffold suspended from the ceiling, during the opening, reenacting, we might say, the postcard in the display window; concealed from the audience, he created a clay relief showing an abstract Napoleon emblem. Leftover clay crumbling off during this procedure fell through a hole in the wall into the display window, where it formed a small heap beneath the postcard presented there, which in turn shows Borglum on a mountain slope. The relief and the scaffold remained in place for the entire duration of the exhibition as relics referring to the action. In addition to the projection of the documentary *Austerlitz I* from Glarus, the room contained three more groups of works.

Ten silver gelatin prints on brass panels entitled *Dante's Inferno* depict motifs that have been found in the alabaster caverns in Woodward County, Oklahoma. This system of gypsum caves, which stretches over 1200 meters (.75 miles), contains a variety of alabaster formations in different colors. More than two hundred million years ago, a large inland sea covered the era, and its evaporation left large deposits containing gypsum. With the title of this work, Germann opens the referential horizon toward Dante's *Divine Comedy*, alluding in particular to the idea of hell (the German words for "hell" and "cave" are very similar). The motifs and aesthetic of the brass panels suggest an association with Gustave Doré's 1861 illustrations of the *Divine Comedy* and in particular with his engravings depicting scenes from the *Inferno*.

In terms of spatial arrangement, the works *Untitled (Austerlitz II)* and *Untitled (Napoleon's Wife)* were displayed on the same table with *Dante's Inferno*. As mentioned above, Germann had spent considerable time growing French and Russian oysters in order to demonstrate an attempted union between oysters of different origin in the context of the exhibition. He once again alludes to Napoleon's invasion of Russia—but now also picks up again on the theme of alabaster, introduced in *Dante's Inferno*. The experiment, in which the blue bracket from *Austerlitz I* is used to bring two different species of oyster together in a nylon container, is meant to show how the alabaster-like calcium deposits the oyster produces will over time cover everything, transforming the material and, with it, the object itself.

Untitled (Napoleon's Wife) unites three silicone casts on nylon pedestals of objects Germann found at Schloss Arenenberg: a cannon barrel, a Rifle ball bag, and a corncob (suggestive of a piece of ammunition) from the chateau's large gardens. The materiality and shapes of these objects, in combination with our awareness of Napoleon's numerous love affairs, transmit quite explicit sexual connotations. Cannon barrel, ball bag, and ammunition are also further references to the armaments and war industries associated with Napoleon. An anecdote that is relevant in this context is that Napoleon had his soldiers plunder the Russians' cannons after the Battle of Austerlitz and bring them to a foundry in France, where they were smelted down for the victory column he subsequently erected on Paris's Place Vendôme. The artist's interest in a similar process of transformation of material is clearly manifest in the component work *Untitled (Napoleon's Wife)*.

Directly related to the alabaster caverns is the work *Ansage (aus den Tiefen der Berge)* (*Announcement [from the depths of the mountains]*), which consists of an old industrial refrigerator, inside which an audio device plays a recording of the Napoleon frog's courtship croaking, recorded by the artist in the cave at Saint-Léonard. *Napoleon's Head/Athanor* is a wooden corpus that, at first glance, suggests an immense musical instrument; looked at from a specific angle, it represents another formal allusion to Napoleon's bicorn. The casting mold on its inside—with so-called casting channels and a small vein allowing air to escape—lends concrete meaning to the work's second title in particular: we are looking at a furnace designed for alchemical procedures. Important processes in alchemy rely on warming or heating. Art terms such as "distillation," "sublimation" and "digestion" describe the three main processes in the maturation of a newly created material that are effected by the so-called philosophical furnace. The mold in this particular instance is shaped to produce spherical objects in two sizes—the dimensions of cannonballs for two historic standard cannon barrels.

With the diversity of materials employed and the importance given to process, Germann's art clearly stands in the Beuysian tradition, with its private mythologies and cult of genius. An understanding of this multifaceted complexity can be secured almost only by considering the work in its entirety; a dissecting analysis is less helpful. One might compare the experience to that of Marcel Proust's *À la recherche du temps perdu*, which leaves the reader, even years later, with a sense of having looked truth directly in the eye, if only for a few seconds. Everyone remembers the scene with the madeleine—a small and inconspicuous scene in this masterwork of world literature. The sudden scintilla of a brief revelation of world history is at the root of our experience of *Saint Helena* as well, even as the work makes no claim to permit, let alone invite, an interpretation that makes sense of every single one of its components.

Does the cycle discussed in the preceding pages complete *Saint Helena/Riches from the Depths of the Mountains*? It depends on whether Germann, not content with tracing the history of Napoleon in metaphorical terms, will realize his plan to produce a dedicated handwritten rewriting of Napoleon's life. For this purpose, Germann chemically reproduced the ink used for what is probably the most famous biography of Napoleon and the one that epitomized his glorification, penned in 1827 by Jacques de Norvins (1769–1854), Baron Marquet de Montbreton, Napoleon's magistrate, companion, and biographer, who wrote: "L'examen de la vie de Napoléon, me disais-je, laisse dominer trois grands caractères: l'excès du génie, l'excès de la fortune et l'excès du malheur."[5]

5—Jacques de Norvins, *Histoire de l'Empereur Napoléon* Dupont, Paris 1827, preface, pp. i–ii.

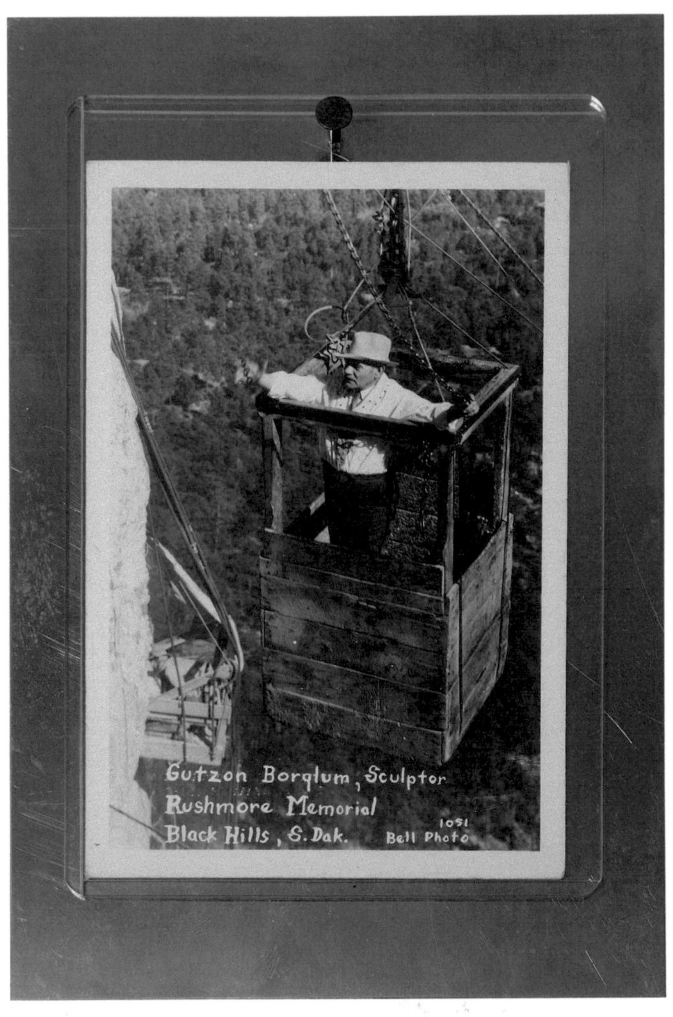
Gutzon Borglum, Sculptor
Rushmore Memorial
Black Hills, S. Dak.
1051
Bell Photo

Table displaying: *Dante's Inferno, 2010; Untitled (Napoleon's Wife)*, 2010; *Untitled (Austerlitz II)*, 2010

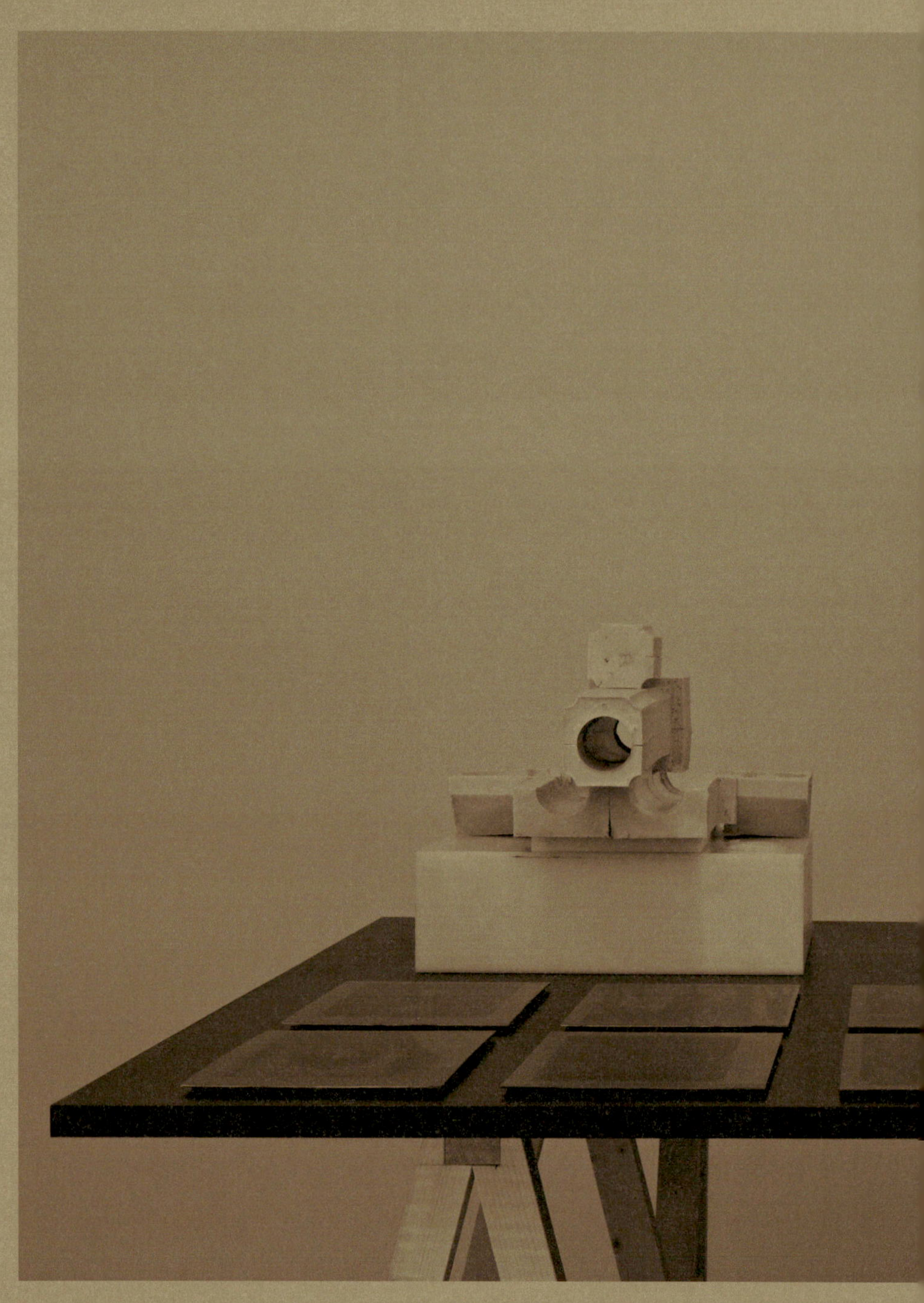

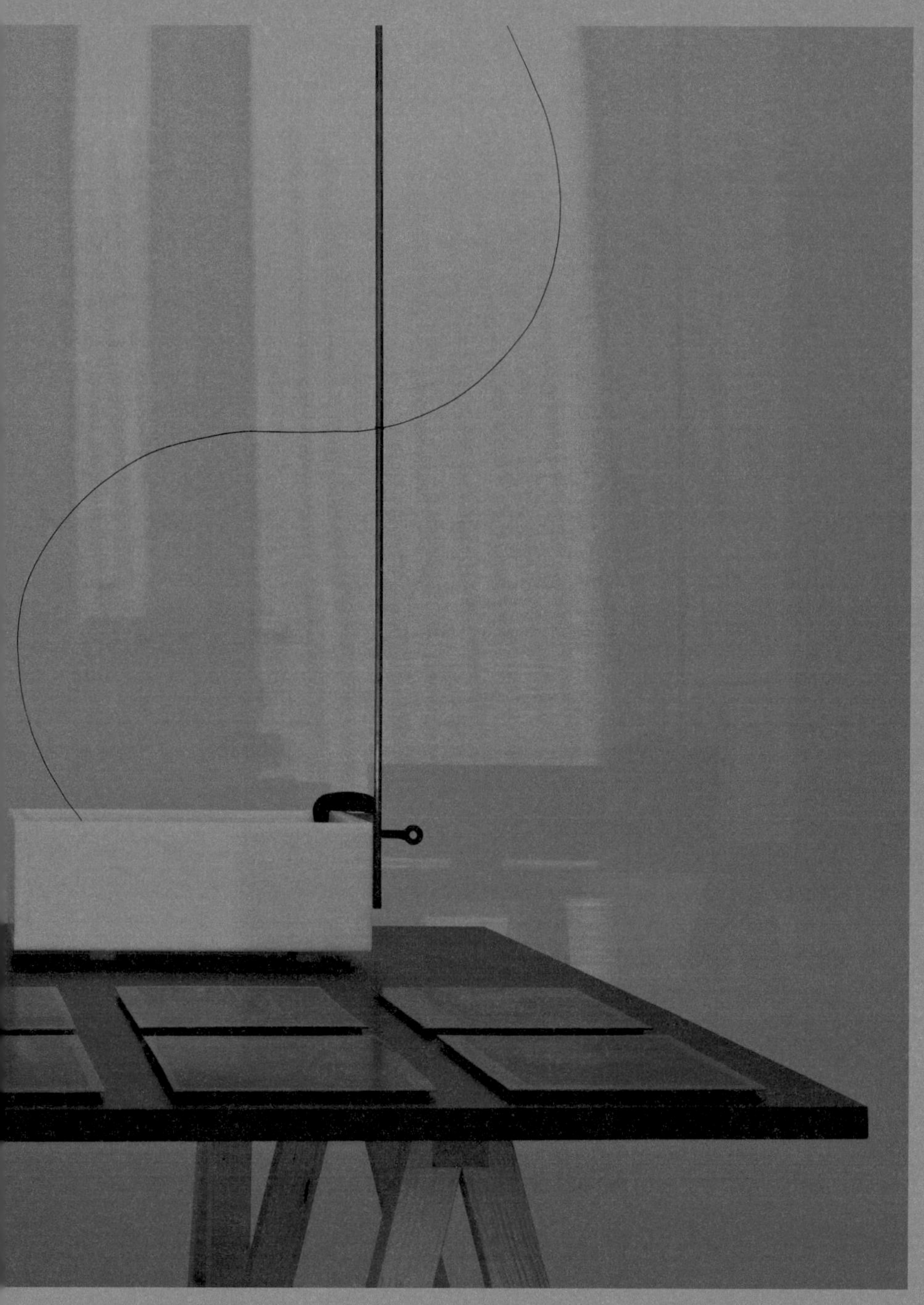

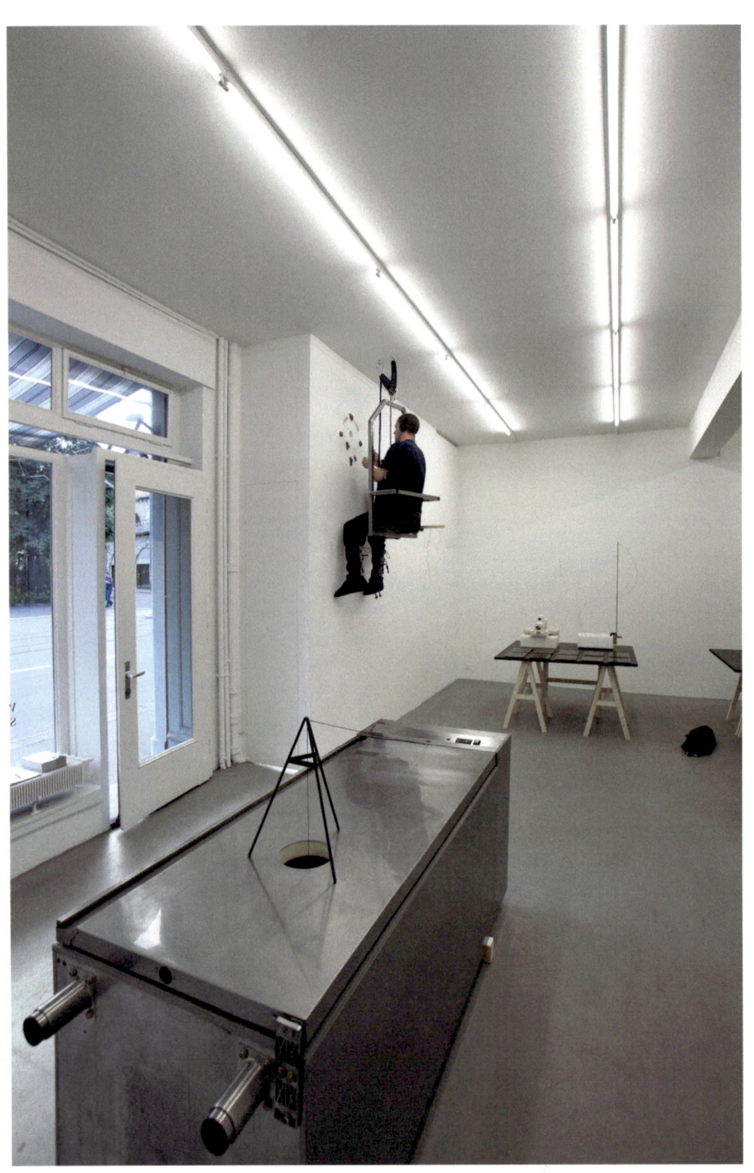

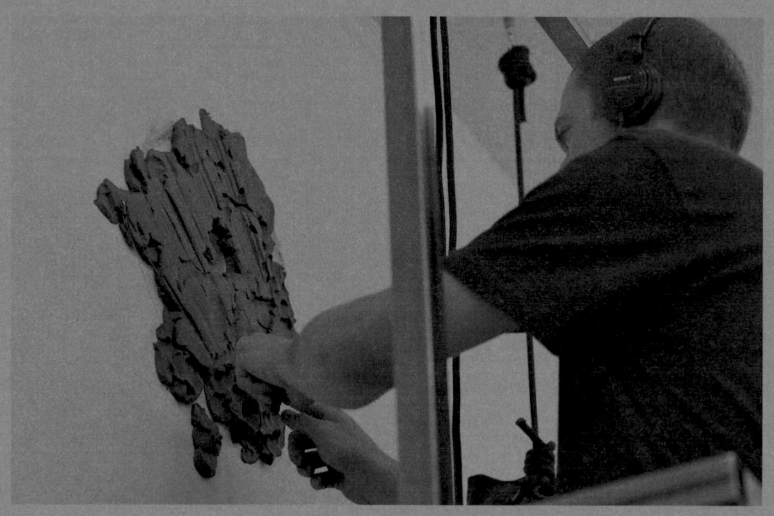

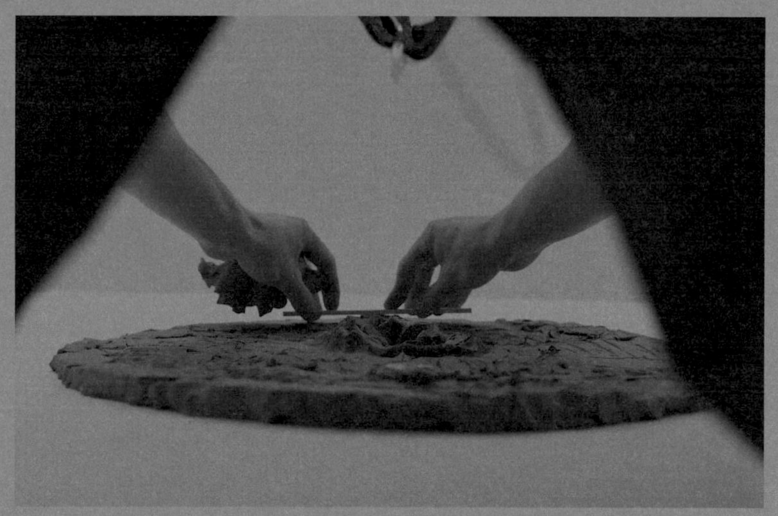

Table displaying: *Napoleon's Head/Athanor*, 2010

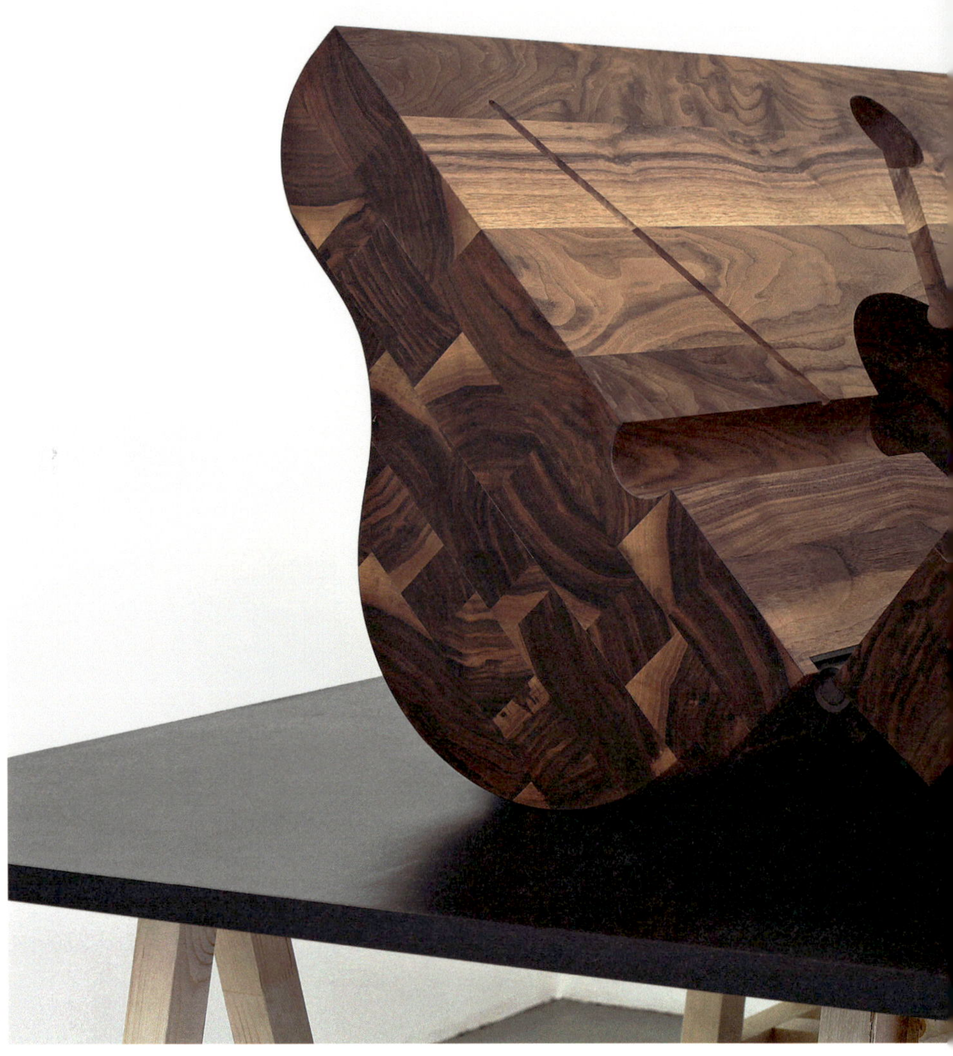

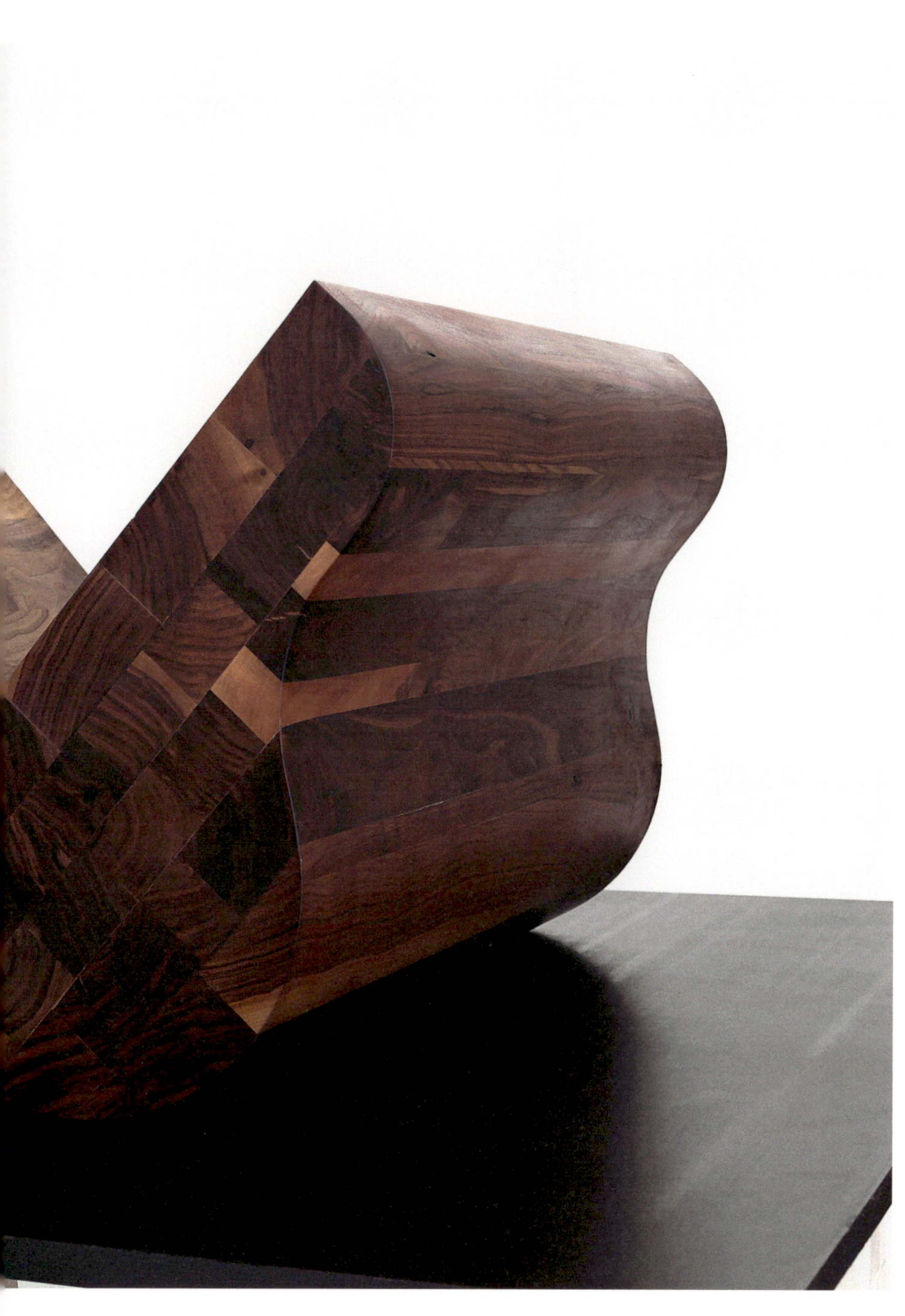

Untitled, 2010

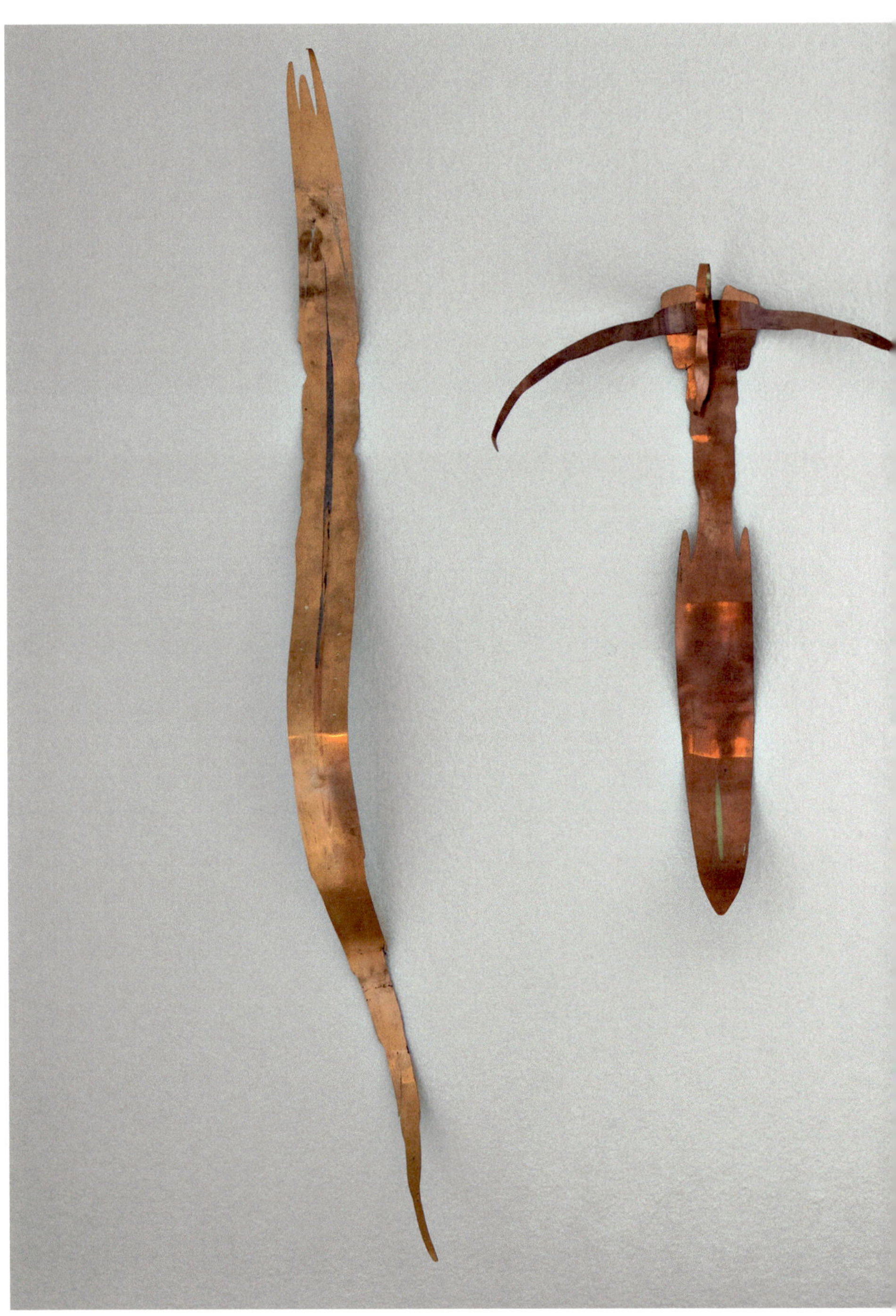

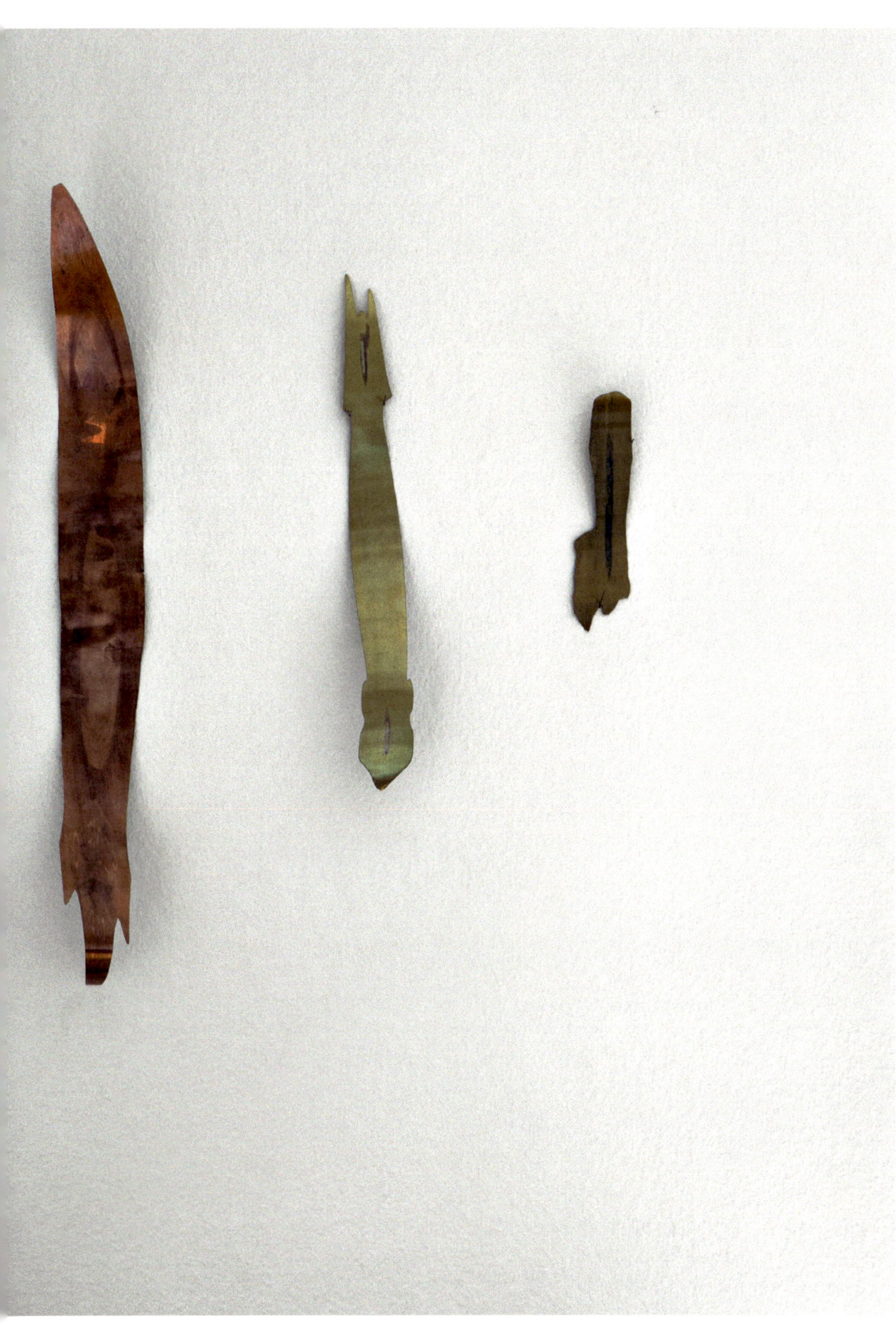

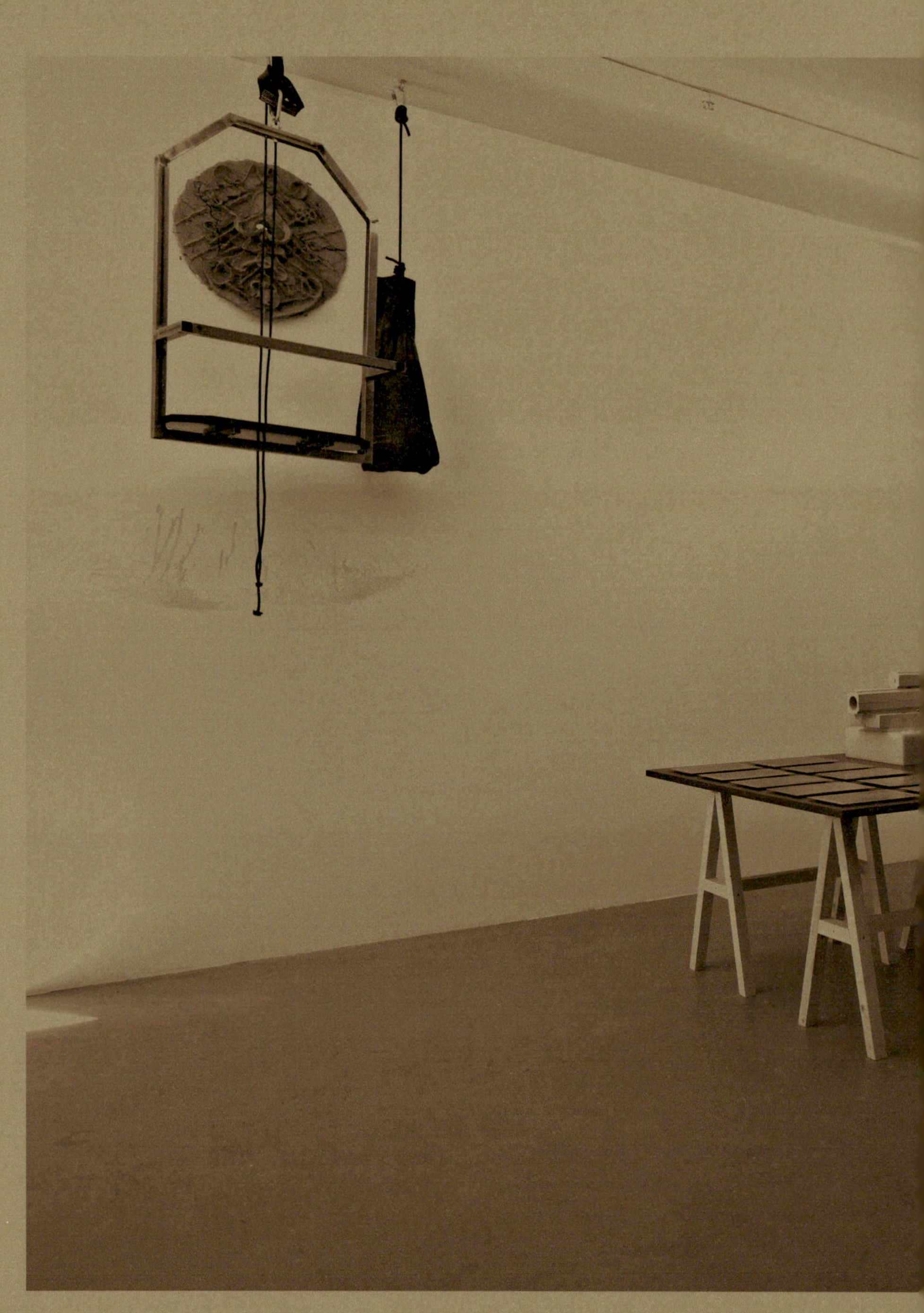

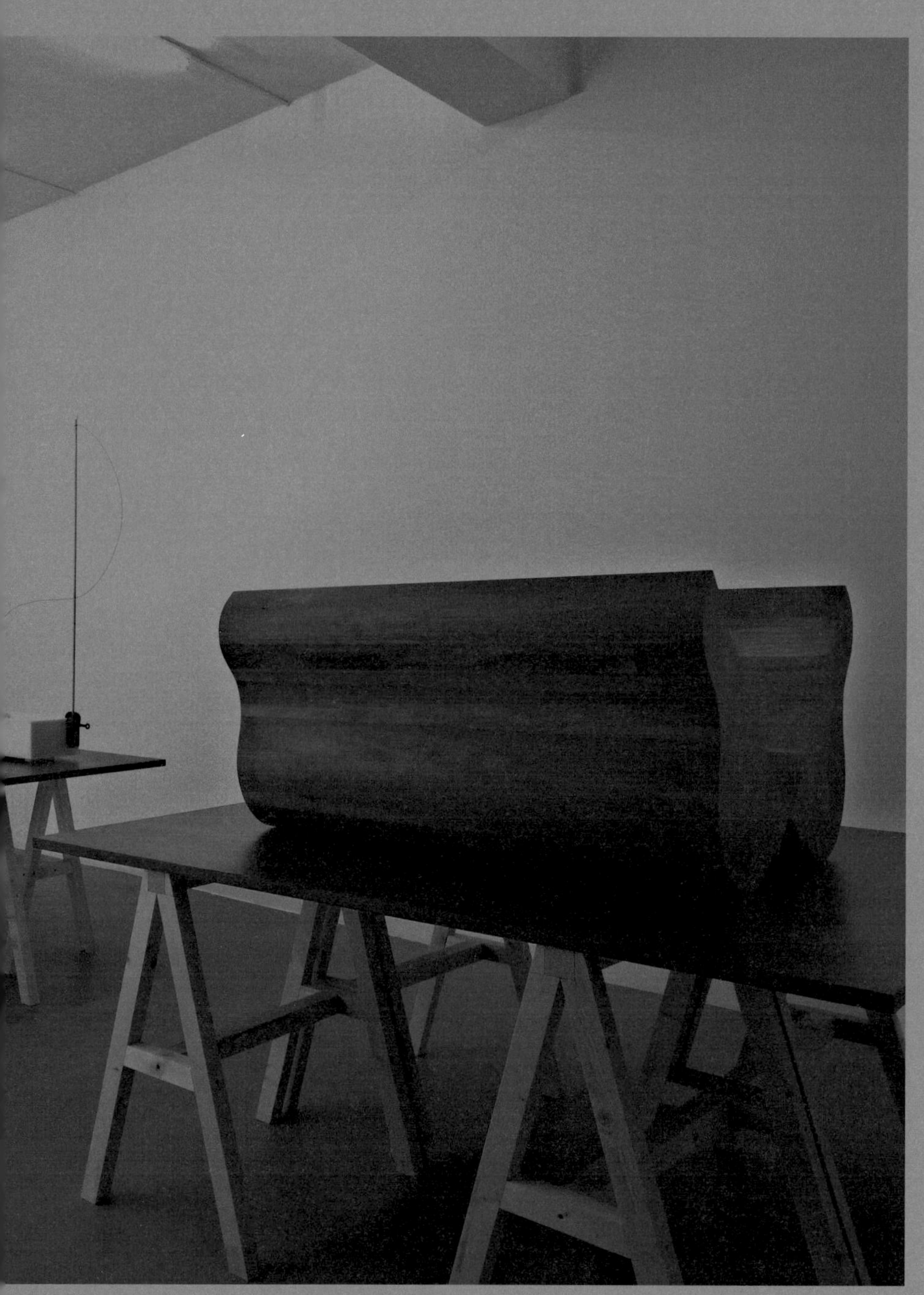

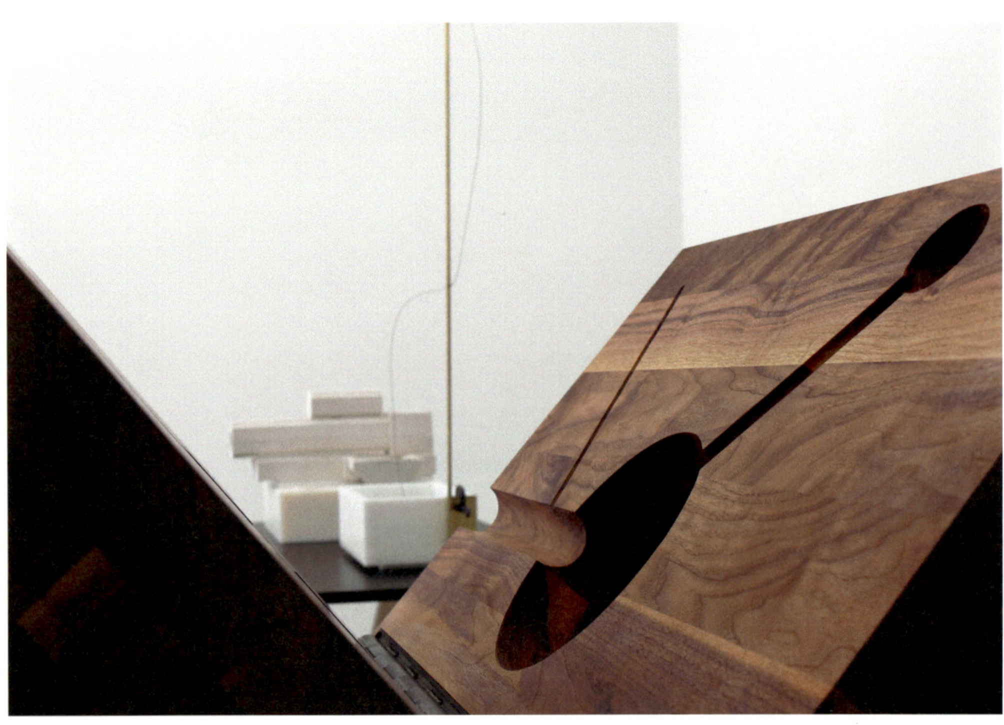

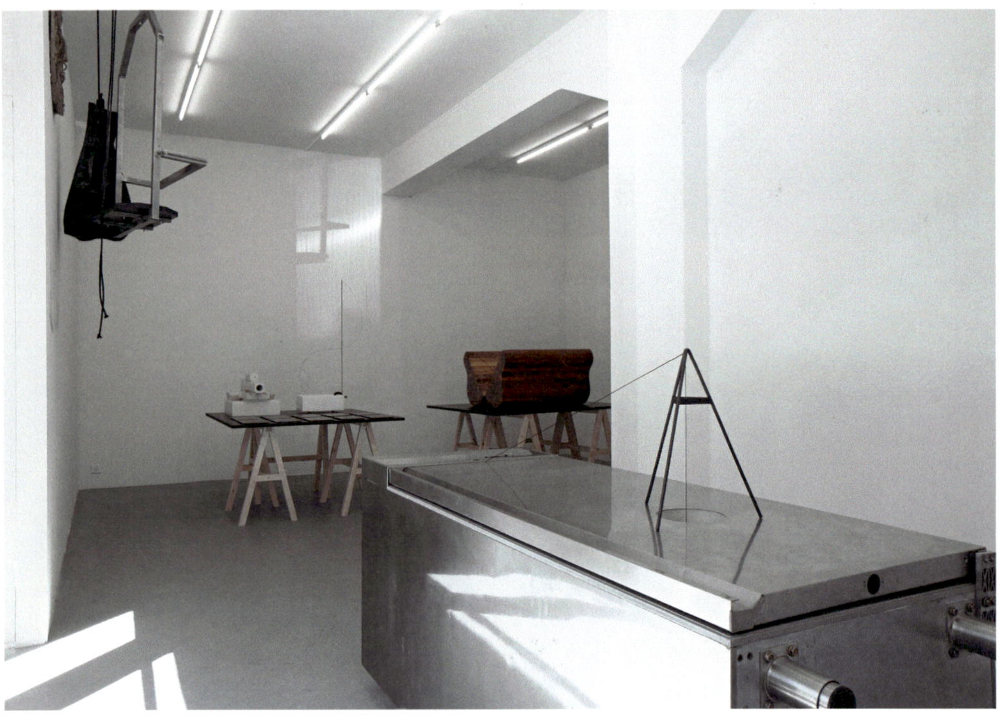

Ansage (aus den Tiefen der Berge), 2010

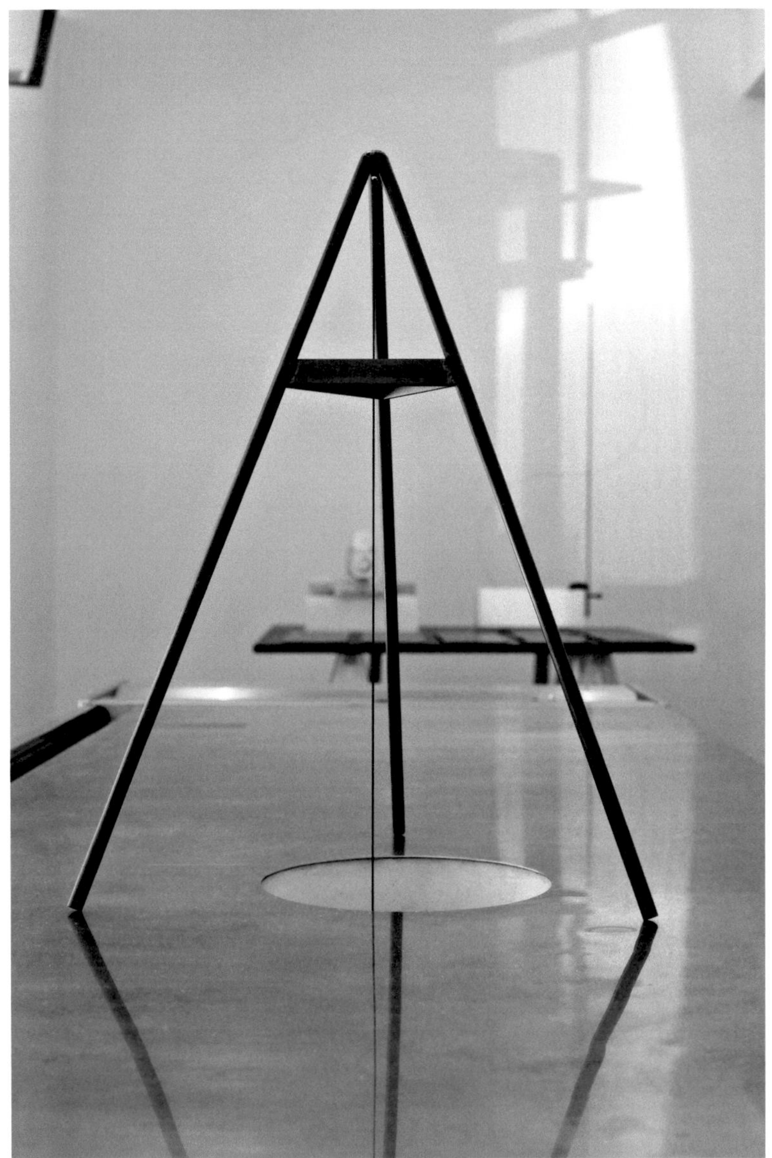

R.A.D.T.D.B., 2010

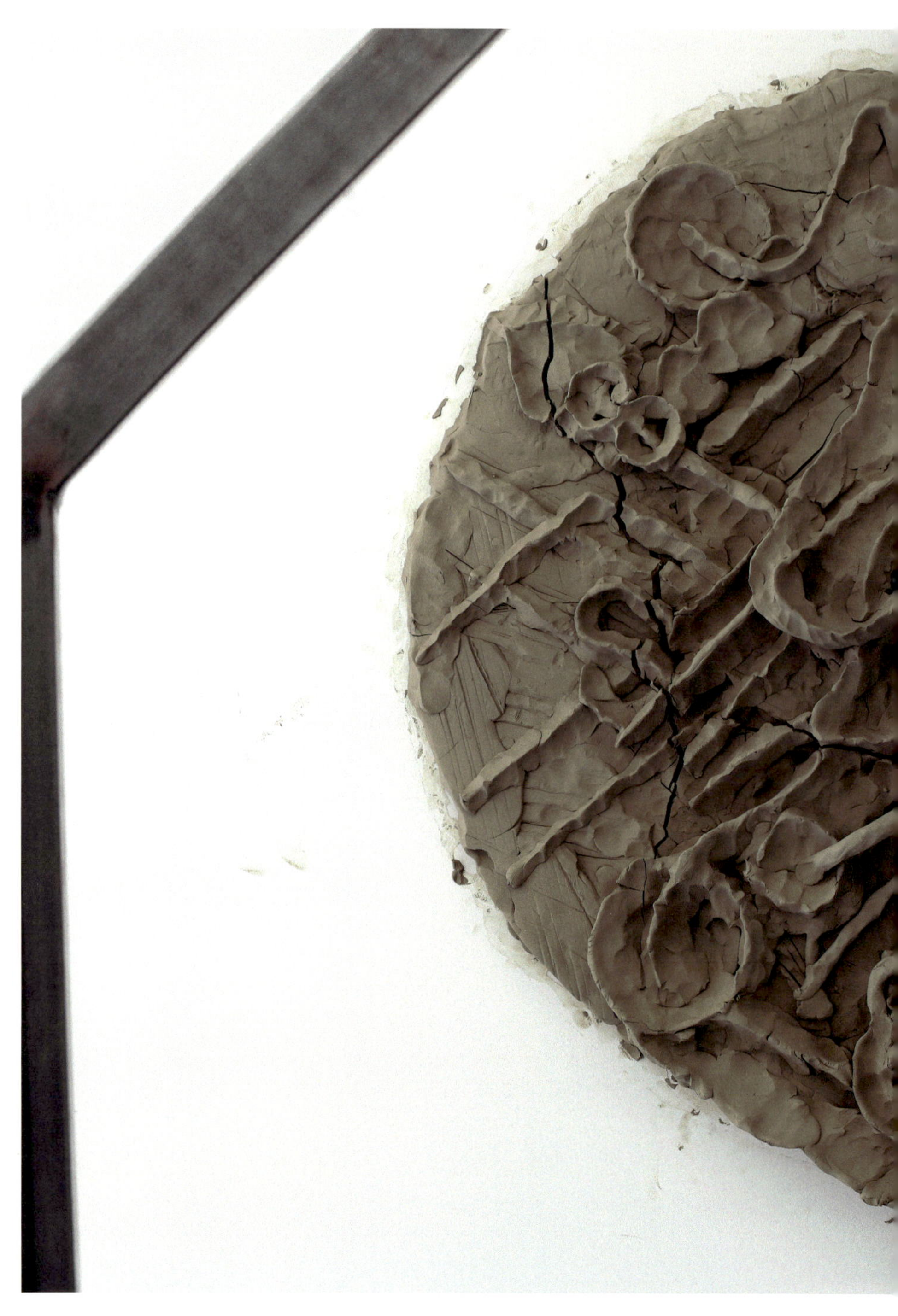

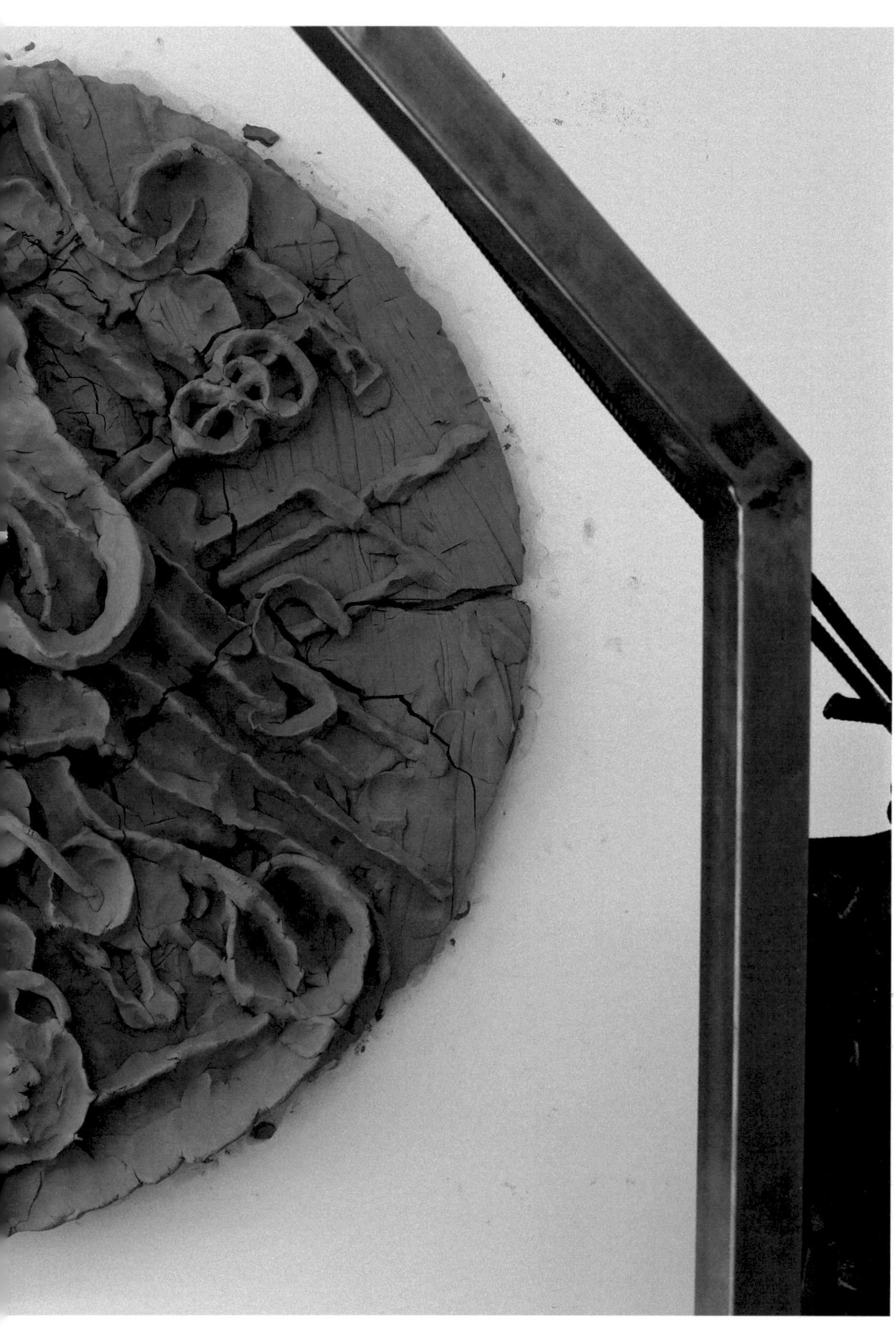

Ansage (aus den Tiefen der Berge), 2010

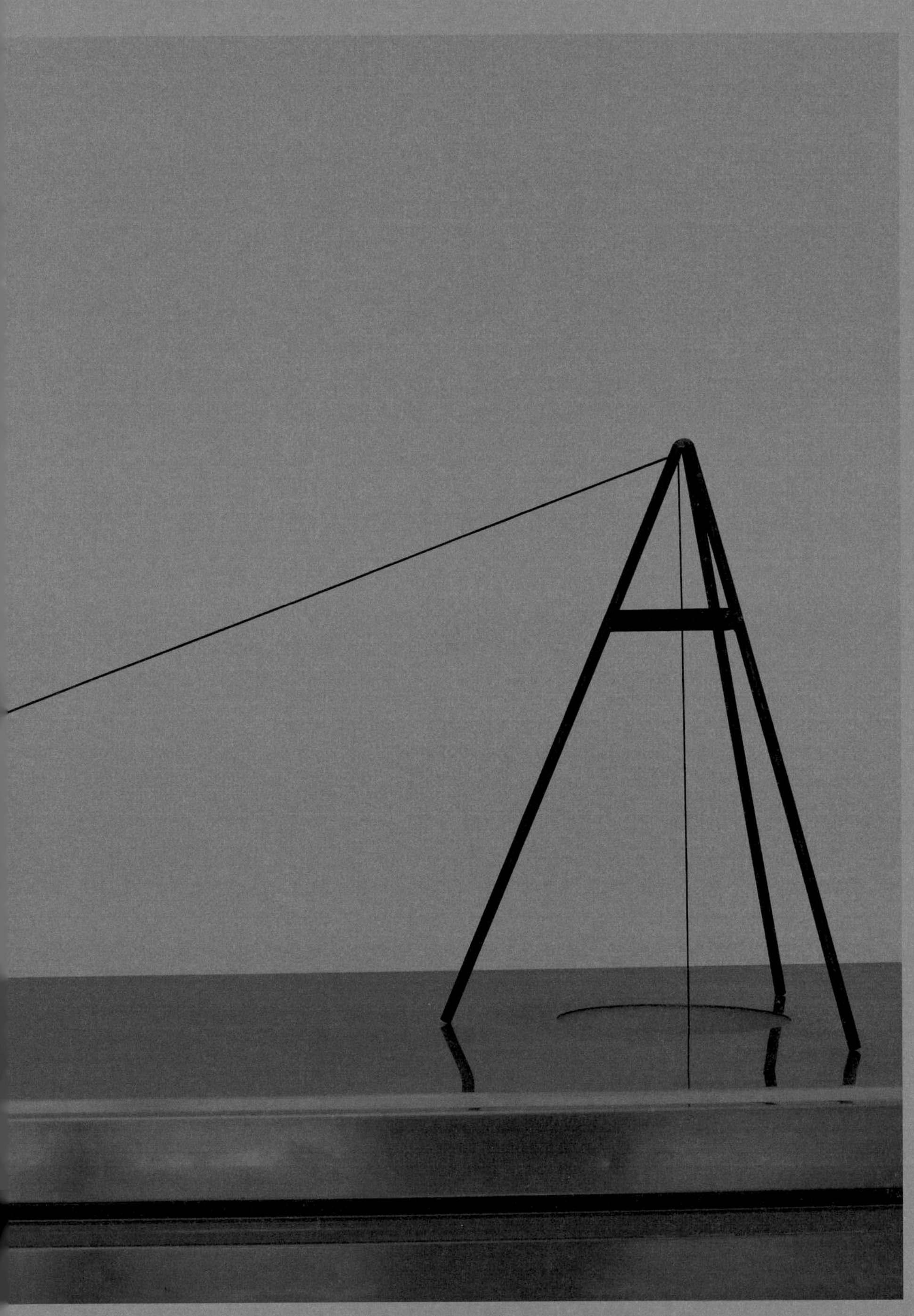

Untitled (Napoleon's Wife), 2010

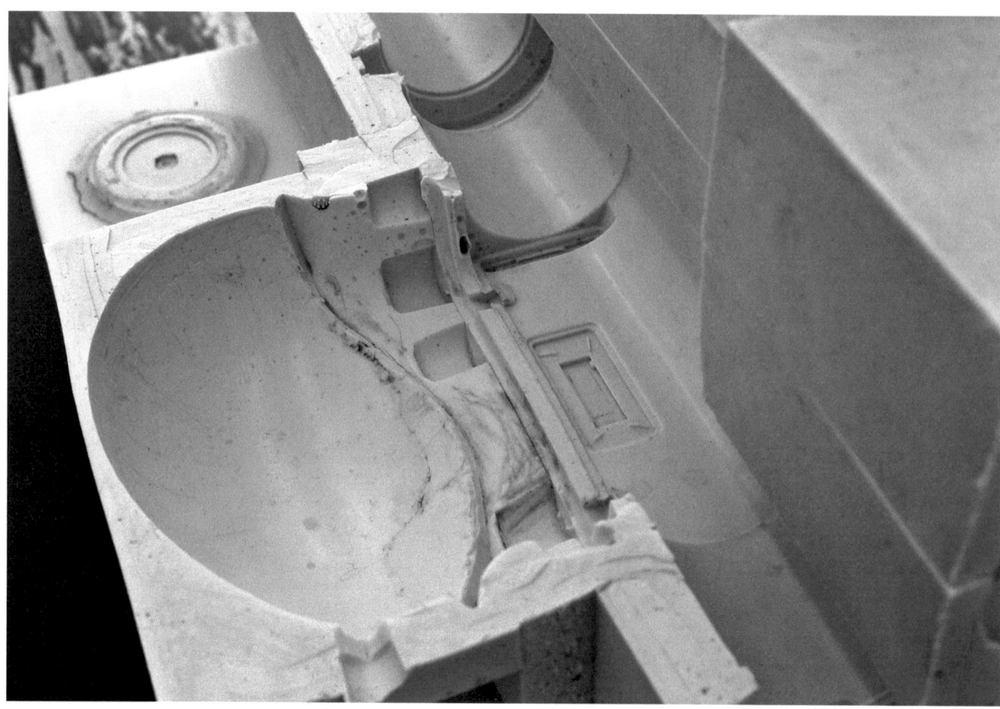

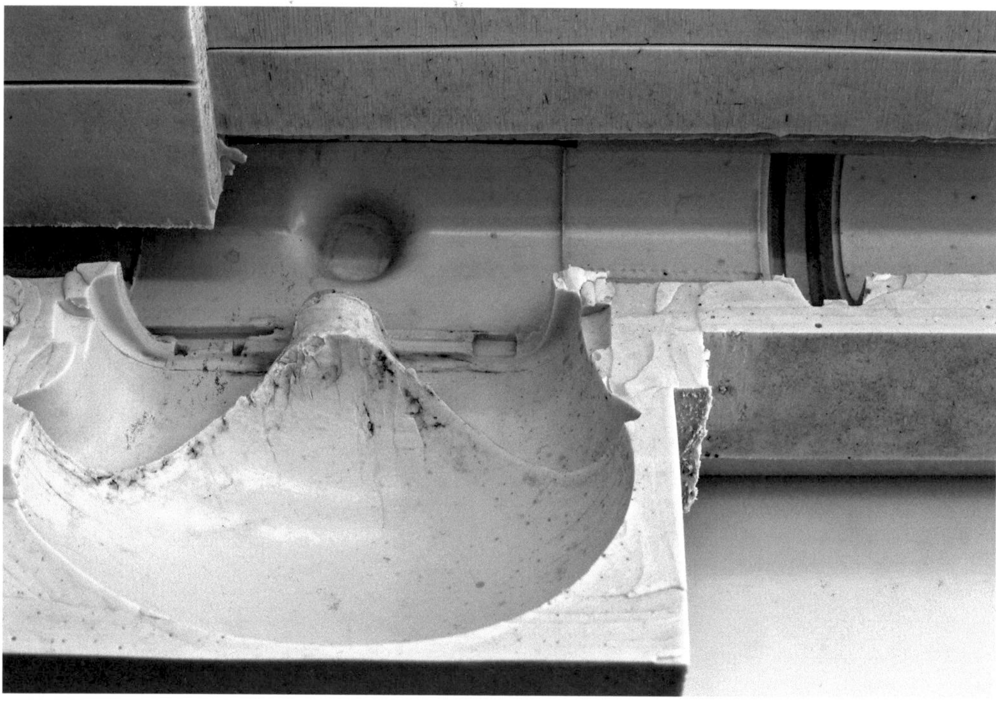

Untitled (Austerlitz II), 2010

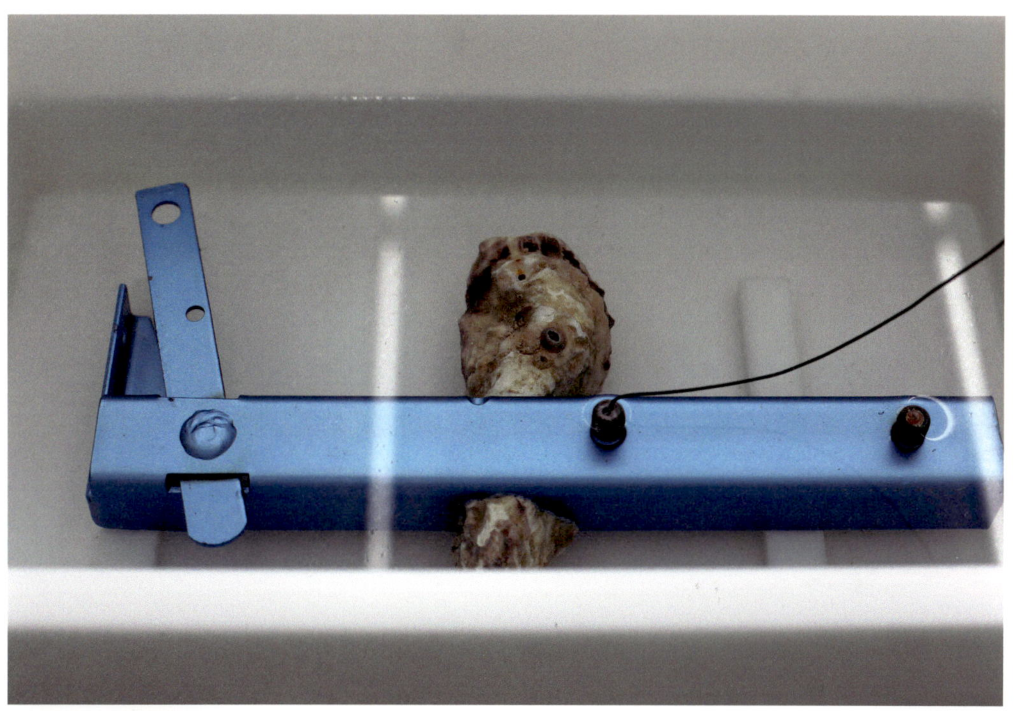

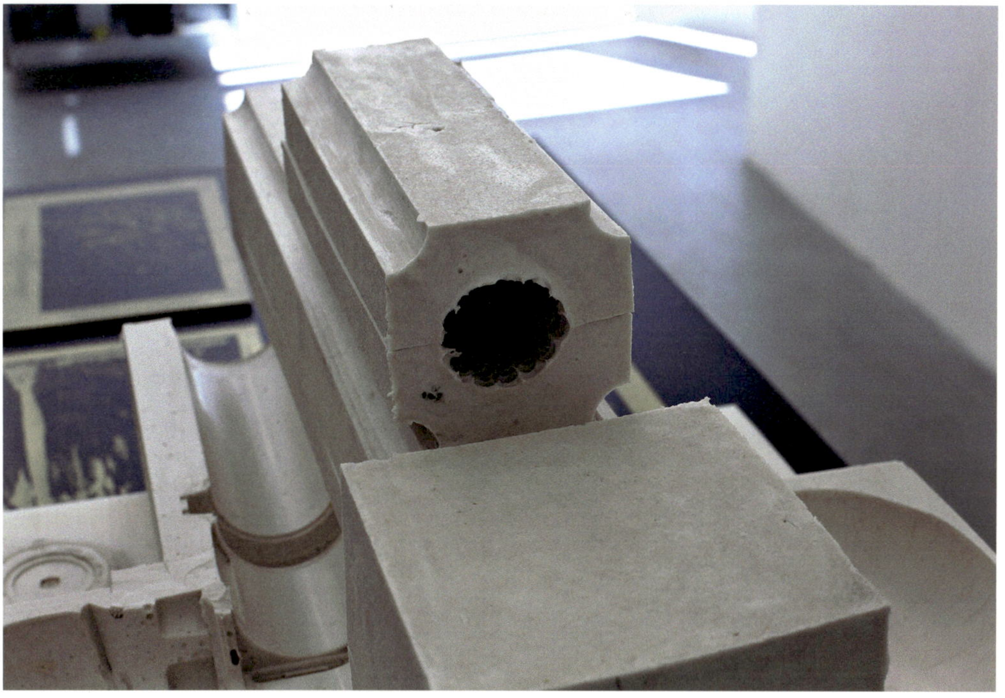

Austerlitz 0, 2010 / *Untitled*, 2010

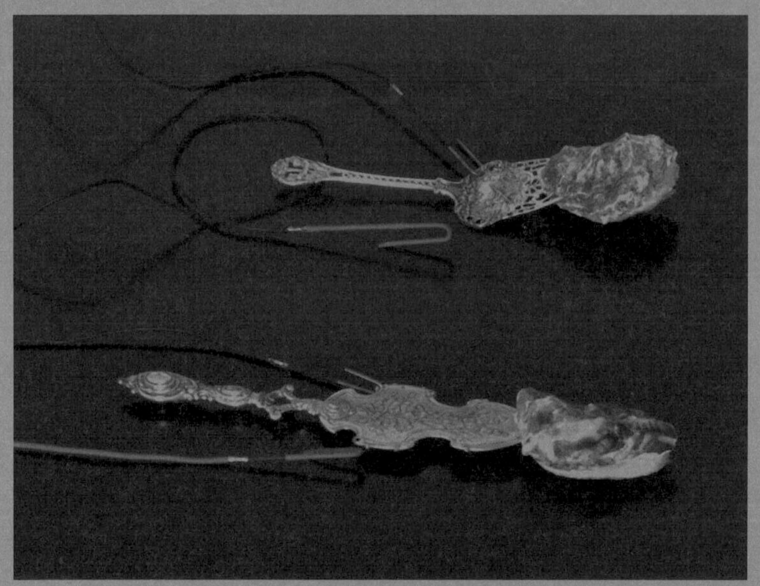

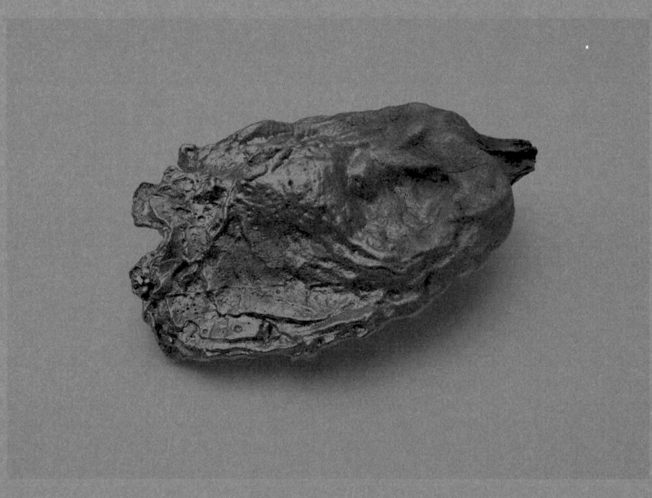

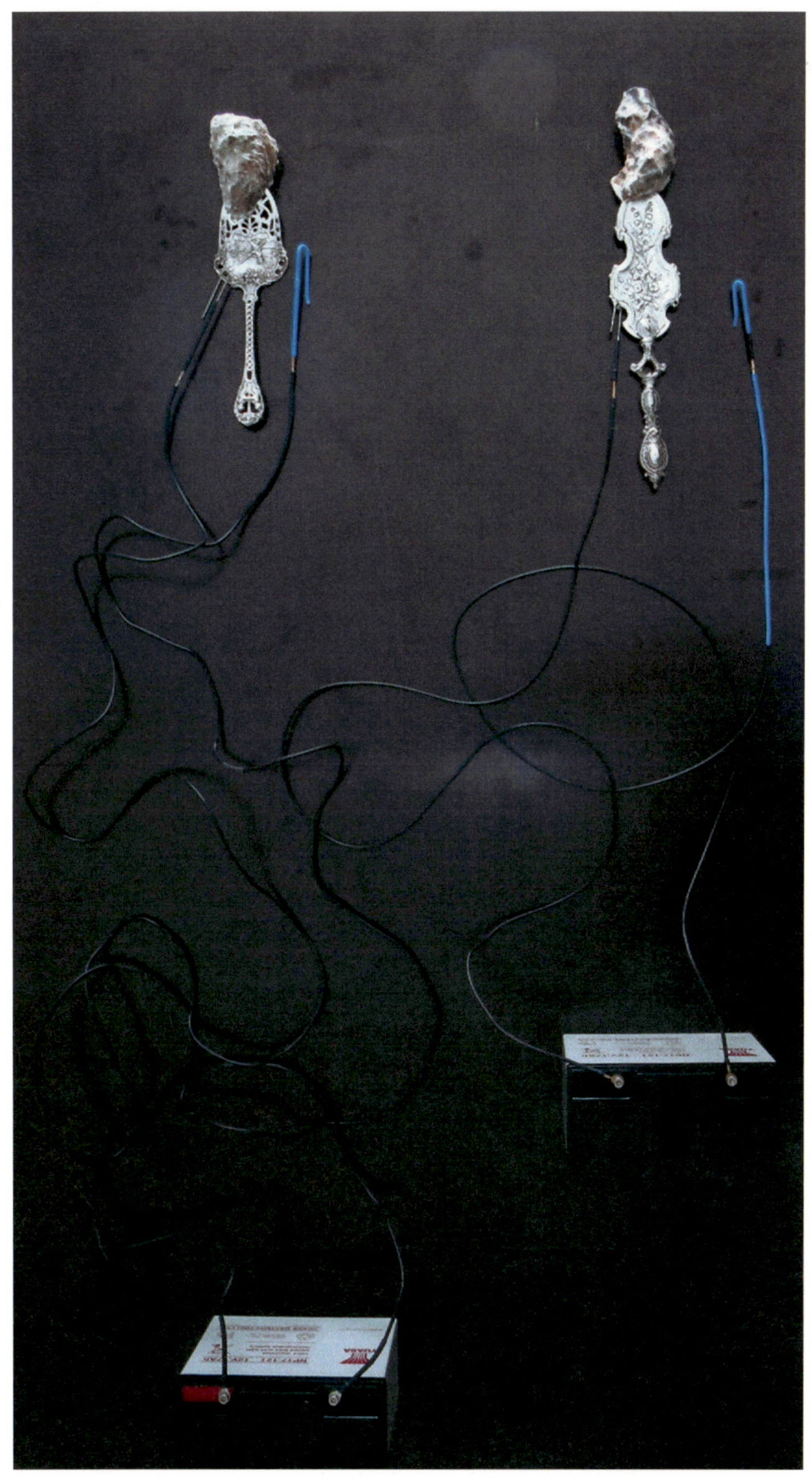

Austerlitz I, 2010

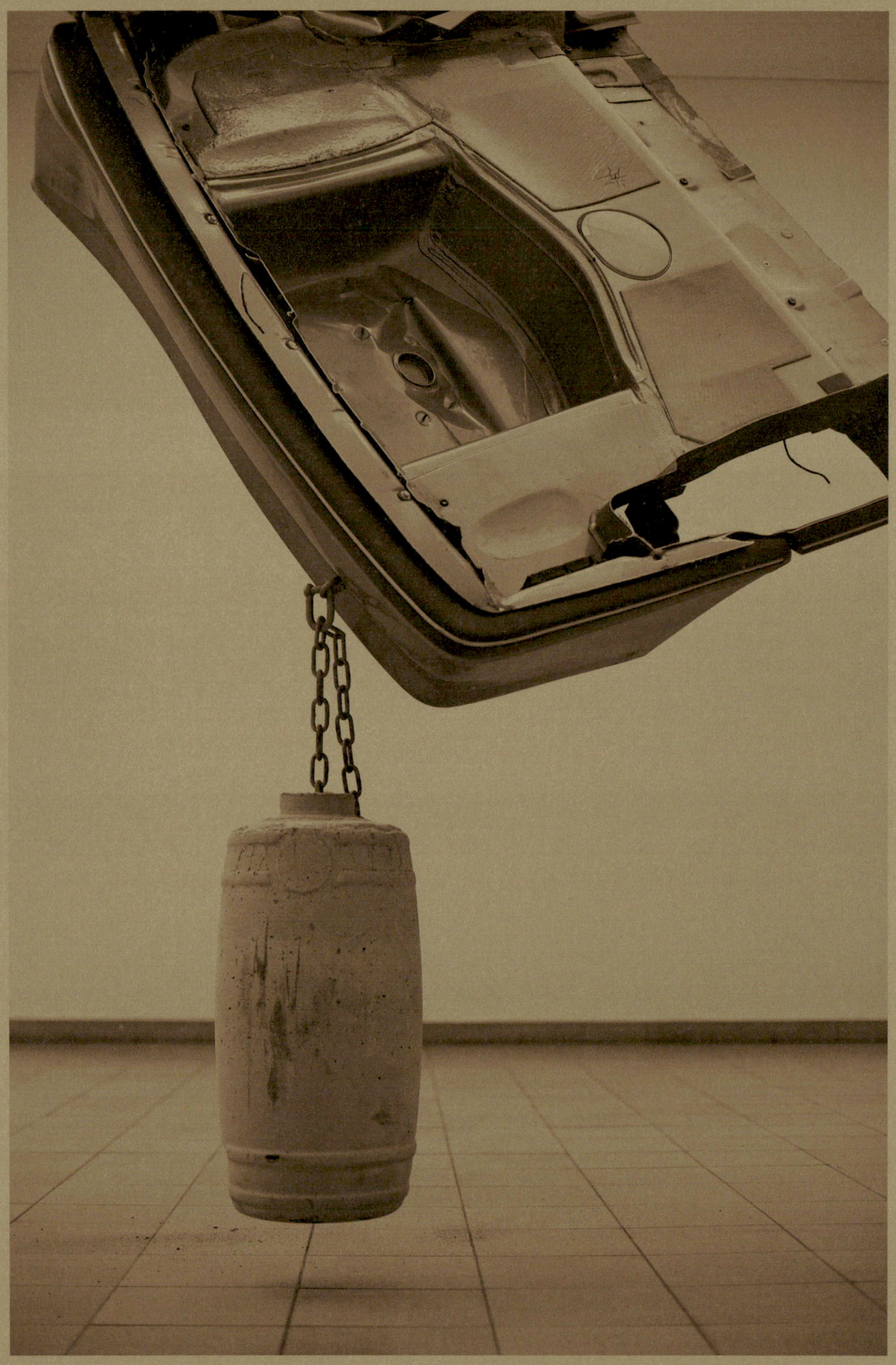

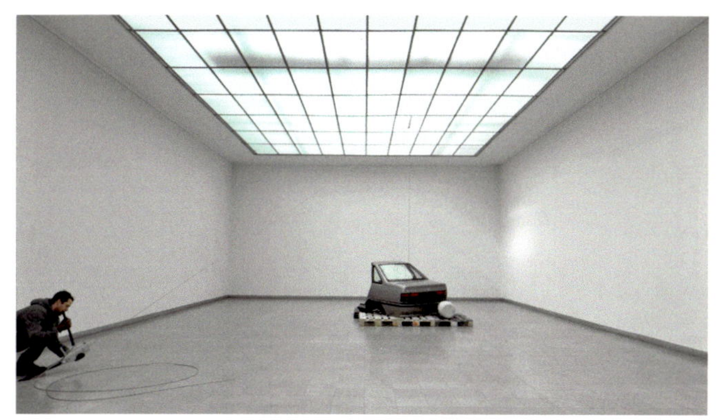

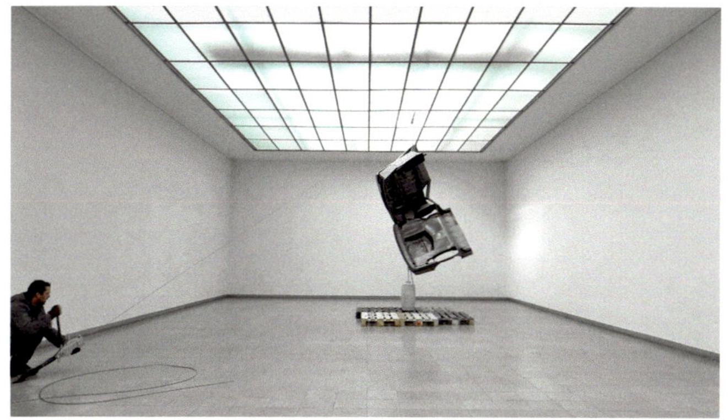

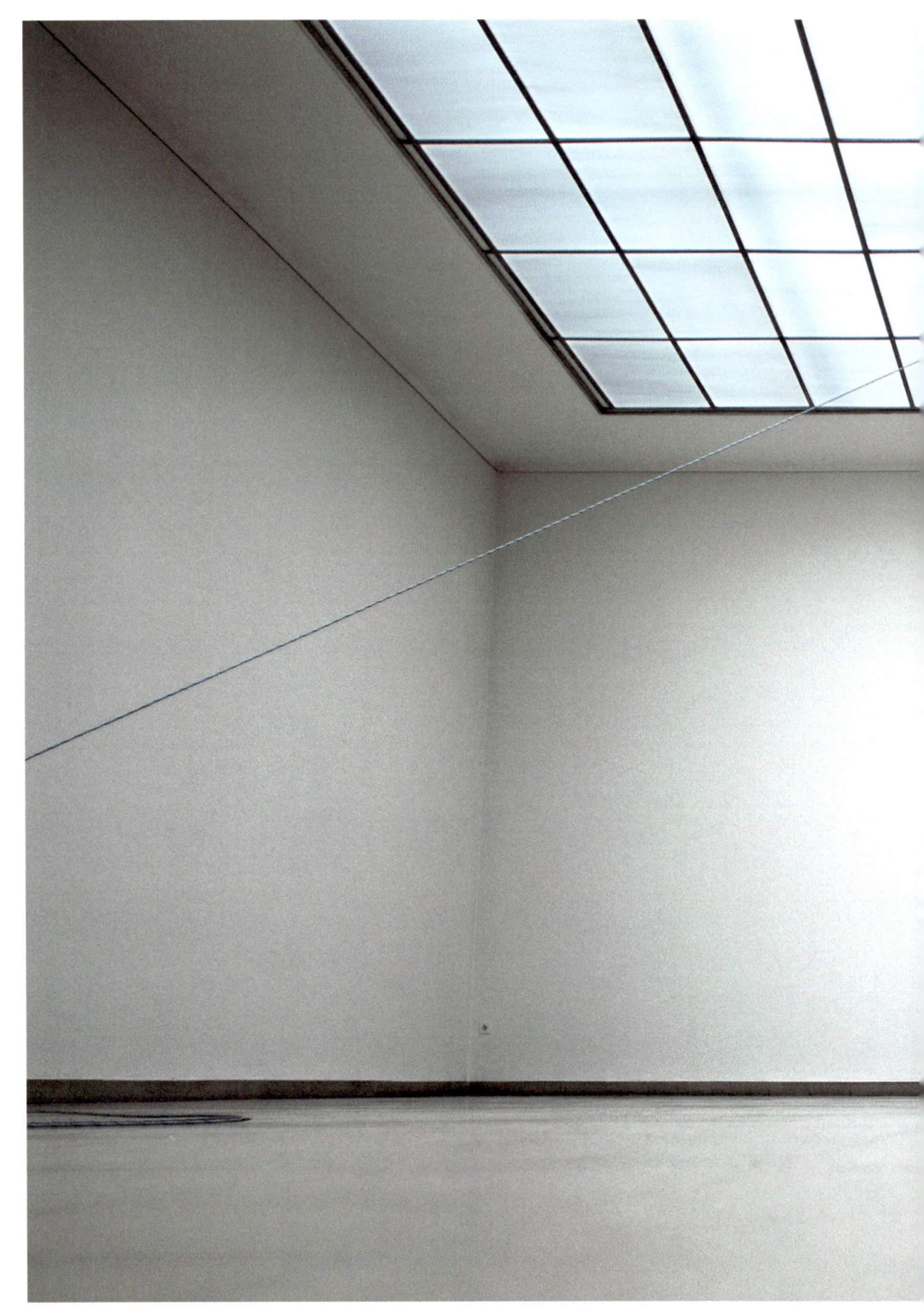

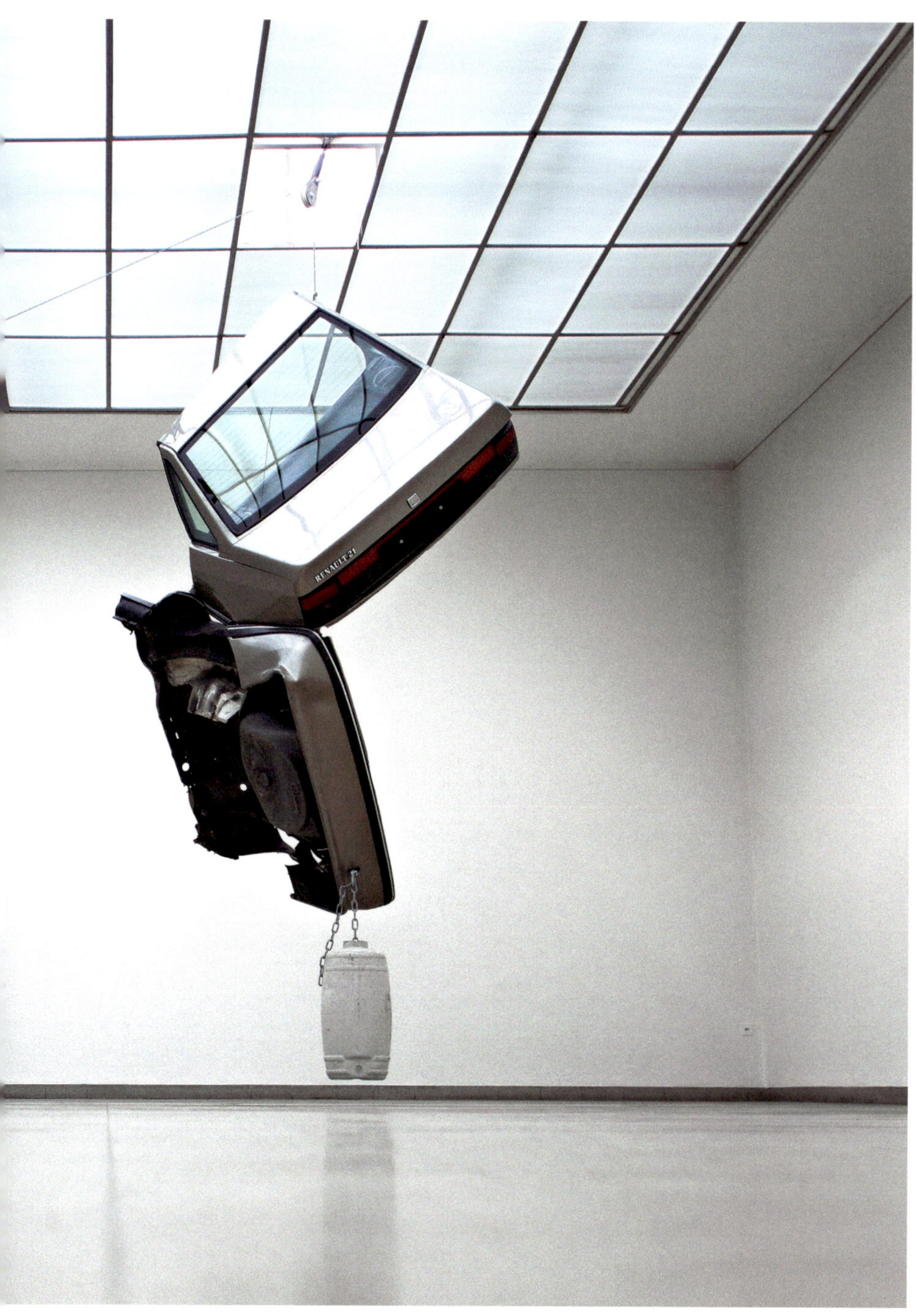
RENAULT 21

Full moon

Full moon is a lunar phase that occurs when the Moon is on the opposite of the Earth from the Sun. More precisely, a full Moon occurs when the geocentric apparent (ECLYPTIC) longitudes of the Sun and Moon differ by 180 degrees; the Moon is then in Oppsition with the Sun. At this Time, as seen by Viewers on Earth, the Hemisphere on the Moon that is facingo the Earth (The near Side) is almost fully illuminated by the Sun and appears round. Only during a full Moon is the opposite hemisphere of the Moon, which is not visible, from Earth, the near Side, completly unilluminated

Silver

Silver has been known since aincent Times and has long been valued as a precious metal, used to make ornaments, jewelry, High-value Tableware and utensils (hence the Terms Silverware) and currency COINS. Today, silver Metal is used in electrical contacts and Conductors, in Mirrors and in Catalysis of chemical reactions. Its compounds are used in photographic Films and dilute solutions of silver Nitrate and other silver compounds are used in Desinfectants. Altough the antimicrobial uses of silver having largely been supplanted by the use of Antibiotics, further research into its clinical potential is in progress.

Der Werwolf von Wien

2009

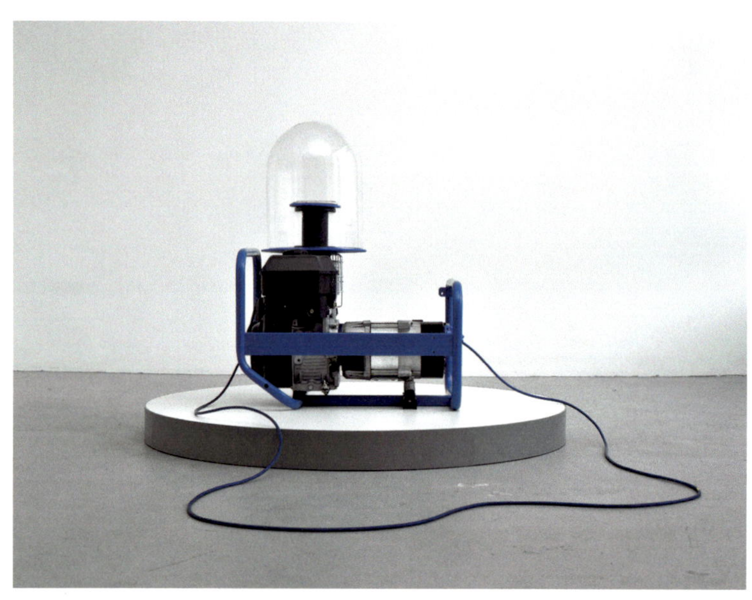

Objekt 9

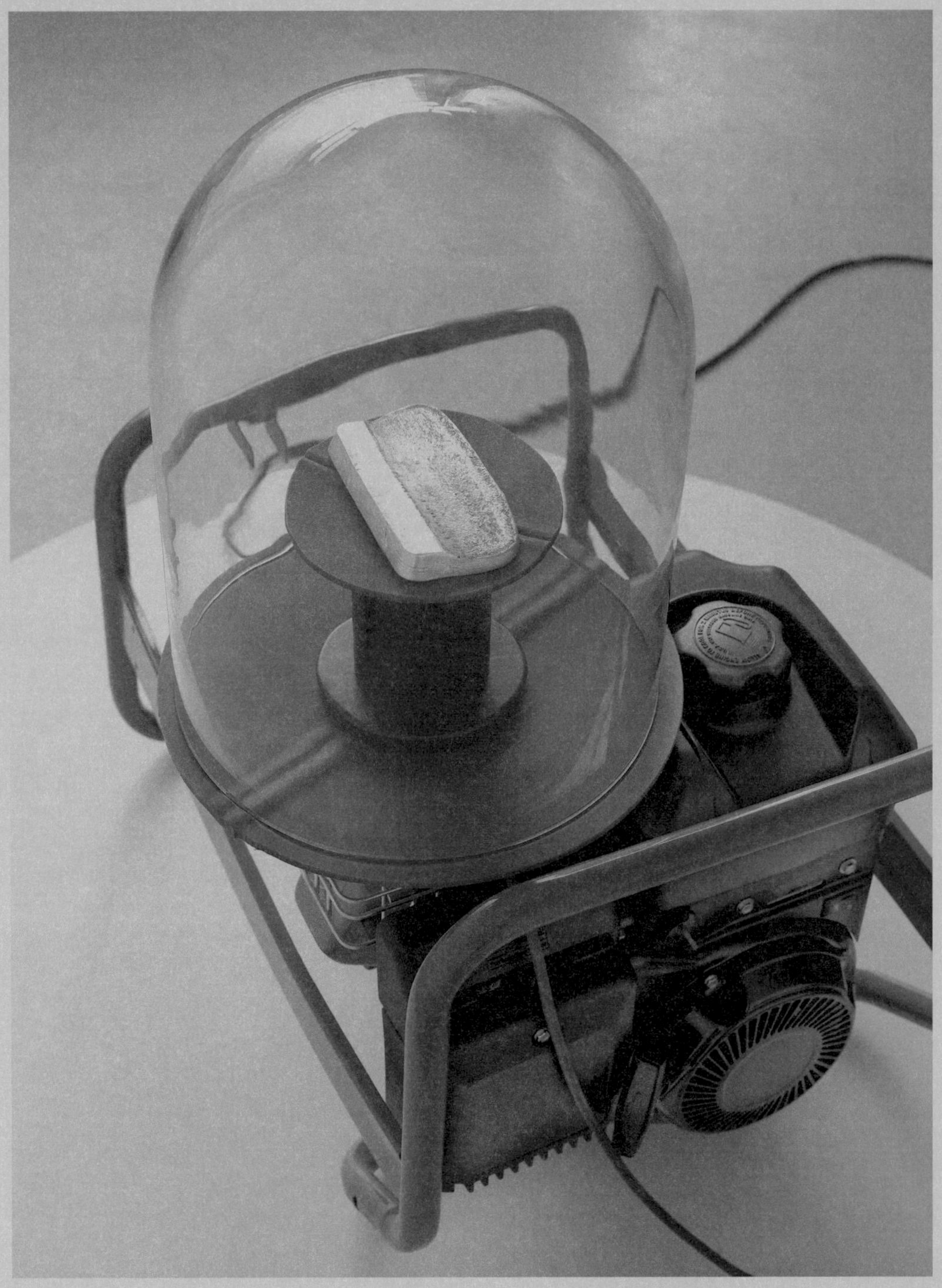

Object 1
Legend:

Traveling in Romania last year, one night I saw someone stealing a sewer cover in the open street. Having attached the loot to a belt, ~~he~~ the person carried it off into the dark. ~~Iron~~ All unattached metal objects are highly popular and quickly turned into cash. In Austria, in particular, unfixed metal objects are often stolen and recycled.

Object 2
Legend:

In the Romanian village of Slatina Timic, the old church was torn down in order to build a new one. The wood from the building was distributed among the residents as firewood (winter) The old organ ended up as garbage. I took the pewter organ pipes to build a heater for my room. The candles inside the pipes heat the pewter, whence the warmth spreads throughout the room.

Object 3
Legend:

The sign covers a grotto in the Jura Mountains I discovered. The entrance hole was originally circular before being deformed by erosion. A time-based installation is being created inside the grotto.

Object 4
Legend:

This installation serves as a beacon attracting werewolves. Silver is used in cryptozoology as an antidote that exorcises lycanthropy (see drawings). 1 audio signal The hammer serves as an instrument that triggers a sound in the silver membrane inside the amplifier. visual The glass sculpture is filled partly ~~filled~~ with a luminescent (phosphorus) liquid causing the silver coin in the upper part of the sculpture to gleam.

Object 5
Legend:

In 1968, the low prices of precious metals led the Swiss National Bank to raise the amount of silver in the coins to 73 percent, producing particularly soft coins whose shape and relief are changed by massive pressure. Every day at 2:11 am, the coins were run over by a German coal train, leaving them deformed.

Objekt 1

Legende:

Als ich Ende letzten Jahres durch Rumanien gereist bin, habe ich des Nachts eine Person gesehen, die auf offener Strasse einen Kanal-deckel gestohlen hat. Mit einem Gürtel befestigt trug ~~er~~ die Person den Deckel ins Dunkel davon. ~~Eisen~~ Alle unbefestigten Metalle sind als Rohstoff sehr beliebt und werden schnell zu Geld gemacht. Vor allem in Österreich werden unbefestigte Metallgegenstände oft gestohlen und weiterverwertet.

Objekt 2

Legende:

Im rumänischen Dorf Slatina Timic wurde die alte Kirche abgerissen um eine neue zu bauen. Das Holz der Kirche wurde unter den Einwohner verteilt um zu heizen (Winter) Die alte Orgel lag auf dem Abfall. Die Orgelpfeifen aus Zinn nahm ich mir, und baute daraus für mein Zimmer eine Heizung. Die Kerzen im inneren der Pfeife erhitzen das Zinn und erwarmen dadurch den Raum.

Objekt 3

Legende:

Dieses Schild dient als Abdeckung einer Grotte im Jura, die ich entdeckt habe. Das Eingangsloch war ursprünglich kreisrund und wurde durch Errosion deformiert. In dieser Grotte entsteht eine Time-based-Installation.

Objekt 4

Legende:

Diese Installation dient als Leuchtturm um Werwölfe anzulocken. Silber wird in der Kryptozoologie als Bannungs-mittel zur Aufhebung der Lykantropie (siehe Zeichnungen) verwendet. 1 Audiosignal Der Hammer dient als Instrument um einen Ton in der Silbermembrane im Verstärker auszulösen.

visuell. Die Glasskulptur ist zum Teil mit einer lumineszenten (Phosphor) ~~gefüllt~~ Flüssigkeit gefüllt. Diese bringt die Silbermünze im oberen teil der Skulptur zum Leuchten.

Objekt 5

Legende:

Die schweizer Bank erhöhte 1968, aufgrund des tiefen Preises für Edelmetalle, den Silberanteil der Münzen auf 73%. Diese sind dadurch besonders weich und verändern durch massiven Druck ihre Form und Zeichnung. Die Münzen wurden täglich um 02.11 AM von einem deutschen Kohlezug überfahren und so deformiert.

Object 6:
Legend:

These basaltic objects are replicas of ~~folk art~~ relics of traditional rituals I have seen; they are used in Romania to keep ~~were~~ strygoi (the undead) away from the house. A photograph of the deceased is attached to the doorpost with a nail in order to bar him or her from entering. The photograph of the dead is tied to a stone and dumped into the water.

Painting 8
Legend:

I commissioned an old Romanian country-style decorative painter to c produce this picture. It is painted ont a stair tread and shows an excerpt from an Austrian cryptozoologist who kept a pictorial diary around 1952. Near the border between Austria and Hungary, he witnessed an attack of the so-called "Tatzelwurm," a worm-like monster. The original is the size of a playing card.

Drawings 10
Legend:

Chapters 7/8/9 were created while I was traveling through Romania by train; they serve as the storyboard for a television series called "The Werewolf of Vienna."

Object 7
Legend:

This object lets the user shoot a bolt against his "NERVUS ULNARIS" (funny bone). You place the elbow on the base plate and use the other hand to activate the bolt gun's trigger. Several repetitions of this procedure lead to an overexcitation of the nerve, which causes a so-called "WOLF'S HAND" anomaly.

Object 9
Legend:

The motor applies 220 volts to the silver sculpture, illustrating ~~that~~ the material's optimum conductivity. The ~~scu~~ installation works, but to protect the viewer, it is not activated.

Object 11
Legend:

Epitaphs, books made of stone, were created in order to transmit stories through time. In Romania, I often spotted the letters "G.U.S.A." Their meaning would seem to be a reference to the union of Russia and America.

Florian Germann, 2009

Objekt 6:

Legende:

Diese Basaltobjekte sind Nachbildungen gesehener ~~Folk-Art~~- traditionsritualrelikte, welche dazu dienen ~~Wer~~ in Rumänien Strygois (Untote) vom Haus fernzuhalten.[1] Ein Foto des verstorbenen wird mit einem Nagel an den Türpfosten geheftet um ihm den Einlass zu verwehren.[2] Das Foto des Toten wird auf einen Stein gebunden und im Wasser versenkt.

Objekt 7

Legende:

Dieses Objekt dient dazu, sich einen Bolzen an den: „NERVUS ULNARIS" (Narrenbein) zu schiessen. Man legt den Ellbogen auf die Grundplatte und betätigt mit der anderen Hand den Auslöser des Bolzenschussgerätes. Die mehrmalige Wiederholung dieses Vorgangs führt zur Überreizung des Nervs, was wiederum in einer sogenannten "WOLFSHAND" Anomalie endet.

Gemälde 8

Legende:

Dieses Bild wurde von einem alten, rumänischen Bauernmaler ~~K~~ in meinem Auftrag hergestellt. Es ist auf einer treppenstufe gemalt. Es zeigt einen Auszug eines österreichischen Kryptozoologen, welcher um 1952 bildlich Tagebuch führte. An der Grenze zwischen Österreich und Ungarn sichtete er einen sogenannten "tatzelwurmangriff". Das Originalbild ist Spielkartengross.

Objekt 9

Legende:

Der Motor führt 220V~ in die Silberskulptur und zeigt ~~das~~ die optimale Leitfähigkeit des Materials. Die ~~Sku~~ Installation funktioniert, wird aber zum Schutze des Betrachters nicht aktiviert.

Zeichnungen 10

Legende:

Die Kapitel 7/8/9 wurden auf meinen Reisen im Zug durch Rumänien hergestellt und dienen als Storyboard für eine Fernseh-Sendereihe, genannt: „Der Werwolf von Wien".

Objekt 11

Legende:

Epitaphien, Bücher aus Stein, werden hergestellt, um Geschichten durch die Zeit zu transportieren. In Rumänien habe ich oft den Schriftzug: „G.U.S.A" gesichtet. Der Bedeutung nach schliesst es auf den Zusammenschluss von Russland und Amerika.

Florian Germann 2009

Objekt 5

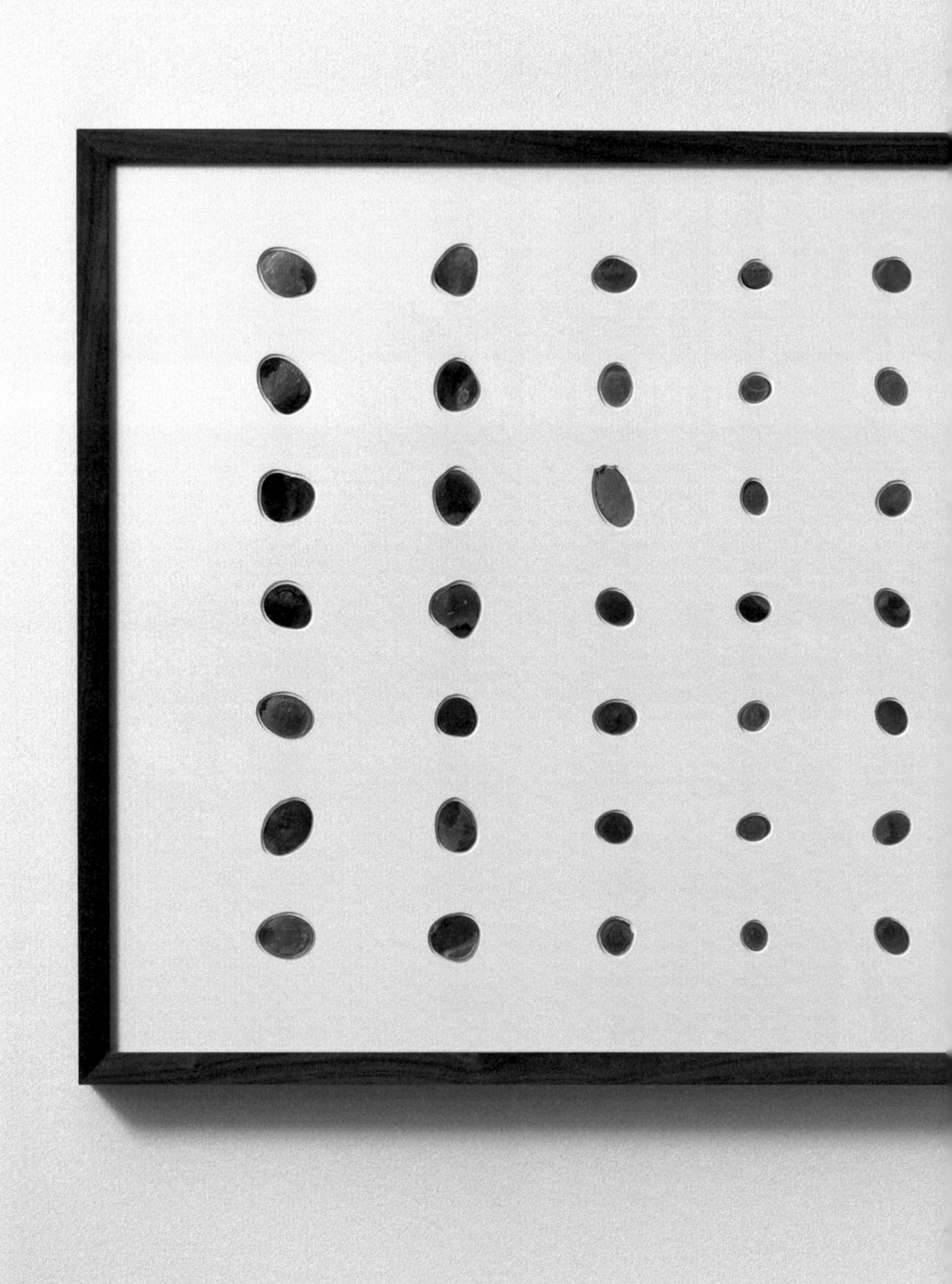

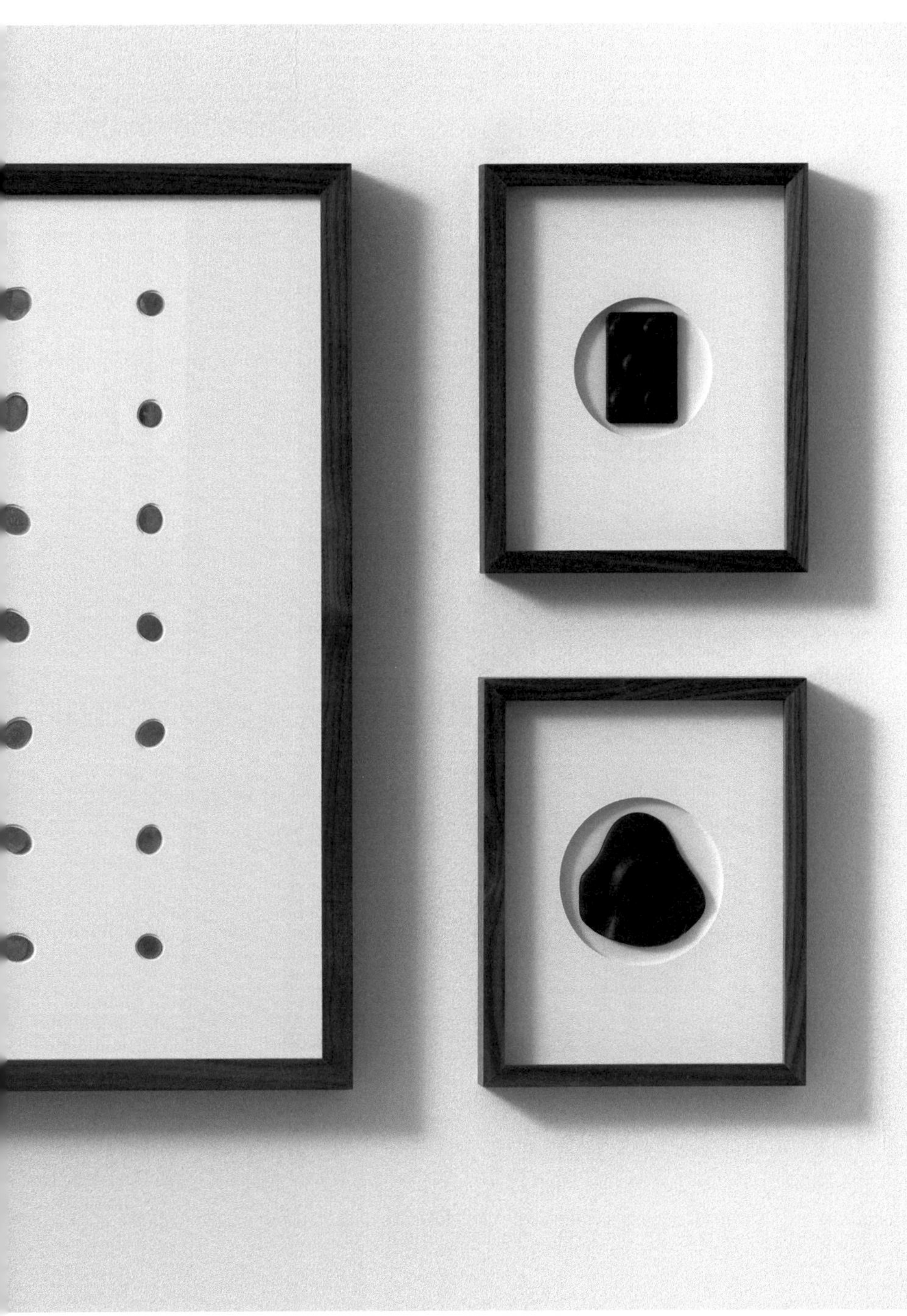

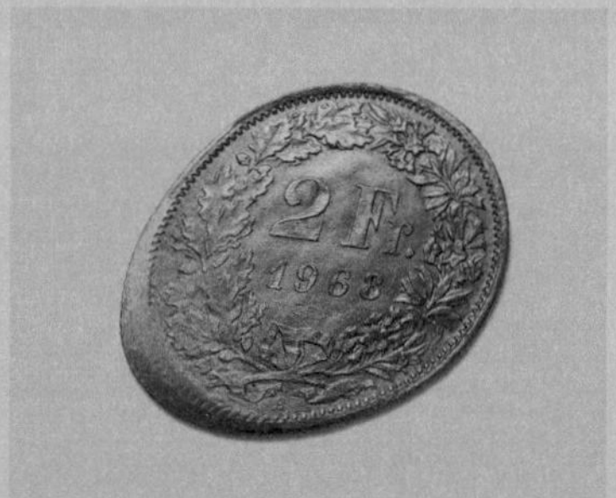
2 Fr.
1968

Objekt 4

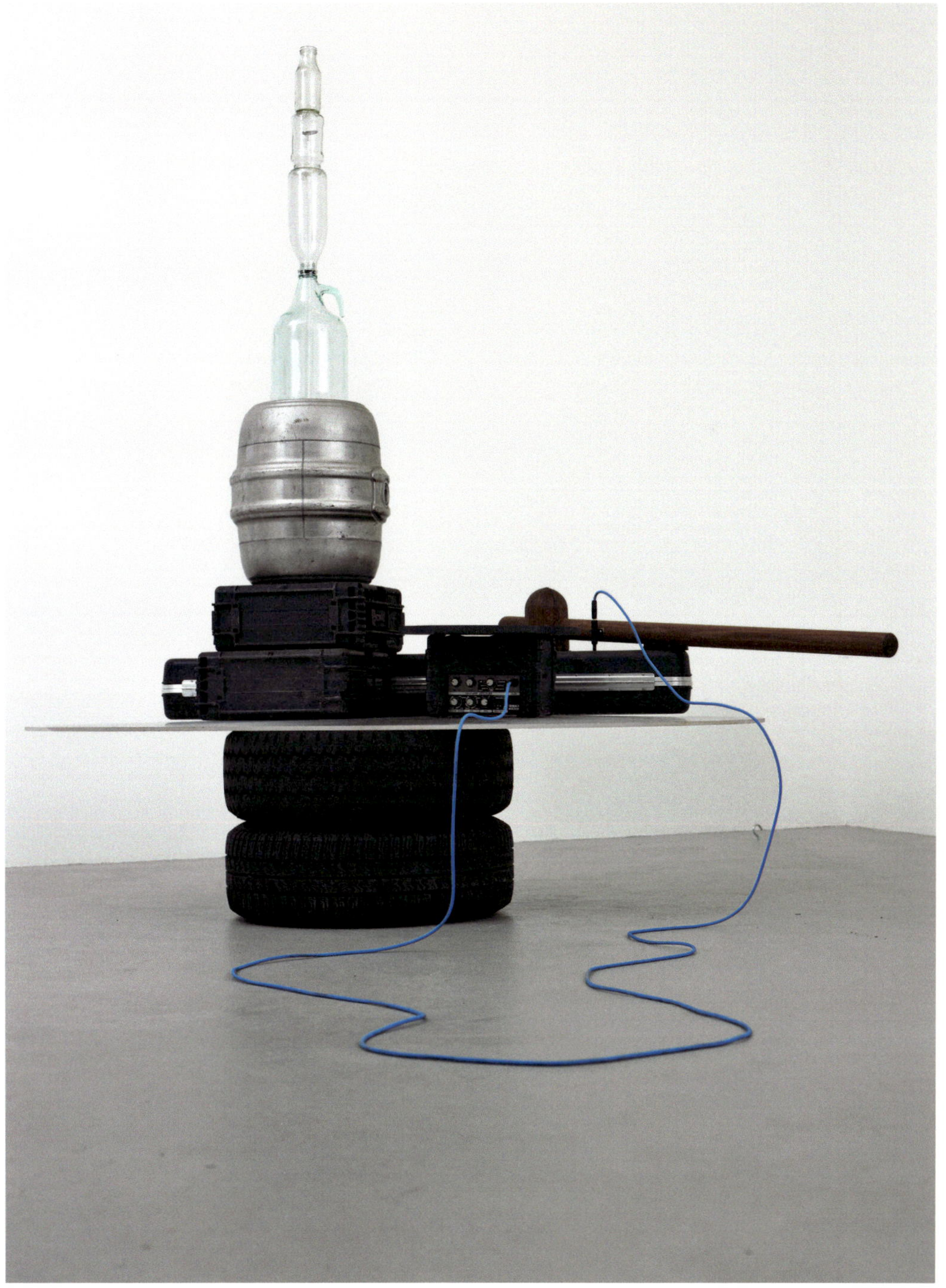

Objekt 11 / Gemälde 8

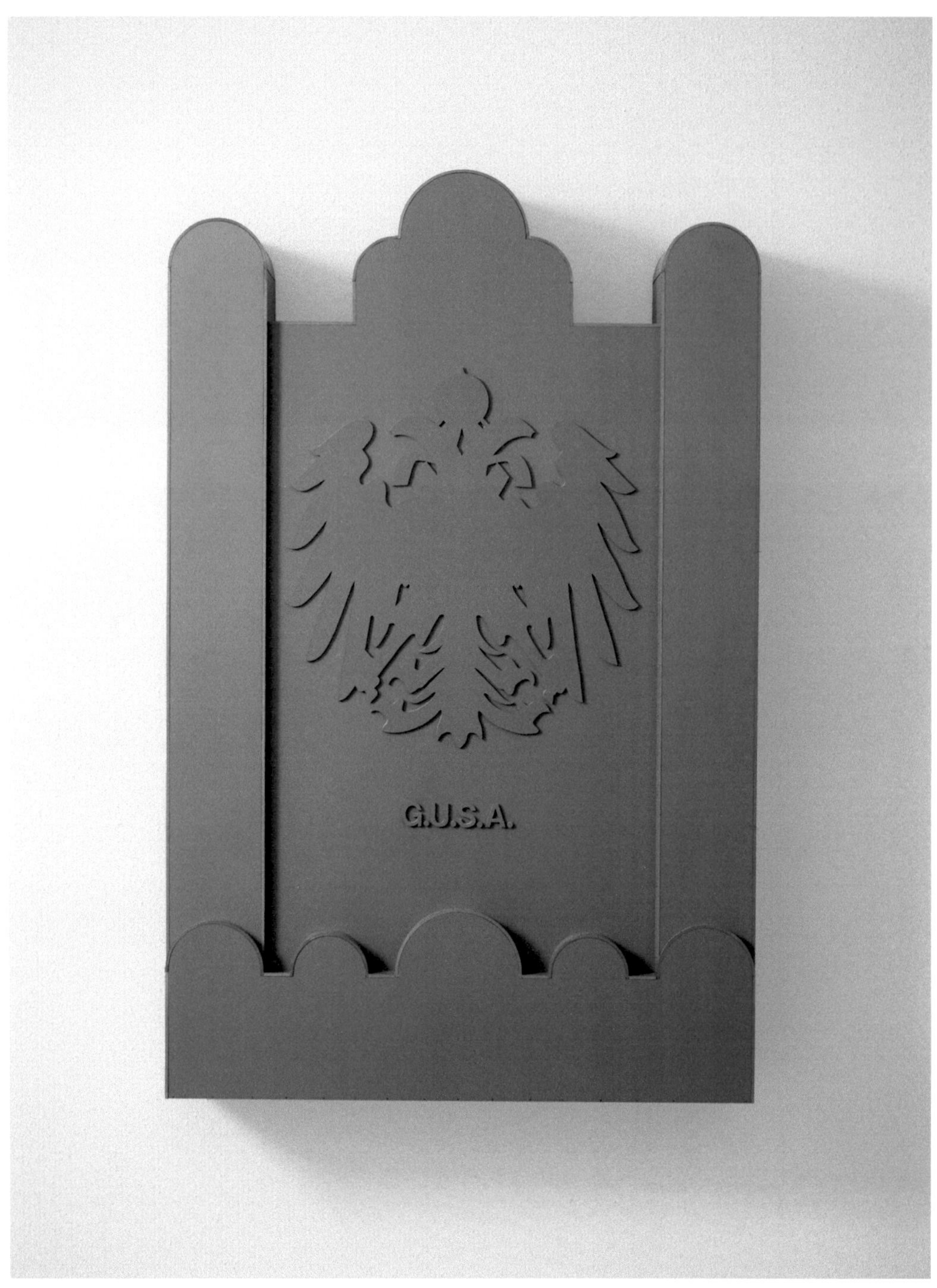

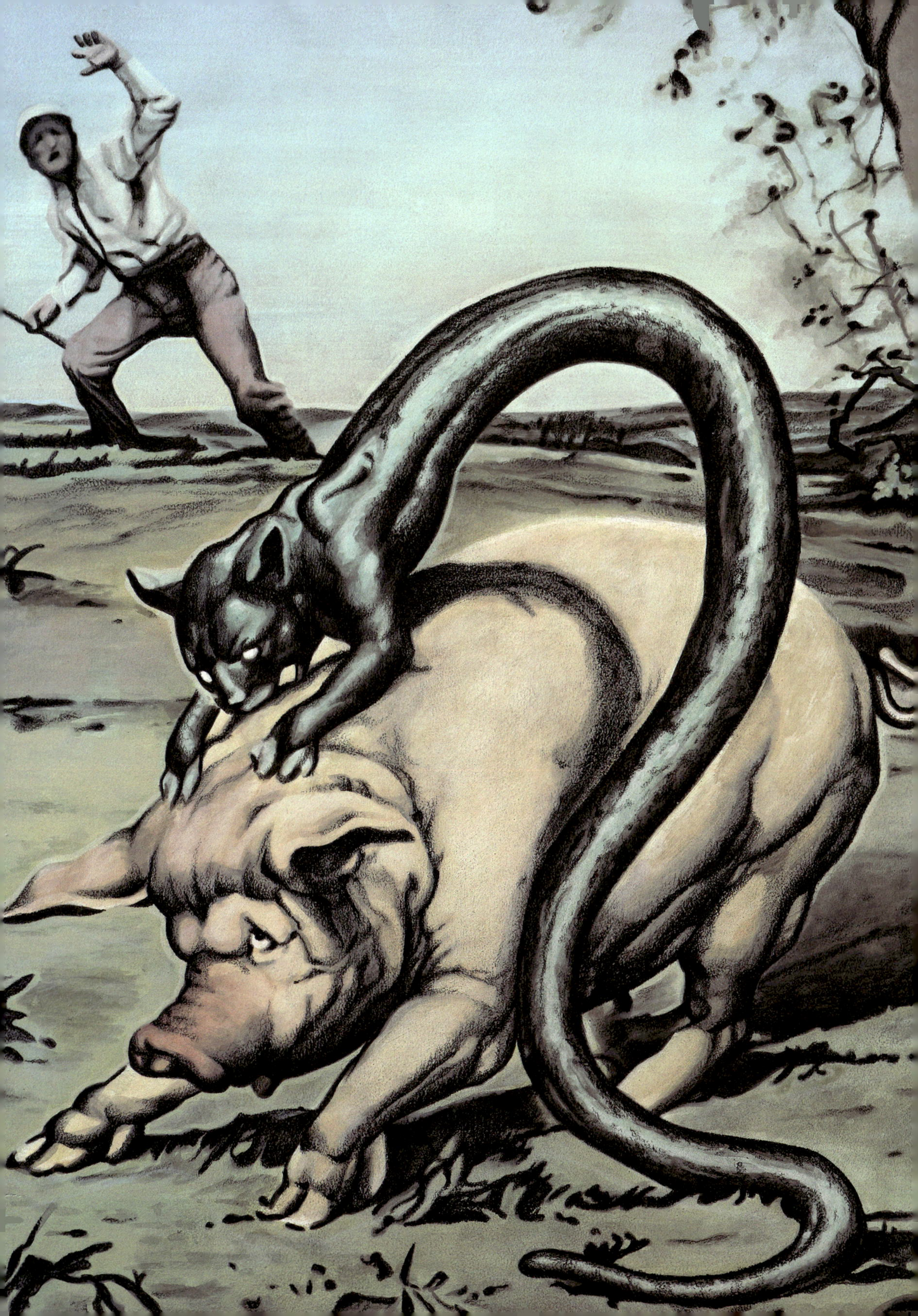

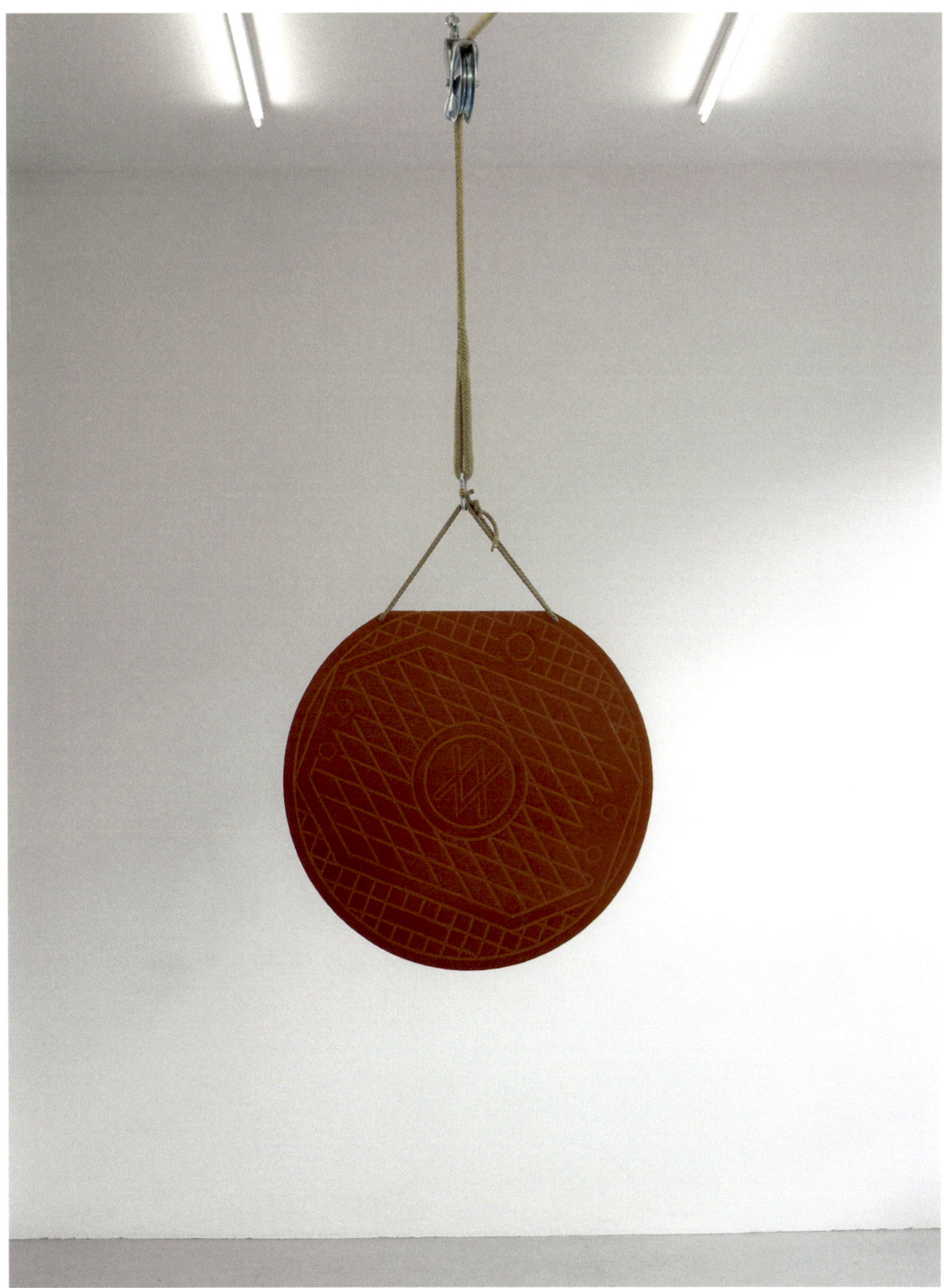

Objekt 2

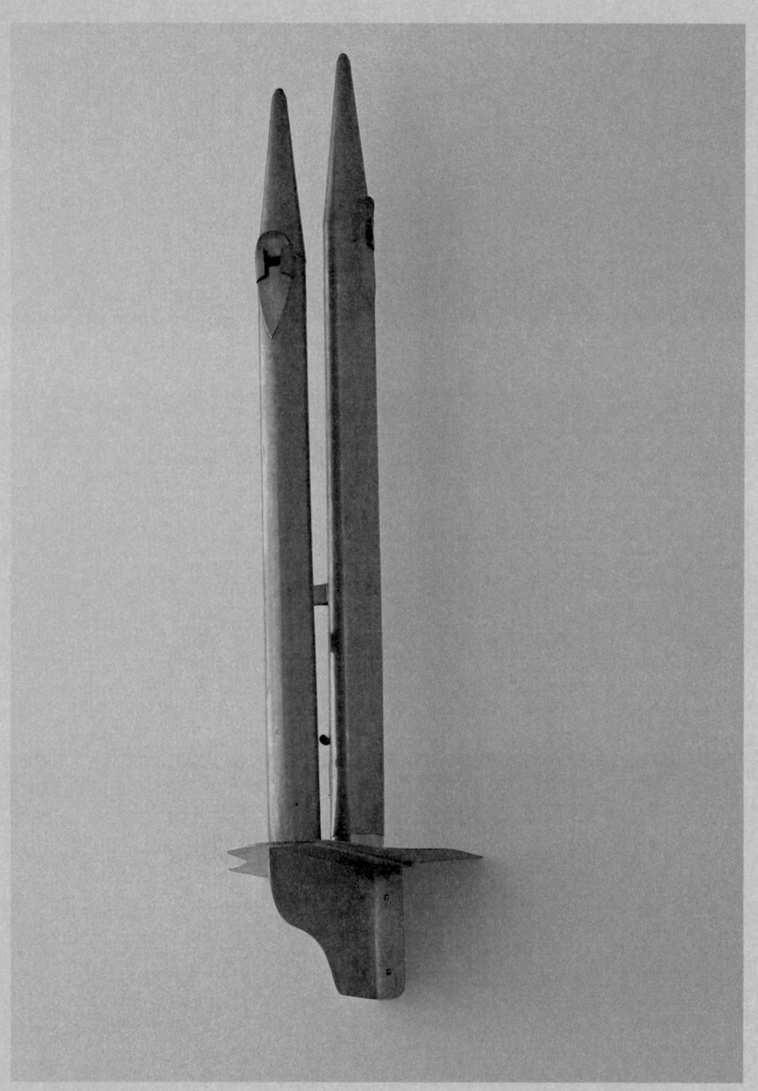

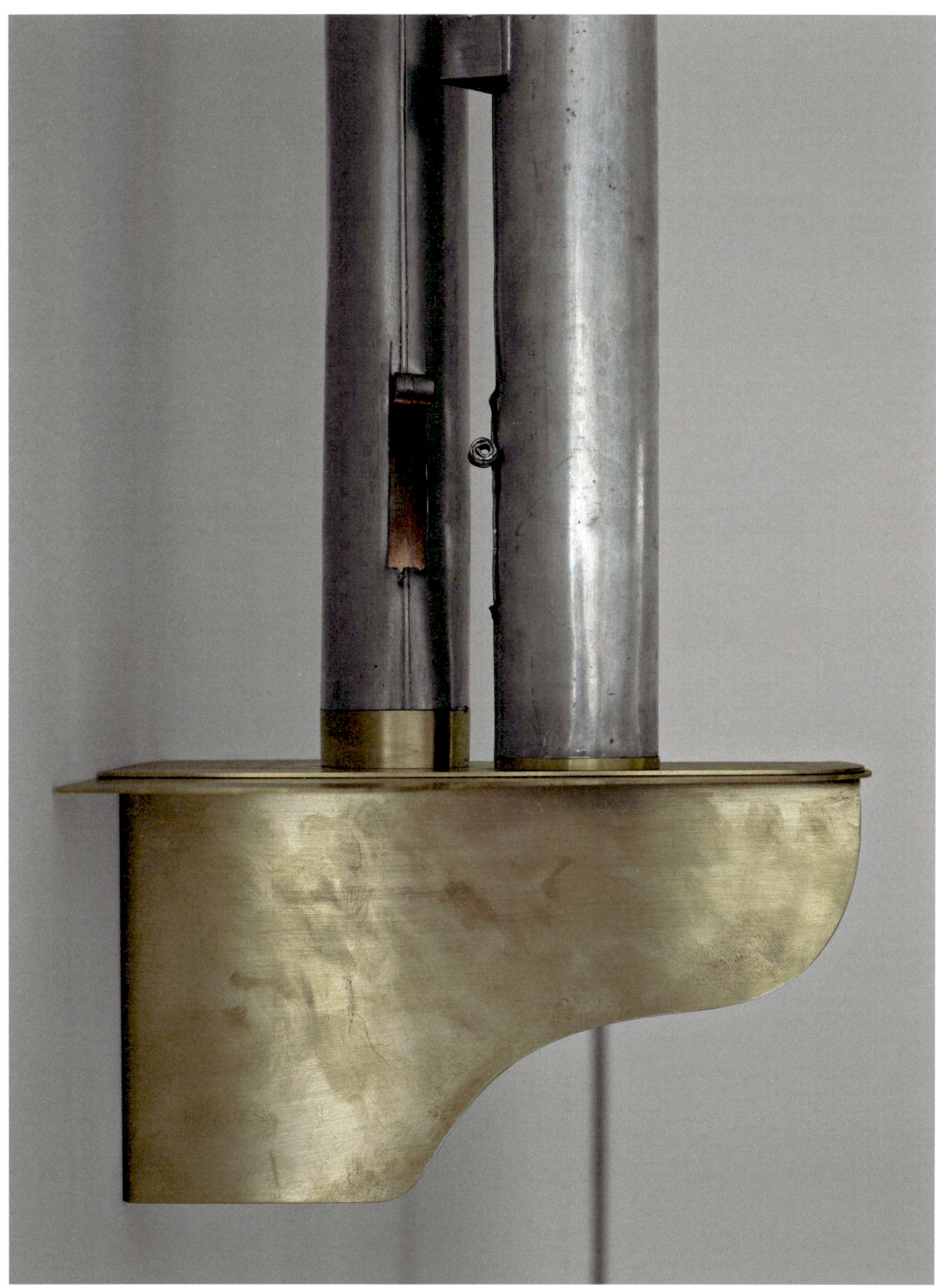

(2) Am 15. Juni 1754 stellte er im Pfarrgarten zu Primetice den ersten geerdeten Blitzableiter der Welt auf, der sich wesentlich vom Stangenblitzableiter Franklins unterschied. Mit Hilfe einiger hundert Spitzen sollte Divischs Blitzableiter einen grossen Teil der elektrischen Ladung aus den Wolken absaugen und damit dem Blitzschlag vorbeugen. Sein Gerät, das Divisch als atmosphärische Maschine bezeichnete, hatte auch eine zentrale Hauptstange, aber daneben befanden sich Querstangen, auf denen Kästchen mit Eisenspitzen waren. Alle Teile der Anordnung waren geerdet.

1756

Die Bevölkerung hatte allerdings Angst vor diesem Blitzableiter. So rissen Bauern, die den Ableiter für den trockenen Sommer verantwortlich machten, diesen wiederholt nieder. Divischs Erfindungen fanden bei seinen kirchlichen Vorgesetzten ebenfalls keinen Anklang. Schliesslich wurde ihm verboten die Wettermaschine neu aufzustellen.

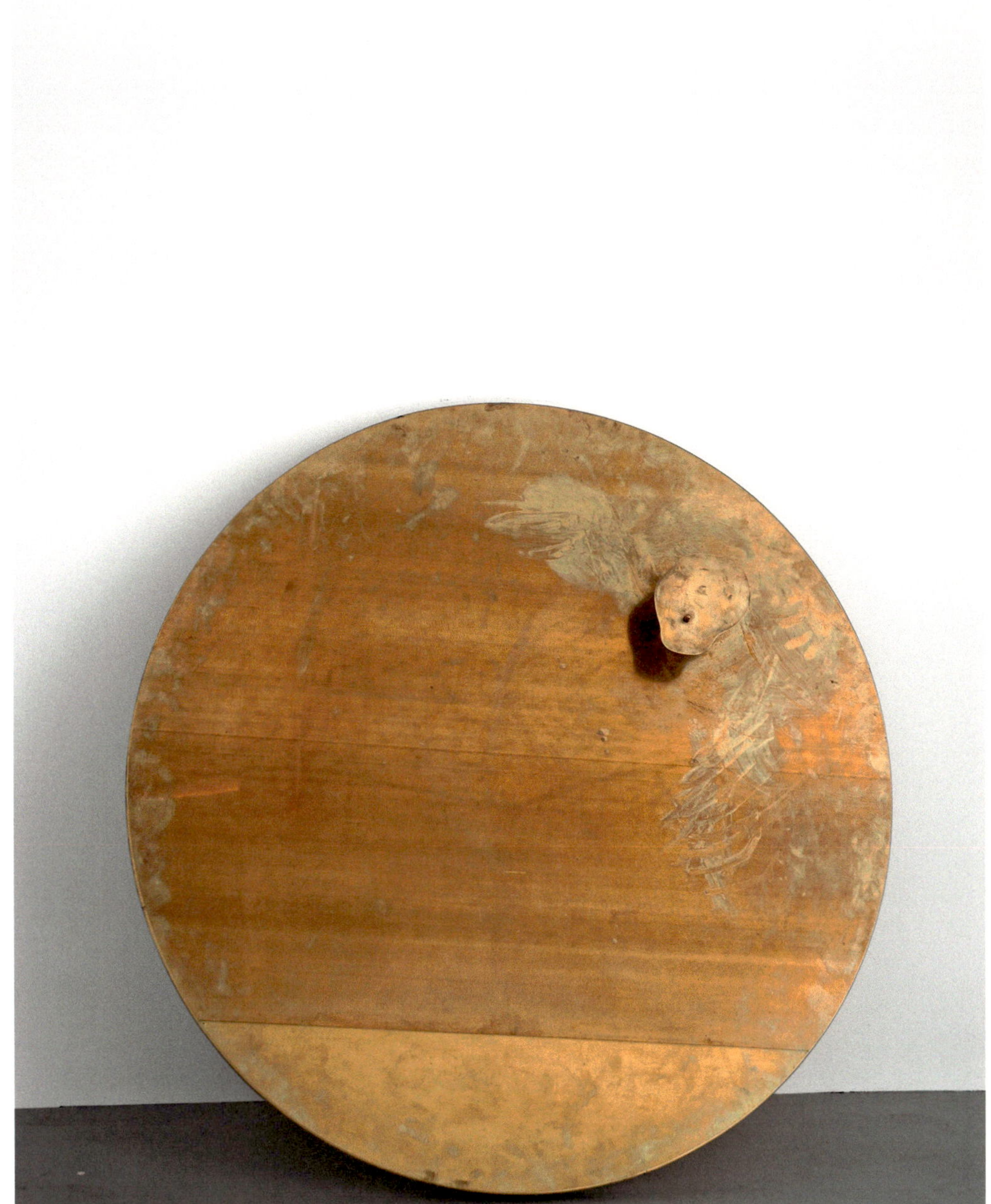

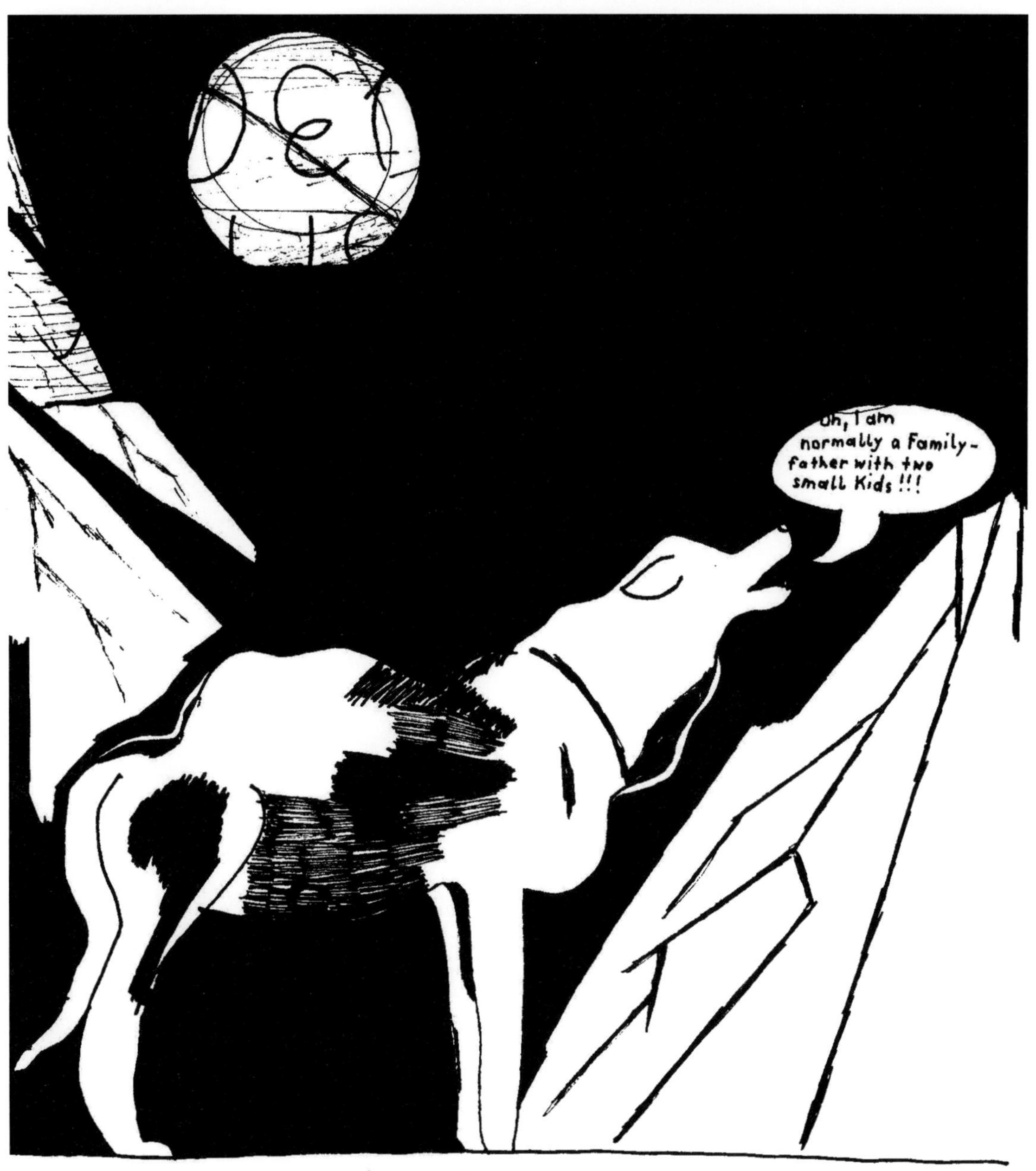

Ein Jahr wie eine Ewigkeit – Take care

PUSHER

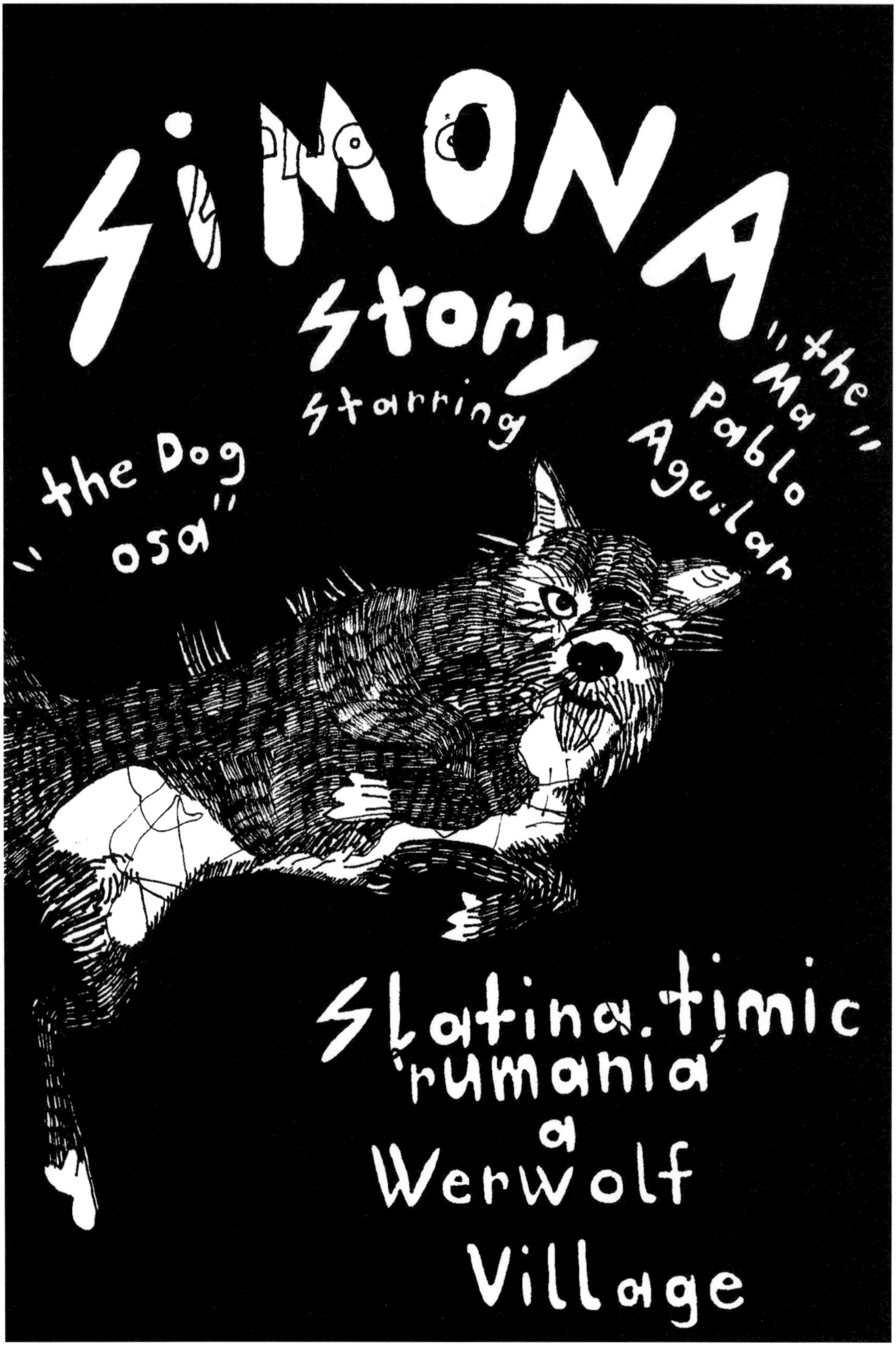

SIMONA

story

starring

"the Ma" Pablo Aguilar

"the Dog osa"

Slatina.timic

'rumania'

a

Werwolf

Village

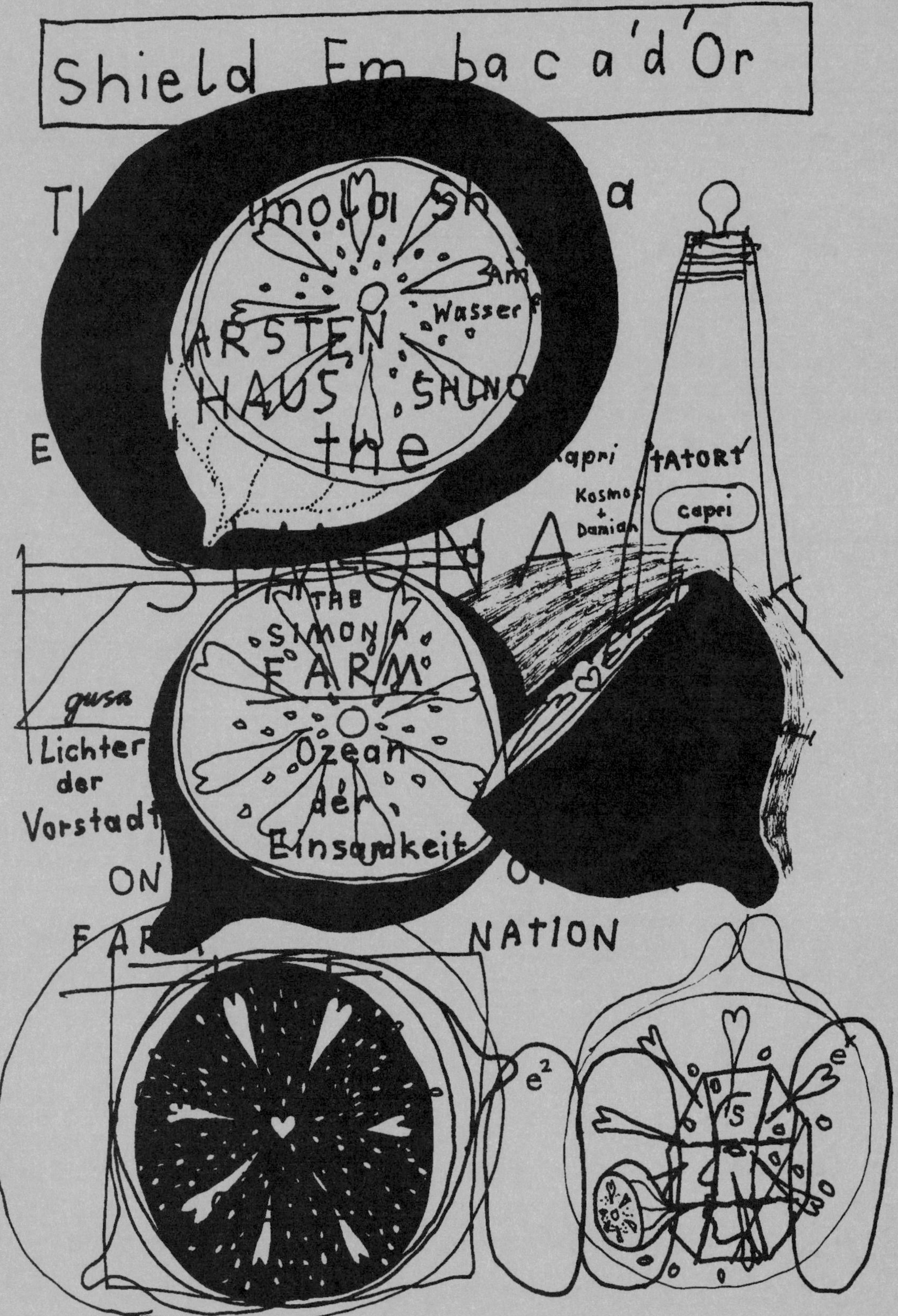
Shield Em bac a'd'Or
Am
Wasser
ARSTEN
HAUS
SHINO
the
Kapri
TATORT
Kosmos
+
Damian
capri
SIMONA
THE
SIMONA
FARM
Ozean
der
Einsamkeit
gusa
Lichter
der
Vorstadt
ON
NATION
e^2
e^x

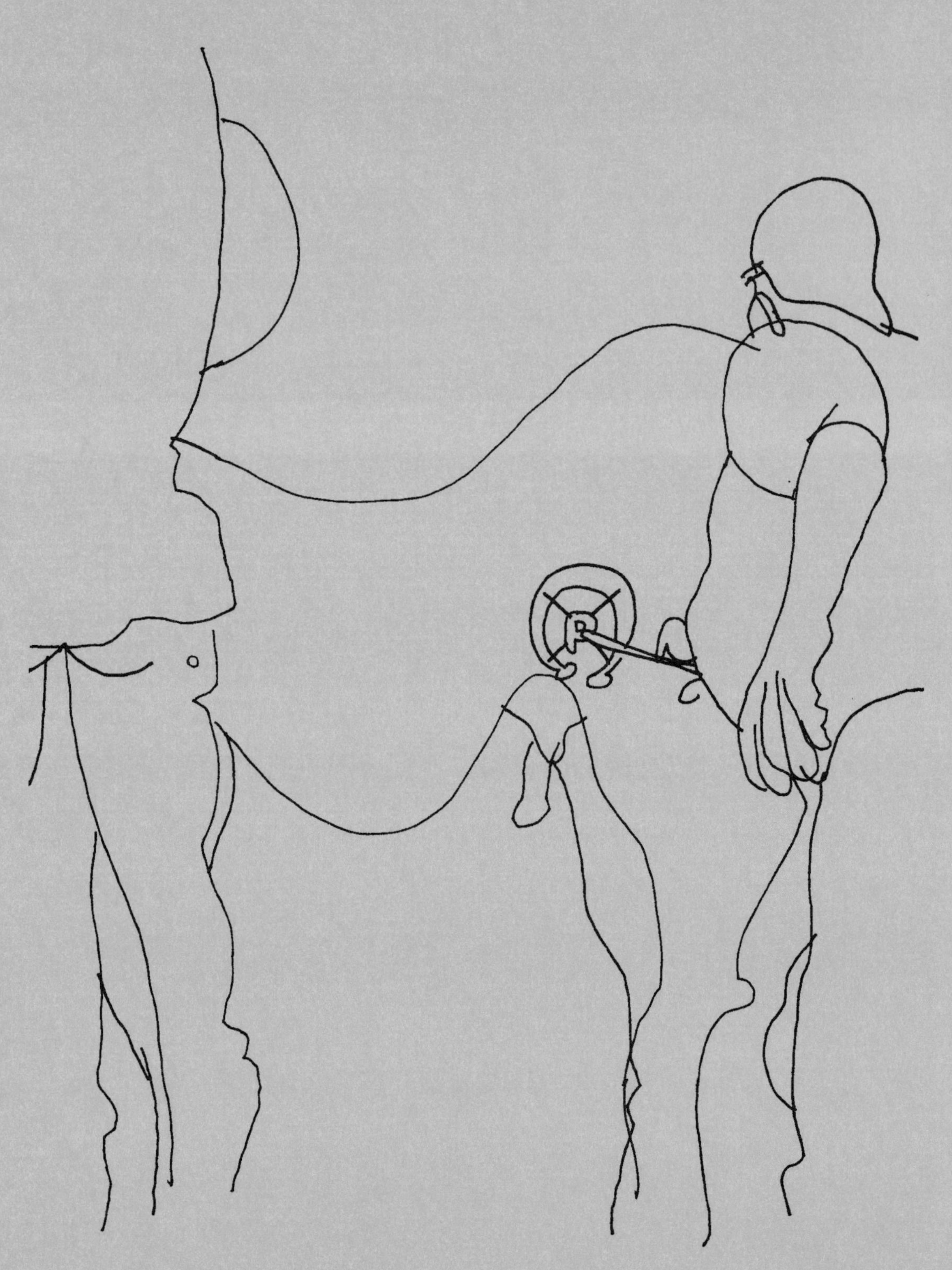
P

C.I.S. Commonwealth of Independant States G.U.S.

The CIS is comparable to a Confederation similar to the original European Community. Altough the CIS has few supranational Powers, it is more than a symbolic organization, posessing coordination Powers in the realm of trade, finance, lawmaking, and Security. It has also promoted cooperation, on democratization and cross-border crime-prevention. As a regional Organisation, CIS participates in UN-Peacekeeping Forces. Some of the Membersof CIS have etablished the EURASIAN Economic Community with the Aim of creating a full-fleged common Market. However, other Member states have shown greater interest in seeking to join Nato and the European Union.

Belarus Russia Ukraine

Vkhutemas

(Higher Art and technical studios)
Vkhutemas was the russian state art and technical school founded in 1920 in Moscow. The Workshops were etablished by a decree from Vladimir Lenin with the intentions, in the Words of sowiet Government, "To prepare Master Artists of the highest Qualifications for Industry and Builders for professional-technical Education. It was a Center for three major movements in Avant Garde Art and Architecture: Constructivism, Rationalism and Suprematism.

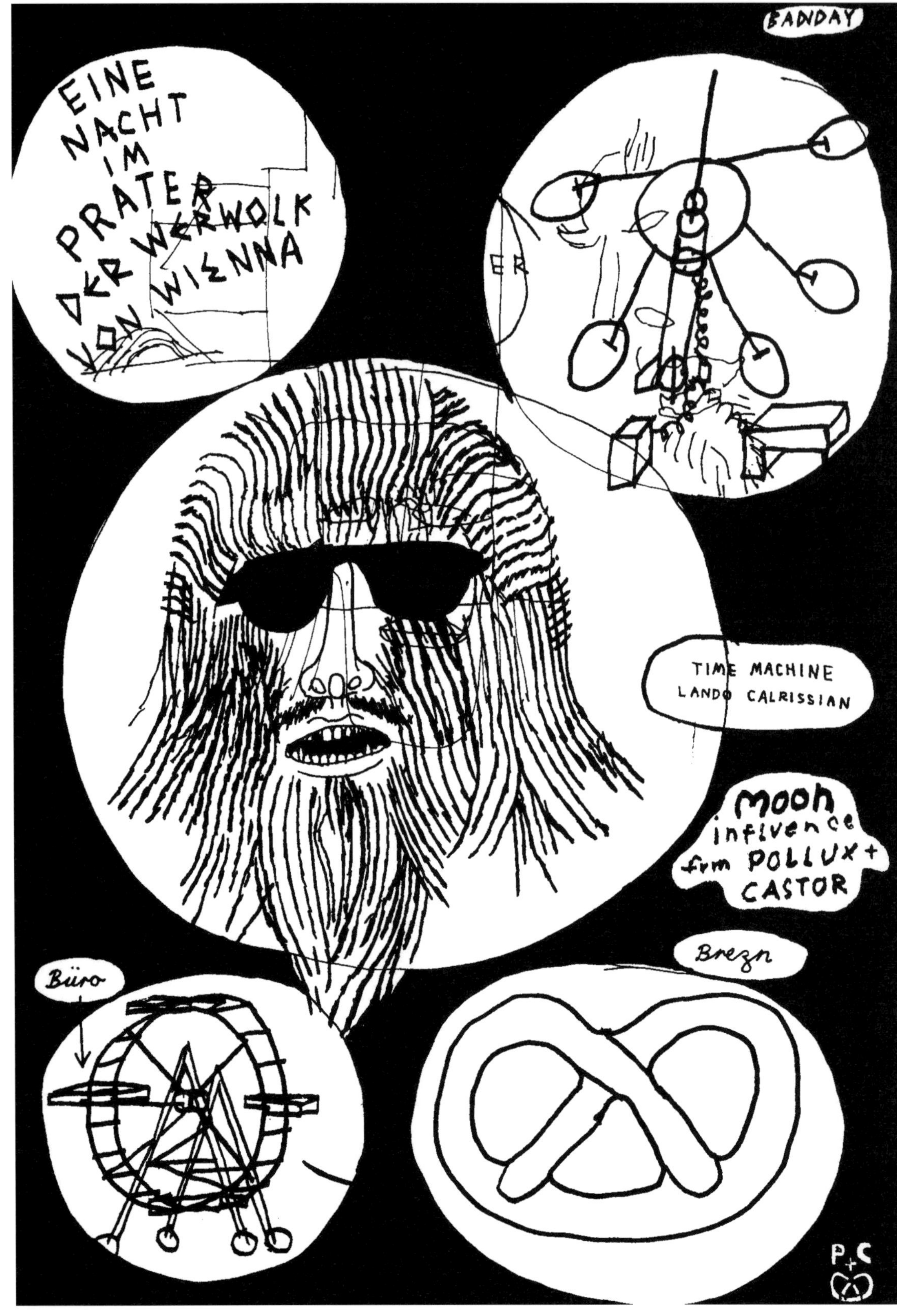
BADDAY
EINE NACHT IM PRATER
DER WERWOLK VON WIENNA
ER
TIME MACHINE
LANDO CALRISSIAN
moon influence
frm POLLUX + CASTOR
Brezn
Büro
P+C

Appendix

LIST OF WORKS

29–53
The Poltergeist Experimental Group (PEG) Applied Spirituality and Physical Spirit Manifestation
2011
Dimensions variable
Various materials
Courtesy of the artist
The actions took place on November 16 and 17 and lasted several hours.
Exhibition views: migros museum für gegenwartskunst / November 19, 2011—January 15, 2012

Cover, 1, 4, 52–53
Blueprints, hot dip compound
325×250 cm

2–3
Silk blanket, brass, polyurethane, rubber, tin, plumb, cable
Dimensions variable

29
Inkjetprint on paper, framed
154.5×110.5×3.5 cm

30, 48
Steel, monitor, cibatool, Bohemian chrysolite, hot dip compound, paper, glass, foam
Dimensions variable

30
Brass, paper, nylon, hot dip compound
15×12.5×2.3 cm

32–33
Silkscreen on brass, copper rust, Schweinfurt green, urine, hot dip compound
14 parts: each ca. 20×30 cm

36–38, 41
Tin, plumb, plywood of birch tree, engine, steel, gas bottle, tubes, blast pipe, chamotte, fuel, glass, plastic, tape decks, audio files
Dimensions variable

38
Blueprint, acrylic glass, walnut wood
52.5×57×9.4 cm

39–40, 46–47
Steel profile, polyurethane, brass, engine, steel
Dimensions variable

42, 45
PVC, rubber, plumb, tin, wood, cloth, hot dip compound, wood
Dimensions variable

44
Phenolic resin, plywood, woggles, rubber
131.5×132.5×9.5 cm

45, 50
Tin plate, polyurethane, batteries, silicone, leather, felt, tin, rope
Dimensions variable

50
Armchair, battery, steel, cable, jack, engine, rope, radio control, crayon
Dimensions variable

51
Copper rust, brass, urine, Schweinfurt green, penny bank
Diameter: 55 cm

Photographs: Patrick Hari (1, 4, 30, 33–36, 38–42, 44–48, 51–53),
Marie Lusa (Cover, 2–3, 32, 36–38, 49–50, 148)

54–103
St. Helena / Reichtümer aus den Tiefen der Berge
2010
Unless other stated: Courtesy of the artist
Unless other stated: Exhibition views: Galerie BolteLang, Zurich / August 28—October 2, 2010

54, 56–62
Dante's Inferno, 2010
Silver gelatin prints on brass plates, 10 parts, each 30×20 cm

79
Gutzon Borglum, Sculptor Rushmore Memorial, Black Hills, S. Dakota, 2010
B/w photograph, framed, 14.8×21 cm

80–81
Table made of plywood and phenolic resin displaying:
Dante's Inferno, 2010
Untitled (Napoleon's Wife), 2010
Untitled (Austerlitz II), 2010

82–83, 88, 92–93
R.A.D.T.D.B., 2010
Steel, plywood, nylon, clay
Relief: Diameter 50 cm, Sculpture: 100×80×40 cm
The action took place on August 27, 2010 and lasted approximately 3 hours.

84–85, 89–90
Table made of plywood and phenolic resin displaying:
Napoleon's Head/Athanor, 2010
Glass blowing mould made of American walnut tree, 100×90×63 cm
Collection Kanton Zürich

86–87
Untitled, 2010
Flattened American police badges (sheriff, sergeant, officer, trooper, deputy), 80×40 cm
Private Collection, Zurich/Berne

82, 90–91, 94–95
Ansage (aus den Tiefen der Berge), 2010
Chrome steel refrigerator, steel crane, hauling rope, dictaphone, microphone, 220×85×85 cm

80–81, 96–97
Untitled (Napoleon's Wife), 2010
Casts made of moulding silicon on nylon blocks, dimensions variable

80–81, 97
Untitled (Austerlitz II), 2010
Nylon, brass, French oysters, wire, steel pliers, 40×40×10 cm

98
Top: *Austerlitz 0*, 2010
French oyster, Russian oyster, silver spoons, electric batteries, dimensions variable
Private Collection, Zurich

Bottom: *Untitled*, 2010
French oyster, aluminum, 8×8×2 cm
Private Collection, Zurich/Berne

100, 102–103
Austerlitz I, 2010
Renault 21, concrete weight with chain, Habegger pulling system, dimensions variable
Exhibition view: Kunsthaus Glarus, *Performative Attitudes*, February 7 — May 2, 2010

101
Austerlitz I, 2010
DVD, 5 min 12 sec
The action took place at Kunsthaus Glarus in relation with the exhibition *Performative Attitudes*, February 7 — May 2, 2010

Photographs: Jon Etter (56–62), Marc Hahn (86–87), Alexander Hana (54, 80–83, 88–89,90–97), Patrick Hari (98–99), Georg Sidler (79, 98), Niels Vije (100–103)

104–130
Der Werwolf von Wien
2009
Unless other stated: Courtesy of the artist

104
Untitled (Kapitel 9), 2009
Ink on paper on pvc, 21x15 cm
Private Collection, Istanbul

106–107
Untitled (Der Werwolf von Wien), 2009
Emergency generator, 1kg silver, glass, cable, 81.5×82×45 cm

108–111
Work descriptions by Florian Germann, 2009

112–114
Untitled (Der Werwolf von Wien), 2009
Silver coins, American walnut tree, 73×103 cm
Burger Collection

Untitled (Der Werwolf von Wien), 2009
Silver coins, nail, Basalt, American walnut tree, 32×26.5 cm
Private Collection, Basel

Untitled (Der Werwolf von Wien), 2009
Silver coin, American walnut tree, 32×26.5 cm
Private Collection, Basel

115
Untitled (Der Werwolf von Wien), 2009
Tire, perspex, PVC, chrome steel, glass, silver coins, American walnut tree, amplifier, 192×160×160 cm

116
Untitled (Der Werwolf von Wien), 2009
Polyurethane, 120×78×20.5 cm

117
Untitled (Der Werwolf von Wien), 2009
Gouache and coloured pencil on wood,
41.5 × 31.2 cm
Private Collection, Zurich

119
Untitled (Der Werwolf von Wien), 2009
Vulkollan, rope, carabiner, 96 × 96 cm
Private Collection, Zurich

120–121
Untitled (Der Werwolf von Wien), 2009
Organ pipes, candles, brass, 111.5 × 28 × 26 cm
Private Collection, Berlin

122
Untitled (Kapitel 8), 2009
Ink on paper on pvc, 21 × 15 cm

123
Messingtisch, 2008
Brass table, Diameter 121 cm
Burger Collection

125
Untitled (Kapitel 9), 2009,
Ink on paper on PVC, 21 × 15 cm
Private Collection, Zurich

126
Untitled (Kapitel 9), 2009,
Ink on paper on PVC, 21 × 15 cm
Private Collection, Zurich

127
Untitled (Kapitel 9), 2009,
Ink on paper on PVC, 21 × 15 cm

128
Untitled (Kapitel 9), 2009,
Ink on paper on PVC, 21 × 15 cm

129
Untitled (Kapitel 9), 2009,
Ink on paper on PVC, 21 × 15 cm
Private Collection, Zurich

130
Untitled (Kapitel 9), 2009,
Ink on paper on PVC, 21 × 15 cm

Photographs: Hans-Jörg F. Walter (106–107, 112–113, 115–116,119–121,123), Georg Sidler (114)

AUTHORS' BIOGRAPHIES

Alexandra Blättler

Studied Art History, French Literature and Linguistics at the University of Zurich, and is currently a PhD. candidate. Since 2004 she has been curator of the BINZ39 Foundation in Zurich (stipendary artists include Stefan Burger, Florian Germann, Elodie Pong), and since 2006 she has been curator at Coalmine – Space for Contemporary Photography in Winterthur (exhibited artists include Fabian Marti, Adrien Missika, Georg Gatsas). In 2010 she received the curatorial grant *KURATOR from the Gebert Stiftung für Kultur. In 2011 she received the curatorial prize *Swiss Art Award* from the Swiss Federal Office of Culture.

Raphael Gygax

Studied Art History, Film and Drama Studies at the universities of Berne and Zurich, and has been working at the migros museum für gegenwartskunst in Zurich since 2003. He is currently a PhD. candidate. Previously curated exhibitions include *Alex Bag* (2011), *Une Idée, une Forme, un Être – Poésie/Politique du corporel* (2010), *Deterioration, They Said – Cory Arcangel, Jacob Ciocci, Jessica Ciocci/Paper Rad, Lizzie Fitch & Ryan Trecartin, Shana Moulton* (2009), *Dawn Mellor* (2008), *Christoph Schlingensief* (2007), *Spartacus Chetwynd* (2007), and *Cory Arcangel* (2005). In 2008, together with writer Sibylle Berg, he curated the theater/art project *Of those who will survive* at the Schauspielhaus Zürich. He writes regularly for several art magazines.

FLORIAN GERMANN

Born 1978 in Kreuzlingen, Switzerland
Lives and works in Zurich, Switzerland

Education

2008
MFA, Zurich University of the Arts

2003
Restoration Assistant, Winterthur

2000
Apprenticeship as stone sculptor, Switzerland

1996
Apprenticeship as cabinet maker, Switzerland

Solo Exhibitions

2011
The Poltergeist Experimental Group (PEG) Applied Spirituality and Physical Spirit Manifestation, migros museum für gegenwartskunst Zürich

2010
St. Helena/Reichtümer aus den Tiefen der Berge, BolteLang, Zurich
Napoleon I., San Kellers Kiosk, Zurich

2009
Der Werwolf von Wien, BolteLang, Zurich

2008
Ballungscenter aller Energien II, Kunsthaus Baselland, Basel

2007
Ballungscenter aller Energien I, Amberg & Marti, Zurich

Group Exhibitions
(Selection since 2004)

2011
New Existentialism: Magical & Poetical Structures, Kunst(Zeug)Haus, Rapperswil-Jona

2010
Performative Attitudes, Kunsthaus Glarus
Stiftung BINZ39, Zurich

2009
Thunders of Epiphanias, Galleria Lanserhaus, Appiano
Helmhaus, Zurich

2008
SIMONA, Schauwerk/Viereck Palast, Appenzell
Summercamp, Galerie Haas & Fischer, Zurich

2007
Ana, der Juwelier. Die Halde am Ende des Ganges, Kunsthalle Lanzarotte
Ballungscenter aller Energien I, Bolzano
Vera Icon, Bad Gallery, Zurich

2006
i.r.u.l.a.n. aka. Spidernet am Reiterbrett, Festival 'Go West', Zurich
i.r.u.l.a.n., Altes Zeughaus, Herisau
Pollux, Sihlquai 125, Zurich

2005
Symposium Contacts, Galerie Klenova, Janovice nad Úhlavou
Stella, Centre Culturel Suisse, Paris
Eat at Joes, Stage Pavillon, Berne

2004
Enduro/Tests and Trainings, Ausstellungsraum Schalter, Basel

IMPRINT

This book was published on the occasion of the exhibition *Florian Germann: The Poltergeist Experimental Group (PEG) Applied Spirituality and Physical Spirit Manifestation*, November 19, 2011–January 15, 2012, at the migros museum für gegenwartskunst Zürich.

Director
Heike Munder

Exhibition Curator
Raphael Gygax

Collections Manager / Exhibitions Coordinator
Judith Welter

Collections Assistant
Anna-Lena Gugger

Head of Administration
Catherine Reymond

Administration
Nicole Sacher

Trainees
Stefanie Kleefeld, Alena Nawrotzki

Head of Technical Services, Exhibitions
Monika Schori

Head of Technical Services, Museum
Roland Bösiger

Technical Support
Gabi Deutsch, Roman Gysin, Nina Weber

Reception
Robin Bhattacharya, Christa Michel, Katharina Rippstein, Monika Stalder, Riikka Tauriainen, Hin Van Tran

migros museum für gegenwartskunst
Postfach 1766
CH–8031 Zurich
T +41 (0) 44 277 20 50
F +41 (0) 44 277 62 86
info@migrosmuseum.ch
migrosmuseum.ch

The migros museum für gegenwartskunst Zürich is an institution of the Migros Culture Percentage
migros-kulturprozent.ch

migrosmuseum
FÜR GEGENWARTSKUNST
ZÜRICH

Published by
migros museum für gegenwartskunst Zürich and JRP|Ringier

Editors
Raphael Gygax, Heike Munder

Editorial Coordination
Raphael Gygax

Trainee
Alena Nawrotzki

Translation from German
Gerrit Jackson

Transcript
Judith Welter

Copy Editing, German
Stefanie Kleefeld, Judith Welter

Copy Editing and Proofreading, German
Doris Senn

Copy Editing and Proofreading, English
Rowena Smith

Visual Concept & Graphic Design
Marie Lusa

Lithography
Georg Sidler, Schwyz

Production
Odermatt AG, Dallenwil

The migros museum für gegenwartskunst Zürich would like to thank

BINZ39, Zurich
Alexandra Blättler
BolteLang, Zurich
Florian Germann

The artist would like to thank

Mirko Baselgia, BINZ39, Zurich; Alexandra Blättler, Anna Bolte, Ilona von Buck, Monique Burger, Florian Bühler, Lucia Coray, Prof. Peter Emch, Patrick Hari, Prof. Bem Höppner, Gianni Garzoli, Götz George, Andreas Germann, Margrit Germann, Stefanie Herrmann, Tomas Germann, Raphael Gygax, Stefan Innauen, Marianne Karabelnik, Prof. Grzegorz Kowalski, Daniel Kurjakovic, Chaja Lang, Henry Levy, Olaf Metzel, Raoul Müller, Heike Munder, Heather O`Rourke, Diego Paris, Reni Paris, Sabine Schlatter (Q.O.E), Roman Signer, Thomas Tobler, Urs Traber, Armando Wehrli, Lukas and Margreth Willen, Olsen Wolf

Special thanks to my father, Andreas Germann

Printed in Switzerland

Distributed by
JRP|Ringier
Letzigraben 134
CH–8047 Zurich
T +41 (0) 43 311 27 50
F +41 (0) 43 311 27 51
info@jrp-ringier.com
jrp-ringier.com

ISBN: 978-3-03764-270-2

JRP|Ringier books are available internationally at selected bookstores and from the following distribution partners:

Switzerland
AVA Verlagsauslieferung AG
Centralweg 16
CH–8910 Affoltern a.A.
verlagsservice@ava.ch
ava.ch

Germany and Austria
Vice Versa Vertrieb
Immanuelkirchstrasse 12
D–10405 Berlin
info@vice-versa-vertrieb.de
vice-versa-vertrieb.de

France
Les presses du réel
35, rue Colson
F–21000 Dijon
info@lespressesdureel.com
lespressesdureel.com

United Kingdom and other European countries
Cornerhouse Publications
70 Oxford Street
UK–Manchester M1 5NH
publications@cornerhouse.org
cornerhouse.org/books

USA, Canada, Asia, and Australia
ARTBOOK|D.A.P.
155 Sixth Avenue, 2nd Floor
USA–New York, NY 10013
dap@dapinc.com
artbook.com

For a list of our partner bookshops or for any general questions, please contact JRP|Ringier directly at info@jrp-ringier.com, or visit our homepage jrp-ringier.com for further information about our program.

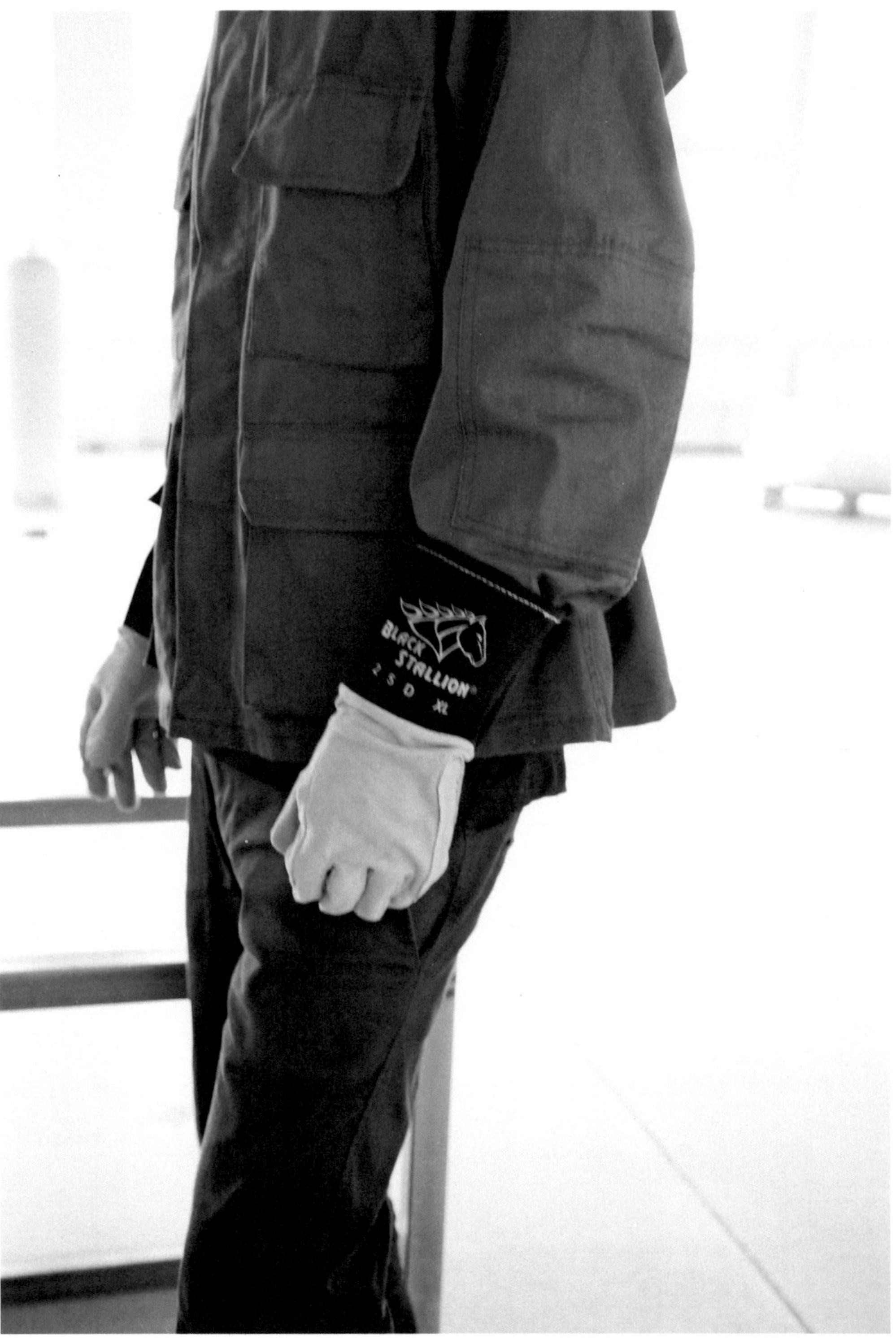
BLACK STALLION®
2 5 D XL